I0824606
OPENING GAME
St. Louis BROWNS
OPENING GAME 1953 SEASON SPORTSMAN'S PARK
BLEACHER
ENTER GATE F
SEC. 21 BOX 311B SEAT 2
1969 NATIONAL LEAGUE CHAMPIONSHIP SERIES
SHEA STADIUM GAME No. 3 1:00 P.M.
UPPER BOX
1969 NATIONAL LEAGUE CHAMPIONSHIP SERIES
ADMIT TO UPPER BOX
SHEA STADIUM GAME 3
18 E 4
BOX ROW SEAT
Pittsburgh Athletic Co., Inc. THREE RIVERS STADIUM
RAIN CHECK The "Pirates"
FRI. NIGHT JUNE 16 1972
FIELD BOX FIRST LEVEL $4.15
CLEVELAND INDIANS
NEW YORK
RAIN CHECK
RED SOX
SEP 10 1978 DAY $5.75
BOX SEAT
ROW 14 SEC. N SEAT 6
RES'D SEAT $1.50 $1.65
WORLD'S SERIES
RAIN CHECK
ADMIT ONE
GAME 1
BOSTON AMERICAN LEAGUE
WRIGLEY FIELD 1962
NATIONAL LEAGUE STARS AMERICAN LEAGUE STARS
RAIN CHECK
UPPER GRANDSTAND $6.00
JULY 30
ENTER GATE 3
FIRST NIGHT GAME 1935
Cincinnati Base Ball Club Co.
RAIN CHECK
Giants
1962 WORLD SERIES
GAME 6
$12.00
LOWER BOX SEAT
ENTER GATE B
MAY 25 1978
BOX SEAT $5.50
FIELD LEVEL
Seattle Mariners BASEBALL CLUB
KANSAS CITY ROYALS
KINGDOME
THURSDAY AFT. - 12:35 P.M.
20 H 9
SEC. ROW SEAT
SAT., APRIL 30 1977
MAIN LEVEL RESERVED $4.50
RAIN CHECK
DAY 9
Yankees
RAIN CHECK
1969
CHAMPIONSHIP SERIES NATIONAL LEAGUE
Atlanta Braves
ATLANTA STADIUM ATLANTA, GA.
RAIN CHECK
Club Level Box $7.00
Oct 30, 2024
WORLD SERIES 2024
YANKEE STADIUM
2024 World Series Home Game 3
SEC 434B ROW 2 SEAT 8
ENTRY INFO / GRANDSTAND 434B
TICKET TYPE / PRICE CODE New York Yankees
BALTIMORE ORIOLES
Championship Series 1969
$7.00
ENTER GATE C or D
15 D 1
SECOND DECK BOX
DELUXE BOX
PHILADELPHIA
San Diego padres BASEBALL CLUB

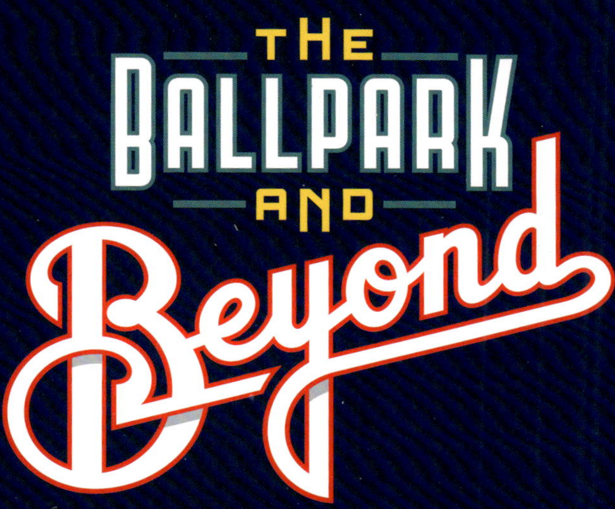
THE
BALLPARK
AND
Beyond

AN ILLUSTRATED CELEBRATION OF BASEBALL'S RICH HISTORY

The Ballpark and Beyond

TODD RADOM

FOREWORD BY BUSTER OLNEY

Sports Publishing books may be purchased in bulk at special discounts for sales promotion, corporate gifts, fund-raising, or educational purposes. Special editions can also be created to specifications. For details, contact the Special Sales Department, Sports Publishing, 307 Fifth Avenue, 4th Floor, New York, NY 10016 or sportspubbooks@skyhorsepublishing.com.

Visit our website at www.sportspubbooks.com.

10 9 8 7 6 5 4 3 2 1

Library of Congress Cataloging-in-Publication Data is available on file.

Cover design and artwork by Todd Radom

Print ISBN: 978-1-68358-514-5
Ebook ISBN: 978-1-68358-515-2

Printed in China

For the Game

CONTENTS

FOREWORD

There are few opportunities in life when you get to see art from its inception, but with this new book by Todd Radom, I was lucky enough to see the concept developed from germination to its brilliant completion. Todd has been a weekly guest on the show that I host, the Baseball Tonight podcast, and he and I—longtime friends—were kicking around ideas for a regular segment. I can't remember the precise form of what I proposed—it probably was some terrible idea involving Wiffleball or cows. Todd responded politely that, no, he was thinking about moving in a different direction. Thus was the first reveal of what you hold in your hands, which fits not only Todd's sense of style, but his curiosity for—and deep understanding of—baseball history. Each of these chapters are hidden doors into what has helped to make baseball great, and Todd guides you to and through them, explaining all of the personalities and the impact of their decisions and contributions.

That Todd could generate something so spectacular is hardly a surprise. He is like the Shohei Ohtani of sports design, uniforms, and logos. Through the years, I have sometimes noticed some particular element of a jersey or hat and asked Todd about its meaning. He has never disappointed, explaining not only the aesthetics behind the choice but also its inspiration.

I was once part of a baseball fantasy league and leaned into my Vermont roots in picking a name for the team: The Green Mountain Boys. I asked Todd if it might be possible for him to design a logo for my squad. Well, within 24 hours, there was a mockup in my inbox that was perfect—a soldier dressed in a colonial-era uniform, guarding an outline of my home state, with a long rifle in one hand and a baseball bat in the other. His expression was of intense resolution and purpose, a full embrace of his challenge laid down in the motto before him: "Get Hits or Die." Of course, I had to have Todd's logo made into a street sign for our home, and I bragged about it so much that it raised the curiosity of then Oakland general manager Billy Beane, who similarly commissioned a logo for *his* football fantasy team from Todd, procuring bragging rights within his league regardless of how his team performed. (I haven't been able to find the invoice for Todd's effort, by the way, but I vaguely remember that it involved a six-pack of lager.)

In my travels, I have always had fun pointing out to acquaintances—or even players—examples of Todd's work, in ballparks and on caps or jerseys. *The guy who did that is known in the industry as The Toddfather*, I might say. Generations from now, some graphic artist following Todd's path will delve into his impact on sports and fan experience, in the same manner as Todd Radom does in these pages.

Buster Olney
December 2025

INTRODUCTION

"Base ball is decidedly the National game of America."
—*New-York Tribune, August 15, 1865*

Four months after the end of America's bloody Civil War, the nation was attempting to bind up its considerable wounds, and baseball was both ascendent and healing. The sport had gained a firm foothold in the national consciousness prior to the conflict, but its status as our "National Pastime" may well have been indelibly cemented during the War, when soldiers from both the north and south organized and participated in ballgames, a welcome diversion from the brutal armed hostilities and harsh prison camps.

It's been a century and a half since the National League was established at a New York hotel in February 1876. The fortunes of both the nation and the sport have waxed and waned along the way, but baseball remains a vital part of our national (and international) conversation, as witnessed by the fact that some 51 million viewers across the United States, Canada, and Japan tuned in to watch the electrifying and decisive seventh game of the 2025 World Series.

How can you not be intellectually curious about baseball? I know I am. The sport has a way of rewarding (or, conversely, torturing) those of us who invest our time it, regardless of whether we are casual fans who flit in and out, grazing on a couple of appetizers here and there, or the diehards among us who want to consume the entire tasting menu, snout to tail, from the first day of spring training right through the final out of the World Series.

There's an entire industry built up around baseball's "Hot Stove League," the annual winter interregnum when pundits and fans alike speculate and swap news and rumors about contract negotiations, trades, free agent signings, and the like. The term "Hot Stove League" is itself an anachronism, a throwback to a time when men (and they were likely *all* men) sat around searingly hot iron pot-bellied stoves in small-town general stores and post offices all across the land, warming themselves up as they kibbitzed about the coming season and reminisced about the past.

Was that aforementioned seventh game of the 2025 World Series the best ever played? How does it stack up against those that took place in 1925, 1975, 1991, 1960, or 2016? Would Babe Ruth and the 1927 Yankees have been able to navigate a four-round postseason, all the way to a world championship? And tell me, which team was the worst ever? Was it the 1962 Mets, the 2024 White Sox, or the 1916 Philadelphia Athletics? These types of conversations serve to fuse together players such as Yoshinobu Yamamoto, Christy Mathewson, and Randy Johnson into a single sub-theme, united across distant ages through the game ... and even though the Dodgers' 2025 uniforms featured a garish advertisement on their sleeves, the club's core appearance was pretty much identical to their Brooklyn ancestors who won the 1955 fall classic seven decades prior. One might have to squint a bit, but it's definitely all connected.

All of which makes me wonder: What was it like at Ebbets Field for the Dodgers' final home game in 1957? Who was the first player to ever ride in a bullpen cart? How incredible would it have been to have seen the 1931 Homestead Grays play? And what did people eat and drink while attending a ballgame in the nineteenth century?

I know and love plenty of folks who are part of the "numbers" crowd, but I've never really fit in there. My personal interests tend to span the entire, vast expanse of the game, both on and off the field. Baseball, above all other sports, lends itself to introspection, discussion, and curiosity, and I've been captivated by the history and culture of the sport since I was a little kid. Back then, I devoured just about everything I could get my hands on—I read books, subscribed to magazines, wrote away to teams for programs and yearbooks, and went to ballgames at New York's Shea and Yankee Stadiums with family and friends. When I was about eight or nine years old, I came across an old 1970 Major League Baseball preview guide, and, lo and behold, there was some team in there called the Seattle Pilots. *Who the heck are the Seattle Pilots?* I wondered. Now remember, dear reader—these were the dark ages, a time well before we could tap our phones and access Wikipedia with one click. Unaided by futuristic technology, I learned something new. Sometime later I read *Ball Four* by Jim Bouton, which gave me greater and even more colorful context on the Pilots' lone season in the Pacific Northwest.

I've worked in baseball for thirty-five years now, designing logos and uniforms, and talking and writing about the game, and my profession and personal interests have converged in ways that I sometimes find hard to comprehend. I've seen Clemente and Ohtani play in person. I've attended a slew of World Series games, starting in 1977, and have been to three Yankee Stadiums, two Busch Stadiums, the Astrodome, and old Comiskey Park. I once shared a cocktail with Babe Ruth's daughter, I knew Buck O'Neil, and I count Josh Gibson's great-grandson as a personal friend. I've signed my name inside the Green Monster at Fenway Park, I've seen baseball played in Cuba, South Korea, and Japan, and I have soaked all of it in, mindful of and interested in just about everything.

Some of you might know me from my weekly in-season appearances on the *ESPN Baseball Tonight Podcast*, which I have been a part of for the past decade or so. *The Ballpark and Beyond* has been a regular, ongoing topic there for the last several years—this book builds upon that, with greater depth, detail, and context—plus, it's got pictures! I am grateful to that podcast's host, my longtime pal Buster Olney, and our producer, Taylor Schwink, for affording me the opportunity to meander through the baseball ages there, veering this way and that, from the Sphinx to Wrigley Field and all points in between. The stories are everywhere, and they are here, in *The Ballpark and Beyond*.

How can you not be intellectually curious about baseball?

TODD RADOM
NOVEMBER 2025

PLAY BALL

HISTORY

PHILA 2
BOS 3
NY 2
MILW 0

INNING 1

0 BALL
0 STRIKE
0 OUT

THE EVOLVING SPHERE

Each season, Major League Baseball uses approximately a million baseballs. The sport's official rulebook outlines the specifications for the ball in detail:

> *The ball shall be a sphere formed by yarn wound around a small core of cork, rubber or similar material, covered with two strips of white horsehide or cowhide, tightly stitched together. It shall weigh not less than five nor more than 5¼ ounces avoirdupois and measure not less than nine nor more than 9¼ inches in circumference.*

It all seems so straightforward, right? Well, not so much. Over the past century, the baseball has evolved in subtle, often invisible ways. However, the interior core of cork, cotton, wool, and rubber remains pretty much unchanged.

The earliest baseballs were all handmade, and the rules that governed the weight, size, and composition of baseballs were constantly changing. In the years shortly before the Civil War, America was in the middle of a transition from an agricultural to an industrial economy, and this new mass production of goods included baseballs. In Natick, Massachusetts, in 1858, the H. Harwood & Sons baseball factory became the first facility to mass produce the two-piece figure-eight stitched ball, the style of which had become the standard by the time the National League was established in 1876. The new circuit adopted the L. H. Mahn baseball, a well-regarded sphere that was manufactured in Boston. Two years later, in 1878, the contract went to the firm owned by Albert Goodwill Spalding, the ace pitcher and nascent sporting goods mogul who had helped organize the new league. In December 1878, the *Cincinnati Enquirer* wrote, "Last year the League paid Mahn & Co. $7.50 a dozen for balls. This year Spalding not only donates the balls free of cost but pays the League $5 a dozen for the privilege of making them. Who says business is not looking up?" Spalding's firm would go on to manufacture the league's official balls for the next hundred years.

When the American League vaulted to major-league status, it adopted the A. J. Reach baseball as its official sphere. Born in London in 1840, Alfred J. Reach was one of baseball's earliest stars—in 1871, he led the Philadelphia Athletics to America's first pro baseball championship. Shortly before he retired as a player in 1875, he opened a sporting goods store in Center City Philly, which eventually expanded and became a manufacturer of sporting equipment. Reach and Spalding entered into a partnership in which Reach focused on manufacturing and Spalding on retailing. Under this arrangement, Reach fabricated balls that bore the Spalding name, as well as its own signature ball.

In 1882, Reach combined forces with Benjamin Franklin Shibe, whose automatic baseball-winding machine was, at the time, cutting edge technology. Their partnership was both agreeable and lucrative. Shibe purchased half of the AL's new Philadelphia Athletics franchise in 1901, and, as was the case with Spalding back in 1878, his proximity to power won his company the contract to produce the league's official baseballs. Reach's manufacturing plant, located in Philadelphia's Fishtown neighborhood, produced all of the AL's official baseballs until 1936, when it closed and consolidated its production into Spalding's own plant in Chicopee, Massachusetts.

The company introduced a revolutionary cushioned cork-centered ball in 1910, which was adopted by both leagues the following season, overtaking the rubber-centered ball as the new standard. This lively ball contributed to a noticeable spike in offense. Not everybody was sold on it, however. As *The Sporting News* noted, "There was never a new thing or principle advanced yet that did not arouse opposition just because it was new. It's a trait of human nature, a kind of human inertia that compels opposition to leaving the beaten track."

The Deadball Era died in the 1920s, a victim of Babe Ruth and the home run. Offenses exploded and, after the National League hit for a cumulative .303 batting average in 1930, the league deadened its ball by thickening the cover of the ball and raising the stitches. The American League raised the seams as well, but didn't adopt the thicker exterior until 1934. In December 1937, the NL voted unanimously to adopt the "No. 4 ball," which featured five strands of thread on the seams, as opposed to four, as their official sphere. This slightly heavier, "slower" ball was seen as a better fit for the Nationals, while the Americans—a league with an surfeit of home run hitters—retained the same "faster pellet" that they had been using. The following spring, government scientists working for the United States Bureau of Standards spent two weeks testing the new balls with a machine that utilized compressed air. Their findings were conclusive, showing "no difference of any practical significance" between the two "different" baseballs. As such, the leagues settled on a new unified ball in 1939, which combined the raised and increased stitching of the NL ball with the AL's thinner cover.

Horsehide covers were replaced by cowhide in 1974, the same year that the Reach label was replaced by Spalding on all American League balls. Then, three years later, Rawlings replaced Spalding as the official supplier for all of MLB. The tradition of facsimile signatures of league presidents on their respective baseballs was eliminated after the 1999 season, when MLB consolidated all its operating functions into the commissioner's office.

Since then, much of the discussion about the composition of MLB's official ball has involved some form or another of controversy. Humidified, mud-covered, juiced, lively, dead, or otherwise, the baseball is an ever-evolving sphere bound by 108 stitches and a century and a half of history.

THE PHILLIES MOVE FIVE BLOCKS WEST

Each year, Opening Day offers up a moment of hope for baseball fans, regardless of just how bad the outlook for their team might be. Until the first pitch is thrown, every team has the same exact record, with the possibility for success at an all-time high. And in Philadelphia, on April 19, 1938, that was exactly the situation. The Phillies' opener featured a parade, which kicked off at Broad and Christian Streets at 12:30. The party moved north along Broad Street to Baker Bowl, the team's longtime home, where, at 2 p.m., both the Phils and the Brooklyn Dodgers gathered in center field for the raising of the American flag and the playing of the national anthem. The Dodgers won that day, 12–5, and the Phils wound up finishing in last place when the season concluded on October 2, ending with a record of 45–105. Even though they lost more than 100 games, and even though this was their sixth-straight losing season, it would prove to be a season of momentous change for Philadelphia: a moribund franchise and perennial loser. For just this one year, the Phillies wore blue and yellow-trimmed uniforms, part of the regional commemoration of the 300th anniversary of the 1638 Swedish landing in what is now Wilmington, Delaware. The Phils' jerseys featured a large sleeve patch which depicted the statue of William Penn—playing baseball—high atop City Hall. Most importantly, the team changed ballparks midseason, shifting operations from the dilapidated Baker Bowl to the Philadelphia Athletics' stadium, Shibe Park, which was located five blocks west.

Negotiations to move the club to Shibe began back in 1911, but the Phillies were bound by the terms of an onerous ground lease which kept them stuck in place until conditions deteriorated to the point that they had no choice but to leave. As *The Sporting News* noted, "More spectators were killed in it than all other big league ballparks put together," adding, "[T]here were many fans who refused to go (to Baker Bowl) because they were in actual fear of the stands collapsing. . . . Women shunned the park because is a foul ball hit the roof, a shower of rust fell on their summer finery."

Baker Bowl served as home to the Phillies for fifty-one-and-a-half seasons, starting in 1887. It was the first ballpark constructed primarily of steel and brick, and the first with a cantilevered upper deck. Its fireproof structure was a major selling point at that time, and the team touted both the safety and beauty of the place. The look of the ballpark was regal—the primary entrance resembled a brick castle, topped with turrets. It was a state-of-the-art facility upon opening, but by the end of its lifespan, it was literally falling apart. In his book *Lost Ballparks*, author Lawrence Ritter wrote, "Baker Bowl began life as a mighty battleship and ended up half a century later as a leaky garbage scow, barely able to stay afloat."

The park occupied a rectangular-shaped parcel, which necessitated some unusual dimensions. Right field was a cozy 279 1/2 feet from home plate, and it was backed up by what eventually became a mammoth 60-foot-high wall. How tight were things on the right side of the diamond? Sportswriter Red Smith wrote, "It might be exaggerating to say the outfield wall cast a shadow across the infield, but if the right fielder had eaten onions at lunch the second baseman knew it." The gigantic right field wall was covered in tin, and the echoes of balls ricocheting off the surface were a familiar sound—the Phillies were terrible in the '20s and '30s, finishing last or next to last sixteen times over the course of their final twenty campaigns there.

A pronounced hump ran across deep center field, evidence of a train tunnel directly below. As the ballpark deteriorated, fans and writers disparagingly referred to it by a variety of colorful names, including "the dump on the hump," the "Toilet Bowl," and "Baker's Bowels."

All joking aside, several truly tragic incidents hang heavy over the history of the Baker Bowl. In 1903, a makeshift balcony that was part of the third base stands collapsed during a Phillies-Braves game, leaving 12 dead and 232 people injured. In 1927, a section of the stands in right field gave way during a game against the Cardinals, killing one and injuring 50. Baker Bowl lacked even the most rudimentary modern amenities of the era—there was no parking for cars, and there was no separate press box or public address system, much less lights for night games.

By 1938, the Phillies had had enough. They negotiated their escape and agreed to be tenants of Connie Mack's A's, who were happy to collect the rent. Baker Bowl's final game took place on June 30, 1938, when the New York Giants beat up on the Phils, 14–1. A crowd of some 1,500 spectators were on hand for the swan song that day, likely relieved to have escaped unscathed. After the Phillies left, Baker Bowl was converted into an auto racetrack, a used car lot, and an ice-skating rink. Outdoor dances were held there. Finally, in 1950, the year that the Phils won their first National League pennant since 1915, what remained of Baker Bowl fell to the wrecker's ball.

SHOWTIME ON LAKE ERIE

The hallowed halls of Cooperstown honor the game's most significant figures, which include a handful of team owners and executives. Some of these individuals are obscure, others are more consequential, but there is only one whose bronze plaque includes the following words: "A champion of the little guy."

When he passed away in 1986, Aaron Copland's "Fanfare for the Common Man" was played at his funeral mass. Bill Veeck has been called many things, including showman, intellectual, maverick, innovator, hustler, and idealist. Conservative members of the baseball establishment described him as a huckster—undignified, combative, and lowbrow.

Along the way he owned the Chicago White Sox (twice) and the St. Louis Browns, but his first foray as the proprietor of a major-league club took place in Cleveland, where he led a group that purchased the Indians in 1946. When he and his consortium, which included entertainer Bob Hope, bought the team, the Tribe's most recent (and only) World Series victory was a distant memory, twenty-six years past. By the time he sold the club only three years hlater, he had helped to restore the faith of Cleveland fans, who celebrated a title in 1948.

Bill Veeck literally grew up in baseball. His father served as president of the Chicago Cubs, and the younger Veeck's first job in the game involved helping fill ticket requests, when he was just eleven years old. He worked his way up the food chain across a number of roles, including office boy, working in the commissary of the concession depart-

ment, and planting the now-familiar ivy on the brick outfield walls at Wrigley Field. He purchased the minor-league Milwaukee Brewers in 1941, then headed off to World War II, where he lost a leg while serving in the Marine Corps. His stewardship of the Indians began at 12:50 p.m. on June 22, 1946, when the thirty-two-year-old Veeck left the office of attorney Joseph C. Hostetler in the Cleveland Union Commerce Building office and declared to the press, "We're in business as of right now." He told the *Cleveland Plain Dealer*, "Baseball has generally been too grim, too serious. It should be fun, and I hope to make it fun for everyone around here." The fun was about to begin.

Veeck immediately set out to modernize the franchise and gin up the fan base. He reinstated radio broadcasts of home games, which had been blacked out. He brought back Ladies' Day, and gave the fans fireworks. In addition, he announced that the club would be shifting spring training to Arizona where the club would continue to train for decades, and moved the Indians into Cleveland Stadium on a full-time basis. At the time, the Indians split their home schedule between League Park—located about three miles northeast of today's Progressive Field—and Cleveland Stadium. Built in 1891, League Park was originally constructed to house the National League's Cleveland Spiders. Due to having been built around a saloon and two other houses—whose owners refused to sell their land—it had the smallest seating capacity in the majors, topping out at 21,400. This also meant that home plate was only 290 feet from right field, which featured a 40-foot high wall that was constructed from three different types of materials. Balls hit off the imposing structure bounced differently, depending upon where they hit, resulting in a pinball effect that the fans loved—even if the right fielders didn't.

By July 1932, the club had shifted their all of their home games to the gigantic new Cleveland Stadium, but they moved back to League Park in 1934, hammered by financial woes in the midst of the Great Depression and unable to sell a meaningful number of tickets at the giant edifice by the lake. Within a few years, the club began splitting their schedule between the two ballparks, playing weekdays and Saturday afternoons at League Park and Sunday and holiday games at Cleveland Stadium. Veeck put an end to this arrangement, moving his team to the larger place on a full-time basis, starting in 1947. League Park hosted its final American League game on September 21, 1946: a 5–3, 11-inning loss to Detroit.

Getting the team settled into a full-time home and creating an atmosphere of excitement around the club paled in comparison to Veeck's greatest contribution. On July 5, 1947, he signed the Newark Eagles' Larry Doby, who that night became the first Black player in the history of the American League. Negro Leagues legend Satchel Paige came aboard the following year as a forty-two-year-old rookie, and the Indians, led by a group of six future Hall of Famers—pitchers Bob Feller and Bob Lemon, infielder Joe Gordon, shortstop/manager Lou Boudreau, and Doby and Paige—won the World Series, shattering attendance figures by drawing 2.6 million fans to their massive stadium. When Veeck's short tenure in Cleveland ended the following year, he was lauded for his contributions to the local community, not the least of which was a world championship. After he signed the paperwork that officially transferred the team to its new owners, he declared, "We've had a lot of fun here, haven't we?"

BASEBALL GOES TO WAR

On the morning of June 28, 1914, a nineteen-year old Bosnian-Serb student named Gavrilo Princip stood in front of Moritz Schiller's Delicatessen on Franz Joseph Street in Sarajevo, Bosnia-Herzegovina. Princip fired two shots into the automobile in which Archduke Franz Ferdinand—heir to the Austro-Hungarian throne—and his wife, Sophie, were riding. The shots killed them both and set the wheels in motion for what we now know as World War I.

Nearly three years later, on April 6, 1917, President Woodrow Wilson led the United States into the conflict in order to "make the world safe for democracy." Baseball opened its regular season just as America entered the war and, as the young season progressed, the sport proved to be an excellent distraction. Patriotic ceremonies and Liberty Loan bond drives were held, American League president Ban Johnson assigned a US Army drill sergeant to every club, and major league squads participated in pregame military drills, swapping out guns for baseball bats.

But as America mobilized, perceptions began to shift. In August, syndicated columnist Grantland Rice, citing baseball's attempts to exempt players from service, wrote that, with few exceptions, "So far there is no questioning the fact that baseball hasn't done its full duty by the nation." Congress had recently passed the Selective Service Act, which required all men between the ages of twenty-one and thirty to register for military service. Boston Braves catcher Hank Gowdy became the first active major leaguer to sign up to fight, when he enlisted to serve in the Ohio National Guard on June 1, 1917. Gowdy spoke about his decision in an essay in *Baseball* magazine: "I had no excuse so far as I could see, for not offering my services ... I wouldn't feel content to stay on this side of the Atlantic in comparative security and know that others were bearing the brunt across the ocean. I don't like to be a target for shrapnel any better than the next man. But that isn't a subject that it does much good to speculate about. Somebody has got to fight and I don't see how I could consistently fail to do my share." He served with distinction and became part of the famed "Rainbow Division," the Fighting 42nd, where he saw heavy fighting in the trenches on the Western Front. In 1942, Gowdy, then a fifty-two-year-old coach with the Cincinnati Reds, enlisted again—this time for World War II. He received a captain's commission in the army the following year and ended up overseeing the physical education program at Fort Benning in Georgia.

Ty Cobb, Christy Mathewson, George Sisler, and Branch Rickey served in the Chemical Warfare Service, an elite combat unit known as "The Gas and Flame Division." They were recruited for their athletic prowess and leadership abilities, as well as for their propaganda value. Working under controlled conditions, they trained soldiers to deploy toxic chemical weapons in combat—troops were to use gas grenades and flamethrowers, which were strapped to their backs to attack the enemy on the battlefield. Mathewson was accidentally gassed during one such training exercise, and spent the next seven years battling

lung issues, including tuberculosis. He passed away in 1925, at the age of forty-five.

The 1917 season concluded on October 15 in New York, where the Chicago White Sox—who went 100–54 during the regular season—defeated the Giants in the World Series. Chicago wore these star-spangled jerseys that October, an expressive display of patriotism in support of the war effort.

While the 1917 season was full of overt patriotic flourishes, 1918 would prove to be a very different year. In May, the Selective Service Division issued a national "work or fight" order, which required all able-bodied men to either participate in war-related work or military service. A few months later, United States Secretary of War Newton D. Baker declared that professional baseball was a "non-essential occupation." "Baseball players are men of unusual physical ability and alertness," he wrote. "The employment of able-bodied persons in nonproductive work cannot be justified on the ground of the social value of the National game." The ruling went on to say that baseball "must bear its share of the burden" of war, and that all players would become draft eligible as of Labor Day, which fell on September 2. Hands forced, baseball's ruling national commission decided to shut the season down early. A fifteen-day extension was granted in order for the World Series to be played, and it began at Comiskey Park in Chicago on September 5. Young Boston Red Sox lefty Babe Ruth tossed a complete-game shutout against the National League champion Cubs, who borrowed the larger ballpark from the White Sox for the fall classic.

War taxes and poor weather, combined with the shadow of global conflict, contributed to what newspapers described as "the indifference of the public," with a small crowd of just 19,274 fans on hand for Game One. A brass band struck up "The Star-Spangled Banner"—which was not yet the official national anthem—during the seventh inning stretch. This marked the first time that the song was played during a World Series game. Boston won the Series on September 11, their last world championship until 2004.

On October 5, 1918, former MLB infielder Eddie Grant, a Harvard-educated lawyer, became the first major leaguer killed in the conflict. He was struck down while leading troops in an effort to rescue members of the "Lost Battalion," the 77th Infantry Division, in France's Argonne Forest. According to the National Baseball Hall of Fame and Museum, "227 major leaguers served the United States through various branches of the Armed Forces" over the course of the war. The conflict concluded on the 11th hour on the 11th day of the 11th month of 1918, November 11, following the signing of an armistice, ending the "War to End All Wars." America celebrated and baseball returned to normal the following year, when the White Sox lost a tainted World Series to the Cincinnati Reds.

THE STREETCAR SERIES

Inntracity World Series are rare events, and the 1944 World Series stands out as perhaps the most unusual of them all: a "Streetcar Series" matchup that pitted the St. Louis Browns against the St. Louis Cardinals, the entirety of which was played at Sportsman's Park. Set against the backdrop of World War II, MLB's talent pool was seriously depleted, which was a seemingly perfect moment for the perennially dreadful Browns to capture their first and only American League pennant. The National League champion Cardinals, on the other hand, were a juggernaut, en route to their third consecutive World Series appearance. The underdog Brownies may have been "the people's choice," but the Cards were a force to be reckoned with. Jumping out to a big lead during the regular season—at one point, they ran up a gaudy 89–29 record—they finished with 105 victories and came into the fall classic as heavy favorites. Their strength was such that the *St. Louis Post-Dispatch* termed the Cardinals "[t]he only club in either league to be rated as approximating pre-war strength."

Sportsman's Park, located at Dodier Street and Grand Avenue in north St. Louis, played host to both clubs from July 1920 until the Browns moved to Baltimore after the 1953 season. The Browns owned the ballpark, which was located on a site that first hosted baseball games in 1866. The Cardinals, fronted by Anheuser-Busch scion August Busch, purchased the stadium in 1953, with the intent to rename it "Budweiser Stadium." The Browns, a franchise in perpetual financial disarray, signed a five-year lease, but would play only one season as tenants before relocating to Maryland where they became the Baltimore Orioles.

Even with the entire Series being contested in one place, wartime travel restrictions and gas rationing were a big theme. *The Sporting News* ran a series of license plate photos (with numbers and letters left unobscured) from states that included Georgia, Indiana, Oklahoma, and Florida, noting "[d]espite gasoline rationing and... restrictions against the sale of tickets to persons outside of the St. Louis area, a number of out-of-state-licenses were noted on cars parked in lots and streets around Sportsman's Park." The *Post-Dispatch* reported, "[a] staff of investigators was busy checking cars from distant points in Missouri, Illinois, and from other states."

There was also a national housing shortage in progress, which necessitated some creative approaches to living arrangements. Browns manager Luke Sewell and his Cardinals counterpart, Billy Southworth (along with their families), shared an apartment at Lindell Towers during the regular season. This situation worked out well; when the Cards were in town, the Browns were on the road. The Sewells temporarily vacated in favor of the Southworths and vice versa, on and off, all season long. Any leftover groceries became property of the incoming family, and the two skippers even shared a clothes closet. Something had to give with both clubs playing at home during the World Series, however, and Southworth and company vacated the apartment for the week. Similarly, the Browns and Cardinals rotated dugouts during the

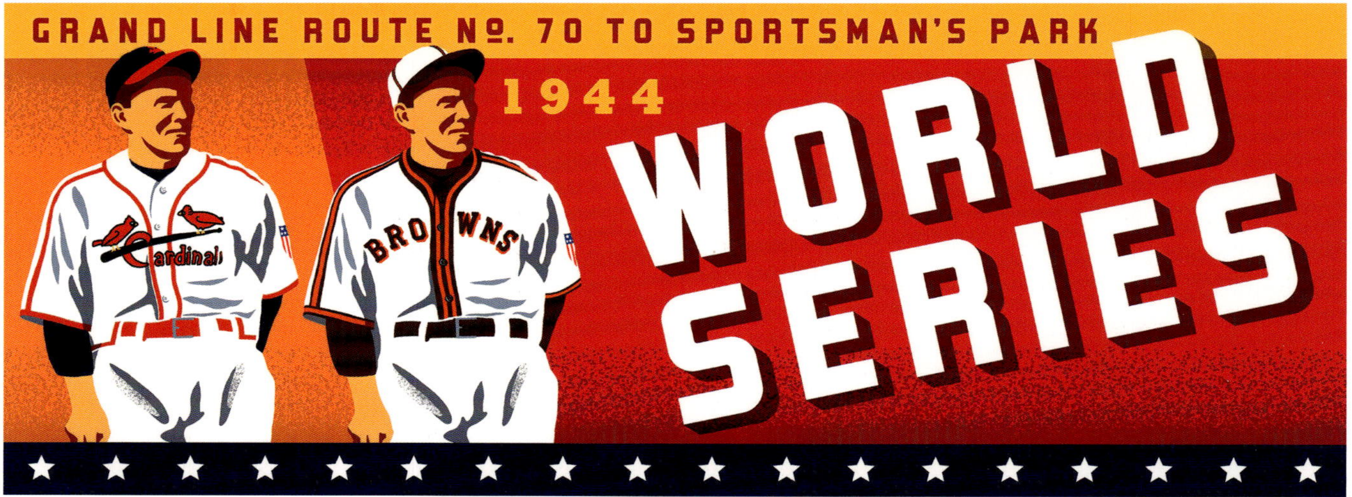

fall classic, with the NL champs designated as the home team for Games One, Two, and Six, and the AL champs gaining home status for Games Three, Four, and Five. Tickets for the Series shared a common design as well, with the Cardinals' home game stubs printed in red and blue and the Browns' in brown and red.

With the 1944 presidential election looming, both Republican vice presidential nominee John W. Bricker and the Democratic vice presidential nominee, Missouri Senator Harry S. Truman, attended the Series.

Interestingly, the 1944 World Series was the first in which every game was played west of the Mississippi River. It was also one of the last that was exclusively White—Jackie Robinson and teammate Dan Bankhead broke the World Series color barrier with the Brooklyn Dodgers three years later, in 1947.

With no travel required, the Series was played across six consecutive days, with each of the games taking place during daylight hours. Oddsmakers tapped the Cardinals as 9/5 favorites to win the Series, but the Browns put up a respectable fight.*

The American League champs took the opening game with a 2–1 victory, winning despite eking out but two hits. The National League champions bounced back in Game Two with an 11-inning walk-off 3–2 win. Game Three went to the Brownies, 6–2, but the Redbirds won the next three, allowing just two runs over those games, wrapping up the Series up with a 3–1 Game Six victory. One way or another, St. Louis was going to win and, for one week in October 1944, it was the undisputed mecca of baseball.

* Though the Cardinals had a decidedly better overall record, both teams had almost identical records at Sportsman's Park, with the Cards going 54–22 and the Brownies going 54–23.

A WAR ENDS, A CURSE BEGINS

By the time the major league season started in April 1945, the end of World War II in Europe was firmly in sight. Historic events seemed to unfold at breakneck speed each and every day that month, including the death of President Franklin D. Roosevelt on April 12, just days before the baseball season was scheduled to begin. For the third straight year, spring training had been held close to the sixteen major league club's home cities, an area confined to the boundaries north of the Potomac and Ohio Rivers and east of the Mississippi, in an effort to cut down on nonessential travel. The All-Star Game, which had been scheduled to be played at Fenway Park on July 9, was cancelled, as many of the game's brightest stars were overseas fighting for their country.

World War II in Europe came to an end on May 8, 1945. The war in the Pacific concluded on August 15, and the formal signing of Japan's Instrument of Surrender took place aboard the battleship USS *Missouri* in Tokyo Bay on September 2. Less than a month later, the Chicago Cubs—who had not won a World Series since 1908—took home their sixteenth National League pennant, the team's last postseason appearance until 1984. They lost the Series to the Detroit Tigers in seven games, and didn't make it back to the fall classic for another seventy-one years. Upon their discharge from active service, three Cubs players—Harry "Peanuts" Lowrey, Paul Gillespie, and Mickey Livingston—wore the honorable discharge insignia, also called the "ruptured duck," on the sleeves of their jerseys, beginning on July 12 at Wrigley Field. Their teammate Hiram Bithorn would join them on September 5. On July 21, New York Yankees pitcher Red Ruffing and catcher Aaron Robinson sported the patches in a game at Yankee Stadium. The Associated Press described the emblems as "Large sized duplicates of the badges former soldiers wear in their button holes."

VICTORY WORLD SERIES
CHICAGO
CUBS
1945

There's one other thing about the Cubs' 1945 World Series loss that needs to be addressed, and it's sort of the goat in the room.

On Saturday, October 6, 1945, William "Billy Goat" Sianis, owner of Chicago's Lincoln Tavern, brought his pet goat, Murphy, to Wrigley Field for Game Four of the World Series. Prior to the contest, Sianis paraded Murphy, who was wearing a blanket that proclaimed, WE GOT DETROIT'S GOAT, around the field. Cubs ushers and team officials, citing the animal's less-than-pleasing odor, denied the pair entrance to the grandstand, despite the fact that Sianis had paid $14.40 for two box seat tickets. After the Series, Sianis sent a wire to Cubs owner Philip K. Wrigley, which supposedly read, "Who smells now?"

Detroit beat the Cubs, 4–1, that day, squaring the Series at two games apiece, and legend tells us that Sianis

put a curse on the team, avowing, "Them Cubs, they ain't gonna win no more." The teams split the next two games, but the Cubs dropped the decisive seventh game, and didn't win it all until 2016, when they defeated Cleveland in an epic seven-game World Series, breaking the Curse of the Billy Goat for always and ever.

But there's an additional piece of information that would seem to indicate that there was actually no curse at all for the vast majority of that seventy-one-year span; just a lot of bad luck and bad baseball. In 1946, the Cubs dropped to third place. They finished in sixth the following year, and were dead last in 1948 and 1949. In September 1950, Sianis publicly declared, "Why didn't owner Phil Wrigley and vice president Jim Gallagher of the Chicago Cubs apologize to my goat and let their team win games again instead of staying in or near the basement? My goat is ready to accept the apology and take the hex off the Cubs." Time, as the saying goes, heals all wounds, and the prospects for a truce were strong. Wrigley wrote back to Sianis, "Please extend to Murphy my most sincere and abject apologies … and ask him to remove the hex." Sianis is said to have read the letter to Murphy, and poof! the "curse" was no more. An optimistic Gallagher said, "There's no telling what might happen in 1951 without the billy goat hex."

The Cubs finished the 1951 season with a 62–92–1 record, good enough for last place.

THE HOMESTEAD GRAYS

When it comes to history, the tiny borough of Homestead, Pennsylvania, punches well above its weight. For a century, it was home to the Homestead Steel Works, a sprawling complex whose employees literally helped build America. Located seven miles southeast of downtown Pittsburgh, Homestead sits on the south bank of the Monongahela River. It is connected to the southernmost tip of Pittsburgh's Squirrel Hill neighborhood by a bridge that was built in 1936 and renamed in 2002 as the Homestead Grays Bridge, in honor of one of the greatest franchises in the history of baseball.

The Grays started out as the Blue Ribbons, an amateur team of Black steelworkers, in 1900. They evolved into the Murdock Grays a decade later, and in 1912 became the Homestead Grays. Pittsburgh was booming at this moment in time, its population buoyed by newly arrived European immigrants and Black Americans who came north as part of the Great Migration. They labored in the steel mills, working unimaginable shifts. In 1911, the federal government reported that one third of steel workers toiled seven days a week, with fully a quarter of them working an eighty-four-hour workweek, which translates to twelve hours a day, every single day. Somehow, some of them found time to play baseball, joining amateur and company teams. The Grays played games against a range of local nines, including the Iron City Giants, the Homestead Steel Works team, the Clay Giants, the Melex Athletic Club, and the McBride Homestead Independents. At the same time, the National League's Pirates were soaring, winning four pennants in the first decade of the twentieth century.

The story of the Homestead Grays is intertwined with that of Cumberland Posey, a Homestead native who is enshrined in both the Baseball and Basketball Halls of Fame. Posey was the grandson of freed slaves and the son of Cumberland Posey Sr., a powerful Black businessman whose financial interests included steamboats, real estate, and coal. The younger Posey was a great athlete and one of the best basketball players of his day, playing collegiately at Penn State, the University of Pittsburgh, and Duquesne University. He began playing outfield for the Grays in 1911 and became the team's captain, manager, secretary, and, finally, owner by 1920.

Under Posey's stewardship, the Grays transitioned from amateur to semipro to pro ball. His club became both powerful and profitable, and his on- and off-field acumen garnered the attention of media and fans alike. At the conclusion of the 1922 season, the *Pittsburgh Post-Gazette* noted, "The Homestead Grays continue merrily on their way, disporting themselves almost daily and booking wherever they can find anyone to play. They have already gone through something like a hundred tilts and they'll probably add at least a dozen to that before they call it quits." The article went on to call Posey "an honest-to-gosh manager" who "deserves all the success that has come the way of himself and his outfit."

Posey's squad ran up gaudy records on an annual basis. Published reports of the time credited them with a record of 106–25–5 in 1923, 108–29–8 in 1924, 130–23–5 in 1925, and an astounding 140–13–10 in 1926. On June 10 of that year a team from Coshocton, Ohio, handed the Grays their first defeat of the season after Homestead opened the year with a reported 40 wins and four ties. One of America's top Black newspapers, the *Pittsburgh Courier*, referred to them as "Pittsburgh's Wonder Team" and openly speculated on whether or not they could beat the world champion Pirates. In October 1926, the Grays took two of three games from a team of American League All-Stars that included future Hall of Famers Goose Goslin, Lefty Grove, and Heinie Manush.

The previously unaffiliated Grays threw in their lot with the six-team American Negro League in 1929, but that circuit disbanded after only one season. The following year, they went back to being an independent club and picked up right where they left off, going 44–15–1. A legend stepped onto the stage for the first time on the night of July 25 of that season, when eighteen-year-old catcher Josh Gibson made his debut against the Kansas City Monarchs at Forbes Field in a 6–5 win. The Grays wrapped up 1930 by beating New York's Lincoln Giants in a 10-game eastern championship series, with the deciding games played at Yankee Stadium.

The 1931 Homestead Grays have been favorably compared to some of the greatest teams of all time. Their roster featured six future Hall of Famers: Gibson, infielder Jud Wilson, outfielder Oscar Charleston, pitchers Smoky Joe Williams and Bill "Willie" Foster, and the legendary hurler Satchel Paige, who pitched in one game for the club. Posey, who was inducted into Cooperstown as an executive, rounds out the group. The Grays are reputed to have won more than 140 games in 1931, winning more than 80 percent of their contests. Hammered by both the Great Depression and local competition in the form of the Pittsburgh Crawfords, Posey founded the East-West League in 1932, placing his team with seven other franchises in the new circuit, but the league folded midseason. The Crawfords were owned by businessman W. A. "Gus" Greenlee, who named them after his Crawford Grill club, located in Pittsburgh's Hill District. Greenlee ran the popular "numbers" game in Pittsburgh, the local street lottery which was estimated to bring $20,000 to $25,000 into his coffers every single day. He used that money to hire Charleston as the team's manager in 1932, and soon added Gibson and Paige, along with other stars such as Cool Papa Bell and Judy Johnson. The team played at the 7,500-seat Greenlee Field, the first Black-owned stadium in the Negro Leagues.

When the 1932 season concluded, *Pittsburgh Courier* journalist W. Rollo Wilson wrote that Posey had suffered "the most disastrous year of his baseball career." "He made enemies of men who had once been his best friends, he saw himself become the mighty somnambulist of a vanished dream when his personal league crashed about his head. He lost his grip on a profitable territory. He saw his club raided by the same ruthless methods which he had employed against other owners in the history years." Battered but undaunted, Posey took on a partner, Rufus "Sonnyman" Jackson, and the Grays joined the second Negro National League in 1933.

Their Pittsburgh rivals, the Crawfords, who once appeared to be an unstoppable force, ran into problems in

THE AMAZING
HOMESTEAD GRAYS

JOSH GIBSON ✵ BUCK LEONARD ✵ OSCAR CHARLESTON

3 X NEGRO LEAGUES
— WORLD SERIES —
CHAMPIONS

1937 when several key players, including Gibson and Paige, departed for the Dominican Republic to play for a team that was assembled by dictator Rafael Trujillo. Within a few short years the Crawfords moved to Toledo, Greenlee Field was demolished, and the franchise was disbanded.

Gibson returned to the Grays in 1937 and was paired with first baseman Walter "Buck" Leonard. The duo was dubbed the "Thunder Twins," and comparisons were appropriately made to Babe Ruth and Lou Gehrig. Just as those two sluggers ignited the great Yankees dynasty of that era, Gibson and Leonard ushered in a golden age for the Grays during which they won an astonishing nine consecutive pennants. The club also played in five of the seven Negro Leagues World Series, starting in 1942, when they lost to the Kansas City Monarchs. The Grays bounced back in 1943 and 1944 with wins over the Birmingham Black Barons, lost to the Cleveland Buckeyes in 1945, and defeated Birmingham in the final Series in 1948.

While Homestead and Pittsburgh represented the franchise's spiritual home, the Grays began splitting their schedule between Forbes Field and Washington, DC's Griffith Stadium in 1940. Just as attendance in Pittsburgh was declining, Washington offered up an enthusiastic and expanding Black community, with Griffith Stadium at the epicenter, located right next to the campus of Howard University. The club called themselves the Washington Grays or Washington Homestead Grays, and fans responded positively. Fate and a changing America would soon, however, intervene. Cumberland Posey passed away on March 28, 1946. Josh Gibson died of complications from a stroke on January 20, 1947—he was just thirty-five years old. Three months later, Jackie Robinson made his debut with the Brooklyn Dodgers, breaking baseball's color barrier. As Black players signed on to play with the previously all-White American and National League clubs, the Negro Leagues sputtered and finally died. The Negro National League closed up shop after the Grays' 1948 World Series win. The team continued to play on after the league dissolved, but on May 22, 1951, the Grays gave up the ghost. Cumberland's brother, Seward "See" Posey, who was running things at the time of the franchise's demise, described his club's diminished attendance and financial losses to the *Courier*. "I couldn't operate on dreams," he said. He died less than three months later.

Today, the legacy of the Homestead Grays remains intact and vibrant, both in Pittsburgh and beyond. Major League Baseball's 2024 decision to incorporate the stats of more than 2,300 Negro League players from 1920 to 1948 into its official records gives us new perspective on just how great Josh Gibson and his peers really were. The Homestead Grays Bridge spans the Monongahela River, connecting Homestead to Pittsburgh, a reminder of past glories and legendary figures.

CUBBIE ISLAND

Santa Catalina Island, located about thirty miles off the coast of Los Angeles, is known for its Mediterranean climate, stunning natural beauty, and charming coastal towns. There's a strong baseball connection there as well—for the better part of three decades, beginning in 1921, Catalina served as the spring training home of the Chicago Cubs.

The story of Catalina Island is tightly intertwined with the Wrigley family, starting with chewing gum entrepreneur William Wrigley Jr., who was part of a ten-person syndicate of Chicagoans that purchased the Cubs in 1916. He became majority owner some five years later. In between, in February 1919, Wrigley bought a controlling interest in the Santa Catalina Island Company, which owned the island. His $3 million investment, the equivalent of about $60 million today, got him 48,000 acres, 10,000 head of sheep, and a hotel. He soon sunk millions more into developing the place, adding infrastructure and attractions in an effort to transform it into a tourist mecca. These improvements included recreation facilities, tastefully designed hotels, and the Avalon Grand Casino, which included a movie theater and a ballroom.

Wrigley's marketing might was substantial, and in 1921 he moved his club's spring training site from Pasadena to Catalina. This arrangement helped to amplify both the Cubs and the Catalina brands, and soon, players were publicized taking part in many of the tourist activities that Wrigley was promoting, including horseback riding, fishing, birdwatching, and golf. "The Cubs Are Here! You Should Come Too" was employed as an all-purpose marketing tagline for the island. He created the all-inclusive spring training road trip experience that fans still enjoy today, more than a century later. Cubs players enjoyed a range of communal experiences there, including barbecues and parties at Wrigley's mansion, as well as an annual mountain-goat hunting expedition.

A revered Cubs tradition owes its roots to Catalina. When Wrigley purchased the island, the assets included the Wilmington Transportation Company, whose fleet ferried visitors back and forth from the mainland. Its logo was a blue flag with a white W. More than a quarter century later, when the Cubs renovated the bleachers at Wrigley Field, they added the now-familiar manual scoreboard, atop which sits a T-shaped naval style "yardarm." Soon thereafter the club began to fly a blue flag with a white W, signifying a Cubs win. While the colors were reversed in the 1980s, the team's famous victory flag originated at their one-time spring training home.

The Cubs' years at Catalina coincided with an era of great success, as the club won five National League pennants between 1929 and 1945. Some of the players who trained there included Hall of Famers Grover Cleveland Alexander, Rogers Hornsby, Dizzy Dean, and Hack Wilson. The island's proximity to Hollywood led to it becoming a celebrity destination as well, and, in 1936, a future president, young radio announcer Ronald Reagan, traveled to Catalina to cover the ballclub.

Wrigley died in 1932, but his love for the island was shared by his heir, Philip K. Wrigley, who continued to expand upon his father's vision. World War II travel restrictions kept the Cubs in the Midwest for three years, when they trained in French Lick, Indiana, and the team shifted their attention to Arizona at war's end. Drawn by the potential for more consistent weather, larger crowds, and easier travel, the Cubs received a sweetheart deal from civic boosters in Mesa and moved their training base there in 1952. It was a stone's throw from the Wrigley-owned Arizona-Biltmore resort and the New York Giants and Cleveland Indians, who had both set up shop there in recent years. In 1972, P. K. Wrigley transferred family ownership of the island to the Catalina Island Conservancy, a nonprofit organization established to protect and restore the island. The organization seeks to balance conservation and tourism, with 100 percent of all donations supporting nature conservancy, education, and recreation programs. Three quarters of a century after they left the island, the Cubs' legacy there remains vivid, if you know where to look for it. The Catalina Island Country Club, which opened in 1929, is still used by golfers who play the adjacent greens, but it also served as the Cubs locker room when the franchise held spring training there. You can enjoy a drink at the bar and take in its display of Cubs memorabilia and imagine what the place was like when the club camped out there, getting in shape, hunting mountain goats, and rubbing elbows with Hollywood royalty.

JACKIE ROBINSON, NEW YORK GIANT?

There are few players in baseball history who are as tightly connected to a single franchise as Jackie Robinson, but on December 13, 1956, the Brooklyn Dodgers did the unthinkable. Not only did they trade away the future Hall of Famer and franchise hero, they sent him packing to their most bitter rivals, the New York Giants. The deal, which shipped Robinson off to the Polo Grounds in exchange for journeyman pitcher Dick Littlefield and $30,000, sent shockwaves throughout the game, especially in New York City. History tells us that the iconic Robinson never played a game in black and orange, and, even now, the very idea of its seems almost blasphemous. When news of the trade leaked out, *The New York Times* quoted an anonymous Dodger fan who said, "I'm shocked. This is like selling the Brooklyn-Battery Tunnel. Jackie Robinson is a synonym for the Dodgers. They can't do this to us." Giants fans were equally stunned. The *Times* also included a comment from a Giants fan named Murray Waldman, who said, "I'm flabbergasted. First Durocher, now Robinson. How many enemies can we absorb?"

Robinson's final official at-bat took place on October 10, a strikeout that ended the 1956 World Series. A few weeks later, the Dodgers embarked upon a 19-game goodwill tour of Japan, which wrapped up in mid-November. On the evening of December 12, Dodgers executive Buzzie Bavasi phoned Robinson at his home in Stamford, Connecticut, to notify him of the trade. Giants owner Charles Stoneham also spoke with Robinson, who said that he was undecided about his future. When the news broke, a shocked Robinson expressed his disappointment, stating that trades were a part of baseball, and, at the same time, telling the *Brooklyn Daily*, "I'm hurt." He said that he would weigh his options, and was quoted as saying, "I'm going to do all I can for the Giants," while also noting that he might also retire. The next day, he invited the press to his home, where he posed for photos with his wife, Rachel, and their four-year-old son, David, while holding a Giants pennant, and said that their oldest child, Jackie Jr., wept at the news.

The Giants planned on playing Robinson at first base as a replacement for Bill White, who was busy fulfilling his military obligations. He would also help bolster the team's sagging home attendance numbers. As for Brooklyn, Robinson, who would soon turn thirty-eight, was the oldest regular on an aging Dodgers club that was looking to retool.

Imagine Willie Mays and Jackie Robinson as teammates? Mays sent Robinson a telegram which read, "I've always admired and respected your wonderful talents and ability. The knowledge that we will be teammates is an indescribable pleasure." It ended with, "It's one of my greatest thrills and happiest moments to be able to say, 'welcome Jackie to the Giants.'"

Unbeknownst to all, Robinson's outward ambivalence was part of a deliberate act of deception. Two years earlier, he signed a deal with *Look* magazine for the rights to his life story, which was to include an exclusive account of his eventual retirement. The pieces started to fall into place the previous summer, when Robinson decided to quit.

The account was to be published in the magazine's January 8, 1957 edition. In the article, which was succinctly entitled "Why I'm Quitting Baseball," Robinson wrote "I couldn't tell Mr. Stoneham I was through with baseball forever because I had agreed long ago to write this story—when the time came—exclusively for *Look*." Another opportunity was sealed just twenty minutes before Bavasi called to tell him that he'd been traded, when Robinson agreed to a full-time position as vice president for personnel relations at Chock Full O'Nuts, a New York restaurant chain.

The media's reaction to Robinson's misleading statements was harsh. He was accused of betraying the local newspapermen who had covered him for years by selling his story to a national magazine. He wrote, "Some people may now feel I haven't been honest with them these past few weeks when they've asked me about my plans. I've always played fair with my newspaper friends, and I think they'll understand why this one time I couldn't give them the whole story as soon as I knew it."

Robinson focused his bitterness on Bavasi, the Dodgers vice president who, in a series of barbed comments to *New York Daily News* columnist Dick Young, said, "That's typical of Jackie ... he tells you one thing and writes another for money."

If there was ever any doubt about his decision to hang it up, Bavasi's attack on the legendarily proud Robinson's integrity permanently sealed the deal. A clearly furious Robinson told reporters, "There isn't a chance in the world I'll ever put on a baseball uniform again." A few days later, he summoned the media to Chock Full O'Nuts' corporate offices, where he publicly dictated a letter to the Giants and Stoneham, expressing "sincere thanks" for their interest and understanding, and noting that his decision to retire had nothing to do with their team. "From all I have heard from people who have worked with you, it would have been a pleasure to have been in your organization."

Jackie Robinson was inducted into the National Baseball Hall of Fame on July 23, 1962. His bronze plaque reads, "Brooklyn, N.L., 1947-1956," with no mention of the New York Giants, the team that the Dodgers traded him to.

MICKEY MANTLE GOES YARD

The address is 434 Oakdale Place in Northwest Washington, DC. It's a tidy, two-story red brick two-bedroom home, built in 1913, with a porch and an ornate wrought iron door. Today, right across 5th Street NW, Howard University Hospital looms large. But on April 17, 1953, the site of the hospital was Griffith Stadium, the longtime home of the Washington Nationals (aka Senators) and, on that day there, Mickey Mantle hit what was purported to be the longest home run in major-league history. Legend has it that the ball carried out of the stadium and came to a stop in the backyard of 434 Oakdale Place. Yankees public relations man Arthur E. "Red" Patterson measured the distance at 565 feet, an attention-grabbing stroke of genius which gave birth to the new term, "tape-measure home run."

Like the legends of the Loch Ness Monster and Bigfoot, Mantle's shot is shrouded in mystery—but here are the facts. The twenty-one-year-old Mantle stepped to the plate in the fifth inning against lefty pitcher Chuck Stobbs and hammered his second pitch deep to left field. Aided by a strong tailwind, the ball sailed over the left field wall, 391 feet from home plate. It continued onward, over the 55-foot-high left-field bleachers—a feat that no batter had achieved in the history of the ballpark. It caromed off the right side of a huge National Bohemian beer sign and then it continued its journey out of the ballpark, giving the Yankees a 4–1 lead. Yogi Berra, who had drawn a two-out walk, scored ahead of Mantle. It was Mantle's first home run of the season, and was witnessed by a sparse early-season crowd of only 4,206 fans.

Here's where mythology enters the story. Patterson, recognizing the significance of what had just transpired, supposedly jumped up and raced out of the press box to follow the ball, declaring, "this one has to be measured." He soon returned, having claimed to have encountered a young man named Donald Dunaway, who was running down the street with a scuffed-up baseball. According to Patterson, Dunaway showed him where the ball landed, and he gave the kid either 75 cents, $1, $5, or $10. Patterson then paced the distance from where the ball allegedly came to a stop, back to the ballpark, and came up with 565 feet. Mantle doubted the accuracy of that number and, as the years went on, so did writers and physicists who assessed the blast. It has been written about and studied in detail and, given the dynamics and the time that has elapsed, it seems as if the truth will never be known. Somehow, applying modern Statcast metrics would spoil the story—as the saying goes, print the legend. Whatever the case, Patterson retrieved the ball and gave it to Mantle, who said that he would put it on display in his Oklahoma home. He soon had second thoughts, however, and the ball was turned over to the Yankees, who put it on view in the lobby of Yankee Stadium . . . where it was stolen a couple of months later. A week after the theft, three boys returned the ball, no questions asked, and the sphere was shipped off to Cooperstown, where it remains to this day.

Washington manager Bucky Harris, who piloted the Senators to their only World Series championship as a rookie skipper back in 1924, said that it was the hardest-hit ball he had ever witnessed. "I just wouldn't have believed a ball could be hit that hard," he told the *Washington Evening Star*. "I've never seen anything like it." Clark Griffith, Washington's eighty-three-year-old owner, broke into the major leagues in 1891—which is to say that, like Harris, he had seen a lot of baseball over the years. He told *The Sporting News*, "No doubt about it, that was the longest home run ever hit in the history of baseball."

The 1953 season was a big year for both Mantle and the Yankees. The Commerce Comet played in his first All-Star Game that summer, and his team won its fifth consecutive World Series, an unsurpassed accomplishment. The Senators relocated to Minnesota in 1961 and were immediately replaced by an expansion Senators club. Griffith Stadium was torn down in 1965, Howard University Hospital took its place in 1975, and Mantle passed away two decades later. A golden aura still surrounds Mickey Mantle, arguably the most celebrated athlete of his era, and while he hit 535 other homers over the course of his career, his colossal 1953 tape-measure home run stands apart as the stuff of legend.

THE END OF THE AFFAIR

In July 1895, the *Philadelphia Times* ran an article that included the following words: "Next to dodging trolley cars and wheeling baby coaches, the chief amusement of the citizens of Brooklyn … is in watching their baseball team play." Six decades later, Dodgers fans' fervor for their ballclub remained intense, even as they stoically faced the loss of their team—a seismic move west that has been grieved over, bitterly denounced, and written about ever since. In twenty-first century Los Angeles, Dodgers fans no longer dodge trolleys, but the relocation of their team from Brooklyn to LA still looms large in the public imagination, even as first-hand memories have faded away.

The Dodgers' final home game at Ebbets Field concluded at 10:17 on the evening of September 24, 1957. Although an official announcement of their impending move to Los Angeles had not yet been made, the die had long been cast. The neighborhood around Ebbets Field began to decline in the late 1940s and early 1950s. At that point, the ballpark itself was becoming structurally unsound, hampered by bad plumbing, narrow aisles, lack of parking, and its small capacity (32,000). Dodgers owner Walter O'Malley moved seven home games to Jersey City in 1956, and sold Ebbets to a local real estate developer for $3 million the same year. O'Malley leaned hard on New York City officials to help him finance and build a new, modern stadium for the club, but they would not play ball. On May 28, 1957, National League owners voted unanimously to allow the Dodgers to move to LA, in tandem with a shift of the New York Giants to San Francisco. This meant that New York would be without National League baseball for the first time since 1882.

Ebbets Field has been celebrated, mourned over, and practically obsessed about since it fell to the wrecking ball in 1960. The Mets' current ballpark, Citi Field, is a direct descendent of Ebbets, with its arched exterior, canopied entrance, and main rotunda directly drawn from its Brooklyn ancestor. While the Dodgers spent forty-five seasons at Ebbets Field, they have played at their current home, Dodger Stadium, for far longer. Regardless, the romance and lore of Ebbets is intrinsically tied to the history of baseball in the twentieth century.

ENTER GATE C
09 24 57
SEC. ROW SEAT
LOWER STAND $2.00
Dodgers
EBBETS FIELD
TUESDAY SEPT. 1957 24
Thank you for coming to Ebbets Field. The Ball club staff will show you every courtesy. Should you have a complaint, however, please give us the particulars.
Brooklyn Nat. League B. B. Club, Inc.
Walter F. O'Malley, President

It was built on the site of what was described as "a malodorous four and half acre slum" in the borough's Flatbush section. Its first game took place on April 9, 1913 (a loss to the Philadelphia Phillies), but what Ebbets represents goes well beyond any box score. Fans entered the ballpark via an elegant 80-foot wide, 27-foot-high rotunda, made of Italian marble. Fourteen ornately decorated ticket booths encircled the area, which was topped off by a chandelier that was composed of twelve baseball bat arms, holding twelve baseball-shaped globes. Its footprint was almost exactly square, and those dimensions came to define the fact that Ebbets Field was, at heart, a true neighborhood ballpark where the fans were always closely tied to the game.

The park was built by and named for then-Dodgers owner Charles Hercules Ebbets. Four days before the first official game at the new stadium, Ebbets penned a piece that was published in the *Brooklyn Daily Times*, in which he outlined the intense local connection between the park and its borough: "Ebbets Field is dedicated to Brooklyn baseball," he wrote. "It is a monument to the game in the cradle of baseball, as Brooklyn was known for years and years. It was built for Brooklynites by Brooklynites; it is essentially a Brooklyn institution."

The ballpark was expanded in the 1920s and '30s, at which time it took on the form that served as home to "The Boys of Summer," Brooklyn's legendary clubs of the post–World War II era. On April 15, 1947, Jackie Robinson stepped onto the Ebbets infield and made history as the first African American player in modern Major League Baseball. His arrival coincided with one of the most storied eras ever, as the club won six pennants over the next ten years, topped off by the franchise's first World Series championship in 1955.

A small assemblage of mourners showed up for the Dodgers' final home game in Brooklyn, a meager crowd of only 6,702 fans. Chris Kieran, writing in the *New York Daily News*, called it, "one of the most poorly attended wakes in the history of baseball." Longtime organist Goodding serenaded the fans with a range of emotional tunes, which included "California Here I Come," "Am I Blue," "After You've Gone," and "Auld Lang Syne." Thirty years later, Dodgers broadcasting legend Vin Scully told Associated Press writer Jim Donaghy, "She played such depressing music that it put a terrifically gloomy feeling on the ballpark." He expanded upon that in 2007, in comments made to the *Los Angeles Times*, saying "Gladys was a very nice lady, known to take a drink or three. . . . The very first song she played was 'My Buddy,' a pretty down song, and it went down from there. . . . The music kept getting more depressing every third out."

For the first time ever, the Dodgers kept the press box bar (itself a vestige of the *Mad Men* era) open until the game ended. When the team announced that it had surpassed attendance of over a million fans, one media wag quipped, "and the only team to leave town after doing it." Roy Campanella threw a little farewell party for the players and writers after the game, and the groundskeepers covered the field with a tarp. They turned out the lights, and the Brooklyn Dodgers slipped into history.

LET THERE BE LIGHT

In October 1879, Thomas Edison staged the first successful test of the electric lightbulb. Less than a year later, employees of the R. H. White and Jordan Marsh department stores played a night baseball game in at Nantasket Bay in Hull, Massachusetts, illuminated by a series of electrical lights that were mounted atop three 100-foot-tall towers. Night games, which were once a dream and then a novelty, are now, of course, a staple of professional baseball. In fact, it's difficult to imagine a world in which all games took place during the day. But, in the late nineteenth century, the official playing rules of the National League stated, "Every Championship Game must be commenced not later than two hours before sunset," and the bold idea of playing a major-league game under the lights would have to wait fifty-five years.

Like many great innovations, this involved a lengthy process and a steady progression of visionary individuals. One of the first was George A. Cahill, an inventor from Holyoke, Massachusetts, who devised a portable lighting system that he called the "Cahill glareless duplex floodlight projector." Cahill staged exhibition games under his lights at big-league parks in Cincinnati and Chicago in 1909 and 1910, which were generally well received. Upon witnessing a night game at his ballpark, Reds president August "Garry" Herrmann noted that some improvements were needed, but that "night baseball has come to stay."

Even with such interest, it took the Great Depression to finally shake baseball out of its daytime torpor. In the early 1930s, a handful of minor-league clubs began to install lights in their ballparks and immediately saw their attendance figures skyrocket. The Negro Leagues—always an incubator for marketing and experimentation—were instrumental in bringing night baseball to the masses. Kansas City Monarchs owner J. L. Wilkinson invested a considerable amount of money in a series of portable truck-mounted light towers that illuminated fields all across the country, transforming darkness into daylight.

Resistance to night games at the major league level continued, even as fans all across the nation were enjoying watching games under the lights. A 1933 *Sporting News* editorial flatly stated, "Night baseball appears to have run its course," adding "baseball is essentially and fundamentally a daytime game." Two years later, however, the paper grudgingly changed its tune, opining that

"Baseball was no more intended to be wholly a night game than daytime was meant for sleeping," but that economic circumstances, fan convenience, technical advances, and increased attendance numbers meant that there was no stopping night games from making it to the American and National Leagues.

The Cincinnati Reds had recognized the potential for night baseball decades earlier and, in December 1934, Reds executive Larry MacPhail led baseball's light brigade forward—his plaque at the National Baseball Hall of Fame in Cooperstown notes his pioneering role. MacPhail received the approval of National League owners to allow his club to play a maximum of seven night games in 1935 as a one-year experiment. The New York Giants, on the other hand, wanted no part of it. Citing the potential for flame-throwing pitchers to injure batters under the unfamiliar lights, Giants owner Charles Stoneham told *The Sporting News*, "I am against night baseball and have no intention of permitting the Giants to play it."

Cincinnati, a struggling club playing in a tiny market with a population of only 450,000, was ripe for experiment. General Electric set about installing a $50,000 system at Crosley Field, composed of eight towers with 632 lights. Finally, at precisely 8:30 p.m., on May 24, 1935, President Franklin Delano Roosevelt—seated in what was described as a comfortable chair at the White House in Washington, DC—pressed a ceremonial key which illuminated the park. A crowd of 20,422 fans, including George Cahill, cheered as the lights came on, after which the Reds defeated the Philadelphia Phillies, 2–1. MacPhail moved over to Brooklyn in 1938, and it was there that the Dodgers became the second club to stage games in the evening. Some teams followed suit, while others continued to hold out. Washington Senators owner Clark Griffith, who once scoffed at the viability of night games, soon came around, as did Philadelphia Athletics owner Connie Mack. The Detroit Tigers finally installed lights at Briggs Stadium in 1948 and, at long last, Wrigley Field got lights four decades later. On August 8, 1988, ninety-one-year-old Harry Grossman, a season ticket holder who attended the 1906 World Series between the Cubs and White Sox, pressed a button that lit up the ballpark, leading the crowd in chanting "let there be light." Much to the disappointment of all in attendance, the game was washed out by rain, but the Cubs played under the lights the following evening, thereby completing the long journey into night that began nearly a century before.

SPANNING THE GLOBE

レフティ・オドール
P
P

THE MAN IN THE GREEN SUIT

Francis Joseph "Lefty" O'Doul put up a season for the ages in 1929. After bouncing around between the majors and minors for the better part of a decade, he completed his first full campaign in the big-leagues in 1928, when he hit .319 in 114 games for the New York Giants. That offseason, New York traded him to the lowly Philadelphia Phillies for outfielder Fred Leach and "a heap of cash." The change of scenery clearly agreed with him. O'Doul's 1929 numbers were otherworldly—he hit for a .398 batting average and set a National League record with 254 hits (which still stands to this day), striking out only 19 times in 638 at-bats while launching 32 home runs and driving in 122 runs. He followed that up with another stellar season in 1930, hitting .383, after which he was traded to Brooklyn. Lefty O'Doul's journey to being an offensive juggernaut, however, was a meandering one. He began his career as a pitcher with the New York Yankees in 1919, but persistent arm injuries eventually forced a move to the outfield. He honed his offensive skills over the course of four seasons in the Pacific Coast League before he was picked up by John McGraw's Giants. Between 1929 and 1933, he recorded an astounding six five-hit games. He won two NL batting titles, appeared in the inaugural All-Star Game in 1933, and retired in 1934 with a stellar .349 career batting average.

Born in San Francisco's Butchertown neighborhood in 1897, O'Doul became one of baseball's all-time great ambassadors after his playing career ended. He was San Francisco through and through, an iconoclast who wore all green from head to toe—green suits, green ties, and green socks. His tombstone reads, "The Man in the Green Suit. He was here at a good time and he had a good time when he was here."

O'Doul opened up a bar and restaurant just as the newly relocated Giants were getting ready to start their inaugural season in San Francisco. Over the decades, it served up countless cocktails and meals to sports fans and celebrities alike, who were surrounded by a sea of memorabilia that focused on the colorful life of its proprietor and namesake.

Lefty's summer months were spent managing in the Pacific Coast League, both in his hometown with the San Francisco Seals, for 17 seasons, and for four other clubs at the tail end of his managerial career. He is credited with helping hone the hitting skills of another San Francisco native, Joe DiMaggio, who he managed with the Seals in the early 1930s, right before the Yankee Clipper achieved legendary status in the Bronx. O'Doul was renowned as one of the game's best hitting instructors—Dominic DiMaggio once said, "He could spot anything you were doing wrong in a minute and show you how to correct it. He was far and away the finest batting instructor that ever put on a baseball uniform."

O'Doul traveled to Japan with a group of major-league players in 1931, and this is where his legacy really took off. He returned the following year to instruct Japanese hitters, and continued to go back year after year, both before and after World War II. He enjoyed working with Japanese college players and wrote a manual that outlined the basics on how to create a baseball team, which included everything from tips on strategy to best practices for uniforms. He later told author Lawrence Ritter, "I kept going back and finally went to work organizing a professional set-up, like we have here. I'm the one who named the Tokyo Giants."

Indeed, almost nine decades later, that pioneering Japanese club still wears black and orange, the same colors worn by the New York and San Francisco Giants. In the late 1940s, O'Doul continued to foster goodwill, leading what was called the first peacetime cultural exchange of the postwar era.

A major celebrity in Japan, he was held in high esteem by everyone, from royalty on down. General Douglas MacArthur, who served as military governor of Japan following World War II, said, "Lefty O'Doul is the greatest Japanese ambassador America ever had." When Emperor Hirohito met with O'Doul in 1949, he told him, "It's a great honor to meet the greatest manager in baseball." An estimated crowd of one million Japanese admirers mobbed O'Doul and his visiting American team, led by Joe DiMaggio, when they arrived in Tokyo in October 1951, shouting, "Banzai DiMaggio! Banzai O'Doul!" In 1954, O'Doul and his wife, Jean, traveled to Japan with DiMaggio and his new bride, Marilyn Monroe, who were celebrating their honeymoon. Lefty's many goodwill tours generated an ongoing stream of contributions for Japanese charitable organizations, which was especially appreciated in the hard years that followed the war.

O'Doul passed away in his beloved San Francisco on December 7, 1969. Friends and admirers from across the globe mourned the loss, the organist played "Take Me Out to the Ballgame" at his funeral mass, and he was lauded as a quintessential fixture of his city, on par with the Golden Gate Bridge. In 2002, he was posthumously inducted into the Japanese Baseball Hall of Fame, becoming the first American to gain entry to that institution.

His globe-spanning legacy continues to resonate, especially in his hometown. In 1980, San Francisco's Third Street Bridge was renamed for O'Doul—it spans what is now McCovey Cove near the Giants' home field, Oracle Park, whose Lefty O'Doul Gate welcomes fans through the turnstiles. Today, more than a dozen MLB players hail from Japan, led by the sport's most celebrated superstar, Shohei Ohtani. It's safe to say that Lefty O'Doul would have approved.

OK BLUE JAYS, LET'S PLAY BALL!

The first words of the Rolling Stones' "Jumpin' Jack Flash" speak to having been "born in a crossfire hurricane." On April 7, 1977, the Toronto Blue Jays were born in a snowstorm, which delayed their first-ever game—against the Chicago White Sox at Toronto's Exhibition Stadium—by 18 minutes. A crowd of 44,649 fans, dressed in gloves and ski parkas and, according to the *Toronto Star*, "carrying thermos bottles full of hot coffee—or something," showed up to witness this auspicious event, regardless of the wintry conditions. Chants of "we want beer" reverberated throughout the ballpark, a protest against Ontario's then-ban on beer at public sporting events.

The weather wiped out the majority of the opening ceremonies, but the visiting White Sox players made the most of the delay. Chicago infielder Jack Brohamer used shin guards as skis and a pair of baseball bats for poles and cross-country skied across the infield, and a group of Sox players lined up in a football formation and threw a pass to outfielder Jerry Hairston, who danced as if he had just scored a touchdown. A five-man color guard of United States Marines came up from Buffalo for the event, but was left hanging in the Chicago dugout as the grounds crew cleared the field with a Zamboni, which had been borrowed from Maple Leaf Gardens.

Singer Anne Murray, bundled up in a red parka, came out and delivered a countrified version of "O Canada." Commissioner Bowie Kuhn was introduced (and booed) and, at precisely 1:48, the Toronto starter, veteran righty Bill Singer, threw a strike to Chicago's Ralph Garr, and the Blue Jays were off and running. All those chilled beer-less fans went home happy that day, as their home team combined for sixteen hits, including two home runs by rookie first baseman Doug Ault, as the Blue Jays beat Chicago, 9 to 5.

The weirdness of this inaugural game was played against the backdrop of the truly weird Exhibition Stadium, formally known as Canadian National Exhibition Stadium (or CNE Stadium), which played host to the Blue Jays for their first 968 home games, from 1977 until May of 1989. A total of 23 million fans attended games there, and most of them probably have stories that involve either the weather, seagulls, or their view (and, quite possibly, all three). Exhibition Stadium included seats with backs along the third-base line, while fans sitting along the top half of the first-base line had to settle for aluminum benches, which froze in the spring and fall and baked in summertime. A new scoreboard was added when the Jays arrived, and it was located 200 feet behind a removable outfield wall. Former Blue Jays team president Paul Beeston once told the *Toronto Globe and Mail*, "It wasn't just the worst stadium in baseball, it was the worst stadium in sports," noting the fact that, despite it all, it represented a home and a fresh start for a brand-new franchise.

The ballpark had a roof over the bleachers, but none over the grandstand, and the furthest reaches of that grandstand included seats that were a whopping 820 feet from home plate, over a sixth of a mile away from the batter. Adding to the strangeness of it all was the Flyer, a wooden roller coaster situated just beyond the right-field stands. Beginning with that first snowy game in 1977, playing conditions at Exhibition Stadium were subject to the varied whims of the weather gods. The ballpark was located hard by Lake Ontario, and the wind coming off the lake was a force to be reckoned with. On April 30, 1984, the Jays were scheduled to play the Texas Rangers, but strong winds coming off the lake caused the game to be postponed after only six pitches. Home-plate umpire Don Denkinger said, "behind home plate was like looking into a sandblaster." A half-inch of infield dirt that surrounded the bases was completely blown away before play was called. Two years later, fog was the star of the game. On June 12, 1986, Toronto's Kelly Gruber lofted a lazy fly ball toward a completely fogged-over outfield. The Detroit Tigers outfielders couldn't see the ball, which rolled all the way to the right -center-field wall for an inside-the-park home run. After a half-hour delay, the game was finally called with two outs in the bottom of the seventh, giving the Jays the win. Throughout the ballpark's tenure, seagulls descended in droves, much to the chagrin of Yankees outfielder and future Toronto World Series hero Dave Winfield, who inadvertently killed one with a thrown baseball in 1983.

Exhibition Stadium was the fourth sporting facility to have been constructed on the site of the Canadian National Exhibition, Canada's largest annual fair. The first structure was built in 1879, and the final version was built piecemeal over approximately three decades, starting in 1948. A multisport facility, the final significant renovation took place in anticipation of Toronto's eventual inclusion into Major League Baseball.

The Ex was meant to be a placeholder until something better could be built, and on May 28, 1989, the Blue Jays played their final game there before moving into the ultra state-of-the-art retractable roofed Skydome, now the Rogers Centre. Exhibition Stadium was demolished in 1999, and much of the site was replaced by the 28,000-seat BMO Field, home to Major League Soccer's Toronto FC. The parking lot just south of the current facility contains a series of plaques that mark home plate, first, second, and third bases—all of which were covered in snow on April 7, 1977, when the Toronto Blue Jays first took flight.

MONTRÉAL EST MAJEUR

On April 8, 1969, New York's Shea Stadium played host to the first international game in MLB history. At 2:12 p.m., Montréal Expos shortstop Maury Wills fouled off Mets pitcher Tom Seaver's first pitch of the season, and Canada officially entered the big-leagues. Opening Day is usually a time for pomp and celebration, but this one was a little different. Montréal Mayor Jean Drapeau threw out the ceremonial first pitch, and five members of the color guard from the College Militaire Royal in St. Jean, Québec presented the maple leaf flag. Canadian opera singer Maureen Forrester sang "O Canada" in both French and English, and Shea organist Jane Jarvis serenaded the crowd with French favorites "La Vie en Rose" and "C'est si bon." A group of fans seated near the Montréal dugout displayed a handmade banner, which read, "Expos Valleyfield, Que, est avec vous!"

Heading into the new season, the Mets had never won on Opening Day, having lost seven consecutive times since they entered the National League in 1962. This one would be no different. The freshly minted Expos jumped all over Seaver and the Mets' bullpen, pounding them for twelve hits—including three homers and five doubles—en route to an 11–10 victory. A total of 44,541 fans witnessed a three-hour-and-thirty-five-minute-long slog, and they could be excused for seeing the glass as half empty considering their team's laughingstock reputation up to that point. Despite the loss, New York manager Gil Hodges was optimistic, telling the press, "I still think this is a much better club than last year." He was proven right six months later, when his Miracle Mets shocked the baseball universe by winning the 1969 World Series.

Canada's arrival to the majors was a long time coming. The Tecumseh club of London, Ontario, became the first Canadian team to win a professional baseball title when they took home the International Association championship in its first season, 1877. The club applied for membership in the National League for the 1878 season, but London's population of 25,000 didn't align with NL requirements of 75,000 or more. Their application to join the NL was tabled, with news reports indicating that the prospects of small gate receipts wouldn't be worth the travel for visiting clubs.

As for Montréal, its baseball history similarly dates back to the late nineteenth century. In 1946, the minor-league Royals served as Jackie Robinson's final stop on his way to Brooklyn and baseball immortality. Long before landing the expansion Expos in 1968, Montréal flirted with big-league status on several occasions, with the first legitimate push occurring in the middle of the Great Depression. The Canadian economy was no different from America's in the early 1930s, but that didn't stop local interests from seeking to draw an MLB team northward. In 1933, the Cincinnati Reds drew an average of 2,763 fans per game, and the St Louis Browns played before an average of only 1,144. Although most teams struggled to draw spectators, clubs that shared a city with another team were hit especially hard as they fought one another for the hearts, minds, and scarce dollars of local

fans. Immediately following the conclusion of the 1932 World Series, rumors began to swirl, concerning a potential shift of the St. Louis Cardinals to Montréal. John McGraw, who had resigned as manager of the New York Giants several months earlier, was supposedly in on the deal. McGraw was whispered to have spent a week in Montréal that summer, advising Montréal Canadiens owners Joe Cattarinich and Leo Dandurand on a potential purchase. McGraw denied any involvement, and the move, of course, never happened.

On June 20, 1933, the *Montréal Gazette* reported that a deal was again in the works to move the Cardinals north of the border. Browns owner Phil Ball also owned Sportsman's Park, which served as home to both St. Louis franchises. He was reportedly willing to release the Cardinals from their lease, "believing that the city of St. Louis can no longer support two major league ball clubs." Again, the move never took place. Ball died on October 22, 1933, thus adding another layer of instability to the future of his already beleaguered franchise. Hector Racine, president of the minor-league Royals, chimed in the following month, stating that he was interested in purchasing a major-league franchise and moving it to Montréal. Two teams seemed to be on his radar—the Reds and the Browns—but both teams stayed put. In 1935, a plan was hatched to shift the distressed Boston Braves to Montréal, which was an attractive market by most measures. It was the largest city in the minors and its ballpark, Delorimier Stadium, was a modern facility that had many advantages over Braves Field. Again, a deal never happened.

By the early 1950s, it became evident that baseball's major-league map, which had been fixed in place since 1902, would soon change. Two-team setups in Boston, Philadelphia, and St. Louis were simply no longer feasible, especially with the postwar economy booming and a host of available cities out there waiting to be filled. The Browns were still floundering in St. Louis, and Montréal was again in the mix as they considered packing up and leaving. Brooklyn Dodgers owner Walter O'Malley, whose Royals held exclusive territorial rights to the city, said, "if Montréal has a chance to become major, I certainly would not stand in the way." A week later, the Browns officially departed for Baltimore. Montréal remained a candidate for big-league ball throughout the '50s and '60s until, finally, on May 27, 1968, it was granted a National League expansion franchise. The Expos' thirty-six MLB seasons ended with their relocation to Washington, DC, in 2005, but hope springs eternal in Montréal for a second act.

expos

BASEBALL AT THE SPHINX

We know that Hank Aaron hit 755 career home runs and that the New York Yankees have won more World Series championships than any other franchise, but can you name the Seven Ancient Wonders of the World?

The list, first complied more than two thousand years ago, consists of some of antiquity's most monumental manmade structures. They are the Hanging Gardens of Babylon, the Colossus of Rhodes, the Temple of Artemis at Ephesus, the Lighthouse of Alexandria, the Statue of Zeus at Olympia, the Mausoleum at Halicarnassus, and the Great Sphinx of Giza. Only the Sphinx, the oldest of the Wonders, survives. Located in the Egyptian desert, the Sphinx, a human-headed lion, was built somewhere around 2575–2465 BCE, which makes it 4,500 years old. It has borne witness to more than a million and a half days and nights, but the afternoon of February 9, 1889, surely stands out above all others.

That day, a group of about two hundred people witnessed a baseball game there, played between members of the Chicago White Stockings (today's Cubs), led by Cap Anson, and an all-star group of players from the National League and American Association, which called itself the All-America team. The game took place with Cheops—the tallest of the Egyptian pyramids—as a backdrop. The ballplayers traveled to the site via a caravan of twelve camels, fifteen donkeys, and three carriages. The Chicago club rode the donkeys, and the All-Americas were conveyed by the camels, which they found uncomfortable and unwieldy. This represented just one stop on a world tour that was organized by former player and sporting goods mogul Albert Spalding. The teams wound up traveling to five different continents and fourteen different countries over the course of their six-month journey, which began on October 20, 1888, and ended exactly half a year later, on April 20, 1889. The tour was designed to promote and popularize the still young sport of baseball, along with Spalding's business interests, and the teams played games in London, Rome, Paris, Hawaii, New Zealand, and Australia. Along the way they met Hawaii's King Kalākaua and the future King Edward VII of England.

The game at the Sphinx was described by Chicago's Jimmy Ryan, whose diary from the tour resides in the collection of the National Baseball Hall of Fame and Museum in Cooperstown. He wrote, "five innings satisfied us for the fine sand blowing into our eyes made them sore so we mounted our camels and donkeys and rode home to Cairo." *Sporting Life* described the game as having been "full of errors and perspiration." For the record, the All-Americas won, 9–6, and afterward the two clubs took turns trying to throw a ball over the ancient landmark, eventually alternating to see who could hit its right eye. "The ball would strike two thirds of the way up and return with vast bounds down the granite sides of the great monolith to the feet of the thrower," wrote New York Giants shortstop John Montgomery Ward in comments that he cabled to the *Chicago Tribune.*

SPALDING'S WOR
1
2
3
4
5
6
7
8
9
A
B
C
D
E
F
G
H
I
PACIFIC OCEAN
NORTH AMERICA
CHICAGO
ATLANTIC OCEAN
SOUTH AMERICA
UNITED STATES
HAWAII
SOUTH PACIFIC ISLAND
AUSTRALIA
EGYPT
ITALY
FRANCE
UNITED KINGDOM
CHICAGO VS. ALL-AMERICA

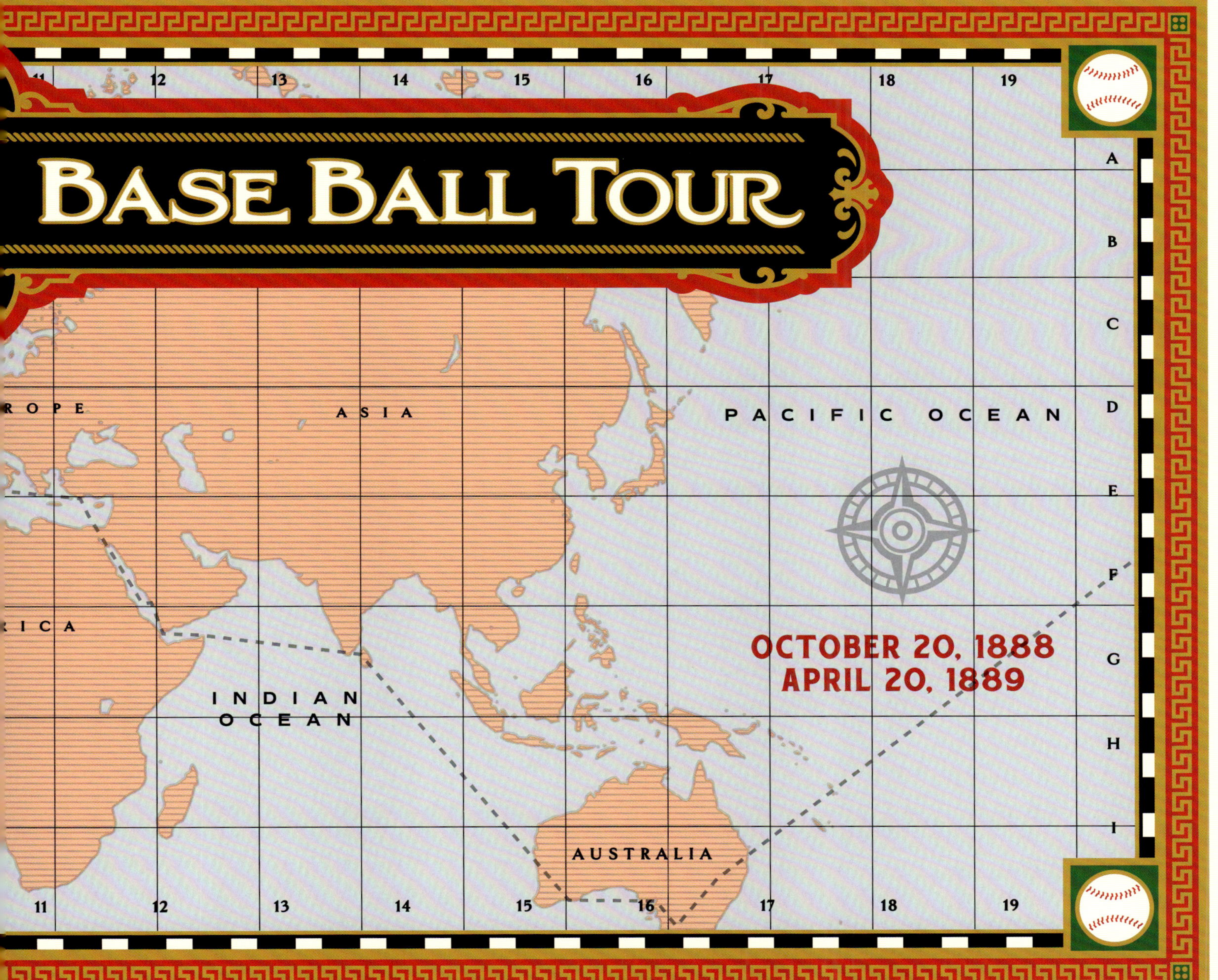

BASE BALL TOUR
ROPE
ASIA
PACIFIC OCEAN
RICA
INDIAN OCEAN
AUSTRALIA
OCTOBER 20, 1888
APRIL 20, 1889

Philadelphia Phillies outfielder Jim Fogarty was the only one to hit the mark.

A baseball from the game resides in Cooperstown, donated by that day's umpire, George Wright, baseball's first superstar, who excelled at shortstop for the Cincinnati Red Stockings twenty years earlier. Wright would go on to be immortalized in Cooperstown as part of its second class of inductees, in 1937.

After the game, the teams traveled to Naples and then on to Rome, where they set up a diamond on the grounds of the Villa Borghese and played seven innings. That match was reportedly witnessed by a crowd of five thousand spectators, including King Umberto I and his wife, Queen Margherita of Savoy. The clubs played a game on the banks of the Seine in Paris on March 8, with the unfinished Eiffel Tower serving as a backdrop. From there it was on to England, where a huge crowd turned out in London on March 12 to see what that city's *Morning Post* called, "the cricket of the United States." The Prince of Wales was in attendance, and when the assembled print media asked him what he thought of the sport, he asked for a pencil and paper and wrote, "The Prince of Wales has witnessed the game of Base Ball with great interest + though he considers it an excellent game he considers Cricket as superior." Chicago's next visit to the UK took place 134 years later, when the Cubs played a two-game series against the St. Louis Cardinals at London Stadium.

The tour continued on through England, Scotland, and Ireland, and on March 28 the group boarded the steamship *Adriatic* and sailed back home, arriving in New York nine days later. Baseball's greatest road trip continued on as the globetrotting squads were lauded with testimonial banquets and speeches. They played games in Brooklyn, Baltimore, Philadelphia, Boston, Washington, Pittsburgh, Cleveland, and Indianapolis, with the final contest taking place at Chicago's West Side Grounds on April 20, 1889. That day, Jimmy Ryan recorded the final entry in his diary:

> *To day we have completed the circumference of the globe, for six months ago to day we bid good bye to Chicago and entered upon our tour Around the World. We have given exhibitions of our National Game in every continent on the face of the globe and also thirteen foreign countries and travelled upward of a distance of thirty thousand miles. This afternoon as tourists we played our last game and a great crowd greeted us as we appeared upon our native diamond. The game concluded and so also did the greatest trip in the annals of sport, namely a Baseball Tour "Around the World."*

When it was all said and done, the Chicago and the All-American squads played 57 games and traveled some thirty thousand miles over half a year, but the most unique venue on the tour was undoubtably the Sphinx, which has silently stood watch over the Egyptian desert for millennia, a survivor of shifting sands, conquering armies, and a baseball that was hurled at it by a Phillies outfielder in 1889.

THE DISTANT PAST

BROOK 4
CINCY 8
ATL 0
ARI 3

3 BALL
0 STRIKE
2 OUT

ALL HAIL THE WHALES

For a brief, shining moment, Chicago played host to *three* major-league teams: the National League's Cubs, the American League's White Sox, and the last champions of the Federal League, the Chicago Whales. The Federal League started out as a six-team independent circuit in 1913, an "outlaw" league operating outside of Organized Baseball's official structure. A year later it added two more clubs and declared itself to be a third major league. The Feds, buoyed by a roster of deep pocketed team owners, raided American and National League rosters and competed against those established circuits in multiple cities, which made the AL and NL very angry indeed. Federal League magnates threw an enormous sum of money into their enterprise, inking established stars to generous contracts and constructing new ballparks.

The Windy City's Federal League franchise was owned by wealthy Chicago restaurateur Charles Weeghman. On December 29, 1913, he announced two splashy moves. Weeghman brought Cubs star Joe Tinker aboard to manage and play shortstop for his club, signing him to one of the largest contacts in baseball history up to that point, $36,000 for three years. Weeghman also announced his intention to construct a concrete and steel ballpark on the city's North Side, near Clark and Addison Streets. The park, originally called Weeghman Park, took less than two months to build, opening its gates on April 23, 1914. We know it today as Wrigley Field. The next day, the *Chicago Tribune* described the scene there, noting that "the windows and roofs of flat buildings across the way from the park were crowded with spectators," a North Side baseball tradition which still carries on well more than a century later.

Prior to the 1915 season, Weeghman's club, commonly referred to as the "Chi-Feds," ran a contest to select a more marketable and memorable moniker. A total of 289 suggestions were submitted, and D. J. Eichoff took home first prize with "Whales," a name that Weeghman liked because of its associations with athletic prowess and power, as well as its uniqueness. The Whales, bolstered by the pitching of former Cub and future Hall of Famer Mordecai Peter Centennial "Three Finger" Brown, beat out St. Louis by a single percentage point to cop the pennant.

The Federal League, not surprisingly, was hemorrhaging money by this point, and a series of negotiations commenced. On December 22, 1915, the three leagues announced that they had signed a peace treaty which effectively bought out four of the Federal League's franchises: Brooklyn, Buffalo, Newark, and Pittsburgh. The settlement took care of Weeghman, who was allowed to acquire a majority interest in the Chicago Cubs, as well as St. Louis Terriers owner Phil Ball, who was permitted to purchase the St. Louis Browns. The Baltimore Terrapins were cut out of the process. Spurned, Baltimore's owners decided to sue Organized Baseball, alleging that the NL and AL had conspired to

Chicago Federal League Baseball Club

monopolize the business of pro baseball in violation of the Sherman Antitrust Act. A jury trial decided in favor of Baltimore, but appeals soon followed. Then, in 1922—seven years after the Federal League had officially disbanded—the United States Supreme Court overturned the verdict, ruling that baseball was exempt from antitrust laws, a decision that has kept potentially competing leagues at bay ever since.

Per the December agreement, Weeghman would purchase 90 percent of the Chicago Cubs from Charles Phelps Taft, half brother of former President William Howard Taft. At precisely 2:31 p.m., on the afternoon of January 20, 1916, Weeghman handed over a check for a cool half a million dollars to John G. Wakefield, the assistant cashier of the Corn Exchange Bank. The proceedings were held up due to the fact that Weeghman's check had originally been made out to Taft, as opposed to the bank, which held the shares in trust. Weeghman and a group of associates walked over to the Fort Dearborn Bank, procured a new cashier's check, and closed the deal. He brought Joe Tinker in as Cubs manager and merged a chunk of his Whales roster with that of the Cubs. The Cubs adopted new uniforms, and they bore an exceptionally close resemblance to those worn by the Whales the previous season—a whale within the "C" was replaced by a bear within the letter "C." Weeghman moved the Cubs from West Side Park, their home since 1893, to his North Side park—now Wrigley Field—where they have played ever since. The Chicago Whales' short lifespan thus gave way to a long legacy, more than a century after they last spouted.

AFTER THE FIRE

On October 9–10, 2024, Hurricane Milton slammed into Florida's Gulf Coast, pummeling the region with sustained Category 3 winds of more than 100 miles per hour. The fiberglass roof of St. Petersburg's Tropicana Field, the home of the Tampa Bay Rays, was torn off in the process, forcing the club to temporarily relocate to Tampa the following season, when they played their home schedule at George M. Steinbrenner Field, the spring home of the Yankees. All of this brings to mind a somewhat similar scenario that played out a century and a half earlier, when the Chicago White Stockings—today's Cubs—had to flee their home after the Great Chicago Fire, which decimated the Windy City precisely 153 years to the day before Milton bore down on St. Pete.

The Rays regrouped, but the White Stockings disbanded for two seasons while Chicago was busy rebuilding. The White Stockings began play in 1870 and became charter members of the National Association—baseball's first professional league—the following season. They rejoined the NA in 1874 after a two-year absence, and, led by club president William Hubert, became founding members of the National League in 1876.

The 1871 White Stockings were strong contenders, right up until the moment that the flames devoured more than three square miles of the city of Chicago, including their ballpark. They had played their home games at the Union Base-Ball Grounds, located right in the heart of the Loop, in what is now the northeast corner of Millennium Park, steps away from "Cloud Gate," the reflective silver "bean" sculpture that is one of the city's most popular tourist attractions. On October 7, the team played its last home game of the year, an exhibition against a local nine. Two days later, the White Stockings were scheduled to play the Rockford Forest Citys, a team led by nineteen-year-old rookie third baseman Adrian Constantine "Cap" Anson, playing the first of his 27 professional seasons. As the Rockford club's train approached Chicago, the players saw a heavy layer of smoke hanging over the entire city. They turned back.

Like so many Chicagoans, the White Stockings' players lost everything but the shirts on their backs. The team decided to leave the city when conditions permitted in order to play a series of games in the east, but the road trip was hampered by bad weather. On October 21, they played a game in Troy against the Haymakers, wearing mismatched, borrowed uniforms and won, 11–5. After a loss to the Haymakers two days later, the White Stockings moved on to Brooklyn's Union Grounds for an October 30 game that would decide the pennant. A crowd of some 2,000 spectators braved a chilly late October afternoon and watched the Philadelphia Athletics defeat Chicago, 4–1, to win the flag. The Chicago team's appearance caught the eye of a writer from the *Cleveland Ledger*, who reported, "One man wore a Mutual shirt and Eckford hose, another an Atlantic shirt, Mutual pants and Flyaway hose, and so on, each man being obliged to borrow a suit from anyone who was willing to lend." The game's final putout was recorded by thirty-nine-year-old Nate Berkenstock, who was playing in his only professional

CHICAGO
EST. 1870
WHITE STOCKINGS
TWENTY-THIRD STREET
GROUNDS

game. Berkenstock, the Athletics' team treasurer and a former amateur player, was called out of retirement to replace an injured outfielder that day. Born in 1832, Berkenstock is the earliest-born professional baseball player.

The White Stockings' stockholders met in Chicago on November 11 and formally decided to disband their club, deciding that "it would be in bad taste" to field a team while the city was still suffering. As the *Chicago Tribune* noted, "The year 1872 will be a season of work in Chicago—hard, unceasing work for everybody, and we shall have little time to devote to amusement, the enjoyment of which takes an entire afternoon." The club then released its players from their contractual obligations and went into a two-year coma.

As the city recovered, a group calling itself the Phoenix Base Ball Association met on the night of April 6, 1872. The purpose of the group, a "copartnership of gentlemen," was to raise capital "to secure and maintain grounds for the playing of base ball" in Chicago, with an eye toward an eventual return to the professional ranks. A week later, they changed their name to the Chicago Base Ball Association. The organization went right to work and their new ballpark, located at 23rd and State Streets, hosted a game between the National Association's Baltimore Canaries and Cleveland Forest Citys on May 29. It was constructed in a mere three weeks. The first baseball game to take place in the city since the fire, it was noted that a crowd of 4,000 "enthusiastic" Chicagoans were in attendance.

On August 16, 1873, a crowd of some 6,000 fans (according to the *Tribune*), came out to watch Philadelphia take on the Boston Red Stockings (today's Atlanta Braves). Most importantly, as the *Tribune* floridly reported, an announcement was made stating that "Chicago was to have next season a nine of her own, worthy of her, and that it was to consist principally of that fine collection of skill and muscle which two years ago fought upon the diamond-field for the supremacy of Chicago in base ball, as her citizens are doing elsewhere for her ascendancy in everything else." In other words, Chicago would be back in the big-leagues in 1874.

Just as the city was being reconstructed, the club made plans for its own revival. The ballpark was readied for the return of the White Stockings, and the *Chicago Weekly Post and Mail* reported that the grandstand would be furnished with 1,800 "settees with backs and arms, and will, in point of comfort, much resemble those of any well-appointed theatre." There was also a press box, which the paper called a "reporter's castle." "A bell will be placed directly over this temple of the gods, and when the time for the game to begin arrives, a cord will be pulled by the bloodthirsty sporting reporter of The Journal, and the nines will at once take their places on the field." The first home game took place on May 13, 1874, and a crowd of between five and six thousand fans watched the White Stockings whitewash the Philadelphia Athletics, 4–0, but the 1874 season proved to be a challenging one for Chicago—they finished with a record of 28 wins and 31 losses.

The 1875 season was not much better, but when the club joined the newly formed National League the following year, they hit their stride, going 52–14 to win the inaugural NL pennant. The White Stockings nickname gave way to Colts in 1890, and then to Cubs a dozen years later. The team's two-year hiatus represents a small blip in their expansive history, one that has survived a conflagration and a curse over two leagues and a century and a half.

HARTFORD & LOUISVILLE'S LAST STAND

The year 1876 was a momentous one for America. On March 7, inventor Alexander Graham Bell received a patent for the telephone. The nation celebrated its centennial on July 4, and, less than a month later, on August 1, Colorado was admitted to the union as the thirty-eighth state. The same day, Wild Bill Hickok was killed while playing poker at Nuttal and Mann's Saloon No. 10 in Deadwood, in the Dakota Territory.

In baseball news, 1876 marked the birth of the National League of Professional Baseball Clubs, with eight teams forming its inaugural roster. The *Philadelphia Times* hailed the news, stating that the new circuit had the potential to help lift "the unfavorable and destructive surroundings" that had been dragging the professional game down. Gambling, franchise instability, and the lack of central leadership all contributed to the demise of the league's predecessor, the National Association. America was in the midst of enormous change at this time, but baseball was already being referred to as the "National Pastime."

On June 25–26, 1876, the Battle of the Little Bighorn—commonly referred to as "Custer's Last Stand"—took place in what is now southern Montana. On the last day of the battle, 1,500 miles away in Louisville, Kentucky, a crowd of 1,200 fans watched the Hartford Dark Blues beat the Louisville Grays, 3–0. Hartford scored all their runs with two outs in the sixth inning, Louisville made seven errors that day, and both teams would be bounced out of the league the following season.

Originally a National Association team, the Dark Blues were principally owned by Morgan Bulkeley, the National League's first president and later governor of Connecticut. Hartford's most celebrated resident, Mark Twain, was a fan of the club. On May 18, 1875, Twain attended a game between his hometown team and the Boston Red Stockings. Boston trounced the Dark Blues, 10 to 5, and to add insult to injury, Twain's umbrella went missing. Two days later he took out an ad in the *Hartford Courant*, which read:

> *TWO HUNDRED AND FIVE DOLLARS REWARD—At the great base ball match on Tuesday, while I was engaged in hurrahing, a small boy walked off with an English-made brown silk UMBRELLA belonging to me, and forgot to bring it back. I will pay $5 for the return of that umbrella in good condition to my home on Farmington avenue. I do not want the boy (in an active state) but will pay two hundred dollars for his remains. SAMUEL L. CLEMENS*

The club was managed by temperamental third baseman Bob Ferguson, whose defensive prowess inspired the excellent nickname "Death to Flying Things." The Dark Blues featured two future Hall of Famers—pitchers Tommy Bond and Candy Cummings, the latter of whom is often cited as the inventor of the curveball. They were also innovators in the ways of cheating, reportedly placing a man in a small shack attached to a telegraph pole to alert their batters to incoming curveballs. Hartford finished with a very respectable 47–21 record in 1876—good enough for second place in the new league—but they were unable to draw fans, so they moved to Brooklyn the following season in hopes of improved gate receipts. In 1877, the team became "The Hartford Club of Brooklyn," which was sort of the "Los Angeles Angels of Anaheim" of its time. The *Hartford Courant* opined that the new moniker was a solid choice, "thus retaining the prestige of the old name and awaiting the prestige which comes from locating in a large city." The team played their home games at Brooklyn's Union Grounds, which was, arguably, baseball's first important ballpark. It was the game's first fully enclosed baseball stadium where, during its debut on May 15, 1862, in the middle of the Civil War, the earliest documented performance of "The Star-Spangled Banner" at a sporting event took place. Whatever the case, the team washed out after a single year in Brooklyn, and were denied readmission by the league after the season, doomed by an absence of fan support in two different cities and the lack of a suitable plan to proceed forward.

*

The Louisville Grays are noteworthy for one very significant event, which resulted in the collapse of the franchise: a game-fixing scandal that involved four players—Bill Craver, Jim Devlin, George Hall and Al Nichols—all of whom were expelled by the league for life. In mid-August of 1877, the Grays were, in the words of the Louisville *Courier-Journal*, "marching on with steady step" toward the National League pennant, consistently winning and playing close to .700 baseball. They held a four-game lead over the St. Louis Brown Stockings and a four-and-a-half-game lead over Boston, but stumbled their way through an eastern road trip that the *Courier-Journal* termed, "disastrous, ignoble, and disgusting." The games included suspicious errors, poor pitching, and bad situational hitting, and the newspaper's August 21 game report was headlined, "!!!-???-!!!"

The Grays wound up going winless over the course of nine games, eventually finishing in second place, seven games behind Boston. Late that month, team vice president Charles E. Chase received a series of anonymous telegrams which advised that he keep an eye on his players. Chase initiated an investigation, which uncovered damning evidence that his players had been tanking ballgames. In October, he called a meeting and confronted the entire team, and the nefarious details rapidly began to unravel. Hall, believing that Devlin had already spilled the beans, confessed. The club's board of directors soon met and heard the evidence and, with the backing of league president William Hulbert, voted to expel Hall, Craver, Devlin, and Nichols. The league then met in early December and permanently barred them from all of professional baseball. The following March 7, the Grays withdrew from the league, "unable to secure a team efficiently strong to cope with other nines." However, the truth is that the franchise was irrevocably tainted by the scandal. The *Courier-Journal* noted, "The disgust created in this community by the development of the rascality of last year's players."

At the conclusion of 1876, *The New York Times* noted, "The year now passing has been a busy one," adding that future generations might remember it "for the beginnings of things therein." A century and a half after those words were written, the National League endures and prospers, despite the unhappy demise of the Hartford Dark Blues and the Louisville Grays.

THEY BROKE THE SPIRITS OF SOME FINE MEN

They were both terrors and innovators on the field, and they were champions of the National League for three straight years in the 1890s. The Baltimore Orioles—no relation to the present team—played hard and dirty, and they perfected and popularized tactics like the hit and run, the cutoff play, and the sacrifice bunt. They leaned into pitches in order to get on base—the 1898 squad combined to be hit by pitches an incredible 160 times in 154 games. Even as they revolutionized the game and dominated the sport, their unsavory reputation remains the stuff of legend.

The Orioles' 1894 roster featured no less than six future Hall of Famers: Hughie Jennings, Joe Kelley, Wilbert Robinson, Dan Brouthers, Wee Willie Keeler, and the heart and soul of the operation, John McGraw. They were managed by another Hall of Famer, Ned Hanlon, who was the father of "inside baseball," emphasizing aggressive play, speed, and a disciplined approach to the game. Part of this style was, in fact, blatant cheating, with some of their tactics including baiting umpires and blocking opposing runners from reaching base. The 1896 club reputedly hid spare baseballs in the outfield, which they snuck into play when a hit got past them. McGraw, playing third base, was known for hooking his hand inside the belt loop of baserunners just as a fly ball was hit to the outfield (at the time, there was only one umpire, so he usually got away with it).

How incorrigible were they? The words of contemporary observers help tell the story. In a June 1894 column in the *Boston Globe*, former player turned sportswriter Tim Murnane called the Orioles out for "playing the dirtiest ball ever seen in this country." Their transgressions included "diving into the first baseman long after he has caught the ball, throwing masks in front of the runner at the home plate," and more. Many years later, author Fred Lieb quoted John Heydler, an NL umpire who later became the league's president: "They were mean, vicious, ready at any time to maim a rival player or an umpire, if it helped their cause. The things they would say to an umpire were unbelievably vile, and they broke the spirits of some fine men."

Their gamesmanship even extended to their groundskeeper, Tom Murphy, who loaded up the area around home plate at Union Park with hard clay. Speedy Baltimore batters were famed for swinging down on the ball, straight into the cement-like infield, which resulted in high bounces that allowed them to reach first base safely before infielders could throw them out—a play which is still referred to as the "Baltimore Chop."

The diminutive Keeler batted .424 in 1897, which included an astounding 239 hits in just 129 games. Renowned for putting the ball in play, Keeler's famous advice for hitting—which he revealed to the *Brooklyn Eagle* in 1901—still rings true: "Keep your eye clear, and hit 'em where they ain't. That's all."

CHAMPION BASE-BALL CLUB OF THE UNITED STATES

BALTIMORE 1894-5-6

Along the way, the Orioles won NL titles in 1894, 1895, and 1896. League attendance dropped sharply in 1898 due to national concerns over the Spanish-American War, which adversely affected the circuit's bottom line. This was an era of "syndicate baseball," whereby owners were permitted to control interests in multiple clubs. In Baltimore's case, they merged with the Brooklyn Bridegrooms in a single 1899 transaction in which nine Baltimore players were assigned to Brooklyn, including Keeler, Jennings, and Kelley. Hanlon went to Brooklyn as well, and the team would soon become known as the Brooklyn Superbas, a play on "Hanlon's Superbas," a world-renowned entertainment troupe. (By this time, the club was already being referred to as the "Trolley Dodgers," a moniker which followed them to Los Angeles nearly six decades later.) Baltimore finished a respectable fourth that year but, ultimately, the only thing that could stop the Orioles was the National League itself. The league consisted of twelve teams at this point, the result of the 1892 merger between the NL and American Association. Very few clubs were profitable as a result of this unwieldy arrangement; travel expenses were bloated and syndicate baseball contributed to the league's extreme lack of competitive balance. Additionally, Ban Johnson and his Western League—soon to renamed as the American League—were making moves to threaten the National League's status as the sole major loop. After the 1899 season, discussions to reduce the NL from twelve teams to eight commenced, and on March 8, 1900, the Orioles, along with the Cleveland Spiders, Louisville Colonels, and Washington Senators, were contracted out of the league. The Baltimore franchise was sold off for $30,000 and was given the right to dispose of its roster. A new century and a new season dawned, but the incorrigible Orioles were relegated to extinction.

GOTHAM CITY

This embroidered emblem was featured on the fronts of the first jerseys worn by the team that we now know as the San Francisco Giants.

The Giants' story begins in New York City, but a number of early clubs preceded them. The sport developed in New York, an urban game that begat teams such as the Gotham and Knickerbocker clubs, two pioneering entries that were formed when the city was undergoing a period of rapid and dynamic growth. Brooklyn, a separate municipality that was consolidated into Greater New York in 1898, played host to the Excelsior Club, the Atlantics, and the Eckfords, who were founded 1855 by a group of shipwrights and dock laborers employed at Eckford and Webb's shipyard. The baseball club evolved into a social club—they played their final game in 1872, but continued on as a social organization until the mid 1950s.

The New York Mutuals, boosted by the patronage of the corrupt Tammany Hall political machine, were charter members of both the National Association—the first professional league—in 1871, and the National League in 1876. The Mutuals were bounced out of the NL after just one season—expelled, along with the Philadelphia Athletics, for their refusals to make late-season road trips through the circuit's westernmost cities.

Six seasons later, New York and Philadelphia—America's two largest cities at the time—still found themselves conspicuously absent from the roster of NL clubs, yet tiny Worcester, Massachusetts, and Troy, New York, were in. Challenged by the upstart American Association, National League owners took decisive action, effectively dumping Worcester and Troy in favor of New York and Philly, and, just like that, today's Giants and Phillies were on their way.

It's an understatement to say that 1883 was a momentous year in New York. The Brooklyn Bridge opened to the public in May, uniting Manhattan with Brooklyn after fourteen years of construction. The Metropolitan Opera

Company was founded, and funds were raised to erect the pedestal that the Statue of Liberty would soon be placed upon, in New York Harbor.

The New York club, commonly referred to in the press as "the New-Yorks," complete with era-appropriate hyphen, wore the emblem of their city on their jerseys, spectacularly embroidered in silk in a dazzling array of colors and laden with a ton of details. The device included, among other things, a shield depicting the sails of a windmill, flanked by flour barrels on either side, beavers above and below, all topped off by a majestic eagle. A sailor stands at left, holding a lead plummet, used for measuring water depths. At right is a Native American, with the words *New York* and *League* anchoring the insignia down. This embellishment was especially noteworthy for its era, a moment when most teams wore uniforms with little or no decoration at all. The club completed the outfit with crimson caps, along with crimson and black stockings, although the press assigned various descriptors to the red color, including maroon, magenta, and "crushed strawberry."

National League baseball returned to New York at 4 p.m. on May 1, 1883, with 15,000 fans—including former President Ulysses S. Grant—packing the Polo Grounds for the festivities. The New-Yorks took the field, the Seventh Regiment Band struck up Handel's "See the Conquering Hero Comes," and the home team defeated Boston by a score of 7 to 5. Two years later, they picked up the nickname "Giants," which they have been known by ever since. The team played more than 10,000 games in New York over the course of 75 seasons before relocating to San Francisco in 1958. Their current uniforms harken back to the ones that they wore when they left New York nearly seven decades ago, but their first set expressed a sense of civic pride in undeniably stylish fashion that would put twenty-first century City Connect jerseys to shame.

THE GREATER NEW YORKS

They are considered the greatest dynasty in the history of the sport, but their beginnings were decidedly humble. The team now known as the New York Yankees emerged from the ashes of the Baltimore Orioles, a club with a short and rather complicated history. While some have directly connected the Yankees to these Orioles, the truth is that these really are two separate clubs. Only five of the thirty-nine 1902 Baltimore players went on to play in New York in 1903, and the Yankees don't recognize the Baltimore Orioles in their official team records.

The American League declared itself a major circuit in 1901, with eight clubs in eight cities—including Baltimore—but the long-term prosperity of the league really hinged upon having a club in New York, which the AL was lacking. The franchise that we now know as the Yankees was officially born on January 10, 1903, following a meeting of the National and American Leagues in Cincinnati. After two years of feuding, the two leagues reached a peace agreement that included a unified set of playing rules, the formalization of contractual arrangements between leagues, players, and teams, and the establishment of an AL club in New York. This was not an easy birth by any means, but the franchise was conveyed to a group of politically connected New York investors for the bargain price of $18,000, the equivalent of close to $700,000 today. The public face of the operation was Joseph Gordon, a Tammany district officer, former state assemblyman, and Manhattan coal broker.

As the saying goes, follow the money. In this case, the parties in question were Frank J. Farrell, who was widely known as "The Pool Room King of New York," and William S. "Big Bill" Devery, the fabulously corrupt former chief of police of the city of New York. A few months before they purchased the ballclub, *The New York Times* reported on a lawsuit involving Farrell: "Frank J. Farrell, whose name has been mentioned often in connection with New York gambling institutions, and who is known as a friend of ex-Chief of Police Devery, testified on the witness stand in the Supreme Court yesterday that he had never been inside a poolroom and did not know what such a place was like."

Led by manager Clark Griffith, the Greater New York Baseball Club made its debut on a raw, chilly afternoon, April 22, 1903, in front of a crowd of some 10,000 spectators in Washington, DC. They lost, 3 to 1.

For their inaugural game, they wore these navy blue road uniforms, which were described by *Sporting Life* as "the swellest things in the business." Pinstripes would come later, but this is the jersey that they sported for the very first game in franchise history. They finished the 1903 season in fourth place (with a 72–62 record), seventeen games behind pennant-winning Boston.

The Greater New Yorks, widely referred to as "Highlanders," played at American League Park, widely referred to as Hilltop Park, located in the Washington Heights neighborhood of upper Manhattan. The hastily constructed new team considered a range of potential

N Y

roped off owing to the ongoing excavation, and fans sat atop rocky outcroppings. The *Washington Evening Star* described the scene: "These fields ended a short distance back of second and first bases in an abrupt decline, the bottom of which was twenty feet or so below the level of the diamond." Regardless of the jerry-rigged conditions, the home team won—defeating Washington, 6–2—and the fans went home happy.

playing sites, including Flushing, Queens—not far from today's Citi Field—as well as several sites in Harlem and the Astor estate at 161st Street and Jerome Avenue in the Bronx—the future site of Yankee Stadium. Instead, they entered into a ten-year lease with the New York Institute for the Blind for the land, and immediately got to work.

The ballpark was a spartan affair, constructed in only six weeks, which included a painstaking excavation of the exceptionally rocky site, which included a swamp in right field. Construction, however, proceeded at a breakneck pace. On March 14, 1903, the *New York Tribune* published a photo of what the site looked like, describing the "trees, some more than two feet in circumference, which dot the field at frequent intervals," but the park was more or less ready for primetime when it opened its gates for the Highlanders' first home game on April 30, 1903. Spectators were handed a small American flag upon entry, and they enthusiastically waved them when their new team paraded across the field prior to the first pitch. The stands were still uncompleted and right field was a mess, necessitating special ground rules. The entire outfield was

At 16,000 seats, Hilltop Park was large for its time, and the views were spectacular. Seats in the top row behind home plate and along the third-base line offered up a scenic view of the Hudson River and the New Jersey Palisades, behind the grandstand and away from the field. This facility would serve the club until they moved in with the New York Giants at the Polo Grounds in 1913. The team's shift from their elevated Washington Heights aerie necessitated a new moniker. "Highlanders" no longer made sense, but "Yankees" filled the void nicely.

The pinstripe-clad Yankees won their first American League championship in 1921, the team's nineteenth campaign. They won the pennant again the following season, as well as the season after that, when they broke through for their first World Series title. That World Series win, in 1923, coincided with Yankee Stadium's first season, and Babe Ruth put up a series of otherworldly numbers that year, posting a 1.309 OPS with 41 homers, 130 RBIs, 170 walks, 151 runs scored, and 399 total bases. Decades of dominance would follow, but it all began, modestly, in their swell-looking jerseys.

FRIVOLITIES

TEX 4
COL 0
WASH 2
HOU 2

INNING 4

2 BALL
3 STRIKE
3 OUT

DAWN OF THE DIGITS

The Cleveland Indians made MLB history on June 26, 1916, when they became the first club to wear numbers on their uniforms. That day, they took the field for a game against the White Sox with large digits—which corresponded to those printed in scorecards—affixed to the left sleeves of their jerseys. This numerical milestone proved to be a fleeting experiment, as the team soon reverted to being number-less, but you can't keep a good idea down. The Cardinals tried the same thing in 1923—they also soon bailed—but in 1929, the Indians and New York Yankees announced plans to wear digits on the *backs* of their jerseys. On April 16, Cleveland shortstop Jackie Tavener, leading off and wearing number 1, became the first big leaguer to bat with a number on his back. Babe Ruth got married the following day, then made his debut wearing number 3 the day after that, in a 7–3 win over the Red Sox. While the Yanks' players were numbered, manager Miller Huggins wore no numeral on his jersey. The team also decided to avoid assigning unlucky number 13 to anyone.

The remainder of American and National League teams soon joined in. Since then, baseball has seen its share of notable uniform number events and oddities.

During the 1934 All-Star Game, players wore large paper numbers that were attached to the backs of their uniforms with safety pins.

The honor of the first uniform to be retired by an MLB club belongs to Lou Gehrig, whose number 4 was permanently set aside by his Yankees in a move announced by team president Ed Barrow, on January 6, 1940.

A bunch of legendary players wore numbers that differed from the ones that they later made famous, among them Willie Mays (who broke in with the New York Giants sporting number 14), Hank Aaron (who first wore 5), Roberto Clemente (who discarded 13 for his now-famous 21), and Mickey Mantle (who originally wore 6 before he shifted to 7).

Al Oliver, who wore number 16 during his distinguished career in Pittsburgh, switched to number 0 when he was traded to the Texas Rangers prior to the 1978 season. "The 0 stands for Oliver," he told *The Sporting News*, "and I decided to make it kind of a symbolic gesture." "Coming to Texas," he added, "means a new career for me in baseball. I'm starting at zero again."

Reggie Jackson's number 44 was retired by the Yankees in 1993, but when he signed his landmark free agent deal with the club before the 1977 season, he said that he intended to wear Jackie Robinson's number 42, which never occurred. Jackson wore 20 during his first spring training in pinstripes as a show of respect to Frank Robinson, who had managed Jackson with Santurce in the Puerto Rican Winter League several years earlier. Jackson wound up settling on 44, a tribute to both Hank Aaron, who had just retired, and Willie McCovey—both of whom were elite sluggers. All of this was precipitated by the fact that the number 9 that he wore in Oakland already belonged to Yankees third baseman Graig Nettles. Speaking of Frank Robinson, his number 20 has been retired by three different clubs: the Orioles, Guardians, and Reds.

Several teams have retired uniform numbers for individuals who never played the game. In 1982, the California Angels honored their founding owner Gene Autry with a retired number, 26, citing his status as the club's "26th man." It was ceded by pitcher Bill Travers, who was on the injured list at the time. Similarly, the St. Louis Cardinals retired number 85 for owner August A. Busch, as part of his eighty-fifth birthday celebration. Milwaukee retired number 1 for Bud Selig in 2015, and in 1993 the expansion Florida Marlins retired number 5 in memory of team president Carl Barger, who died suddenly the previous year. The digit was a nod to Barger's favorite player, Joe DiMaggio. In 2012, however, the team *unretired* the number and gave it to outfielder Logan Morrison. When the Montréal Expos moved to Washington, DC, in 2015 and became the Nationals, they opted to reissue the three different digits that the franchise had retired in Canada: 8 for Gary Carter, 10 for both Rusty Staub and Andre Dawson, and 30 for Tim Raines.

Baseball lifer Don Zimmer was honored by the Tampa Bay Rays with a retired number, 66, which signified the number of years he spent in professional baseball. Zimmer was affiliated with fourteen different major-league clubs along the way, but spent 11 years in uniform as a coach in Tampa, his longest stopover over the course of his long baseball career. The Pittsburgh Pirates retired former manager Billy Meyer's number 1 at some point in the 1950s, but there's no evidence to indicate why. Meyer skippered some awful teams in Pittsburgh and finished with a record of 317–452 (.412) over his five seasons as manager, starting in 1948.

Jackie Robinson's uniform number 42 was retired across all of Major League Baseball in 1997, on the fiftieth anniversary of his historic debut. But before breaking the color barrier, he wore number 5 during his short stint with the Kansas City Monarchs in 1945. The Los Angeles Dodgers retired Robinson's 42—along with Roy Campanella's 39 and Sandy Koufax's 32—in a ceremony at Dodger Stadium on June 4, 1972.

Knuckleball pitchers Tim Wakefield, Charlie Hough, and Tom Candiotti each wore number 49 in tribute to Hoyt Wilhelm, the pioneering knuckleballer who wore that number at the outset of his Hall of Fame career.

There are a number of Japanese-born pitchers who have worn number 18, the revered "ace number" in Japan: Kenta Maeda, Daisuke Matsuzaka, Shota Imanaga, Hiroki Kuroda, and Yoshinobu Yamamoto are among them.

Dick Allen played 35 games for the 1977 Oakland A's, where he wore "Wampum"—the name of his Pennsylvania hometown—along with number 60, which signified the year of his high school graduation. Pitcher Bill Voiselle also paid tribute to his hometown when he wore number 96 while playing with the Braves and the Cubs, a numerical nod to his native Ninety Six, South Carolina. History was made in 2020 when Yankees pitcher Miguel Yajure made his debut with the number 89—representing MLB's last unused uniform number—affixed to his pinstriped uniform.

Finally, there are those occasions where players were called upon to work out accommodations with respect to uniform numbers. When the Philadelphia Phillies acquired Mitch Williams from the Chicago Cubs in April 1991, his usual uniform number, 28, was already taken, worn by new teammate John Kruk. A trade was called for. Kruk ceded his number to Williams and switched to 29 in exchange for two cases of beer.

3
OLIVER
0
CARTER
29
ORTIZ
34
44
9
ECKERSLEY
37
24
PALMER
22
JOHNSON
51
BRETT
5
24
HARPER
34
26
WALKER
33
CAREW
29
FISK
72
45
5
WINFIELD
31
8
20
5

PERRY
36
JACKSON
9
RYAN
34
6
TROUT
27
7
14
42
9
GRIFFEY
24
14
BENCH
5
CHMIDT
20
KALINE
6
RIPKEN
8
41
WAMPUM
60
2
IBSON
45
19
6
BOGGS
12
21
NIEKRO
35

TRASH RINGS

Dysfunctional. Triumphant. Colorful. The kelly green and gold-clad Oakland A's of the 1970s evoke a range of apt descriptors, but "dynasty" should rightfully be the final word for this legendary team that won five consecutive division championships, with three straight World Series wins sandwiched smack in the middle—one of the most dominant stretches in modern baseball history. The mustachioed "Swingin' A's" fought with one another and against their opponents, and are also remembered for being united by their many grievances against owner Charles O. Finley, who was famed for his frugality and reputation for micromanagement. Despite his many shortcomings, Finley was the one who was responsible for building the A's roster, just as he is remembered for letting it all fall apart as the sport transitioned into the era of free agency.

A championship ring is, of course, a powerful and historic symbol that marks a memorable season. It's often the benchmark against which fan bases judge one another, and, for players, it represents a forever moment that sometimes defines a career. Charlie Finley's approach to the A's first two World Series rings was typically bifurcated.

On March 3, 1973, Finley dropped in to his club's spring training facility in Mesa, Arizona, to parcel out the spoils for having won the 1972 World Series. The gold rings were, by all accounts, masterpieces. Described as the most extravagant World Series baubles ever created to that point, the rings sported a full one-carat diamond set atop a green oval-shaped stone, flanked by "1972 World Champions." One shank called out the A's World Series triumph over the Cincinnati Reds, while the other celebrated their American League Championship Series victory against Detroit. A facsimile of Finley's signature was included, as was the notation "S+S=S," a Finley motivational catchphrase that stood for "sweat plus sacrifice equals success." The rings were reported to have cost $1,500 a pop, and each player also received a half-carat diamond pendant for their significant other—which was valued at $600 apiece—along with a half-sized replica of the Commissioner's Trophy. Finley's well-deserved notoriety for cheapness was cast aside for this one fleeting moment. He came through for his team in style and, looking forward to their coming championship defense, he told his players, "Get out this year and bust your rears and go all the way again and I'll make these things look silly."

The 1973 Oakland A's did just that, overcoming dissention, drama, and the New York Mets in a seven-game World Series. They were led by Reggie Jackson, who garnered American League and World Series MVP awards, and Catfish Hunter, who went 21–5 in the regular season and 3–0 in four postseason starts, including a win in Game 6 in the fall classic.

As the club gathered in Mesa the following March, players received their 1973 World Series rings via Parcel Post, a departure from the previous year when Finley doled out the bling personally while promising something even more lavish if his team repeated. The quality of the rings, to put it mildly, was not what the team was expecting. Where a diamond had appeared the previous year, there was now a gaping void, leaving just a gold ring with a synthetic emerald-colored stone.

"I think the rings are horsemeat," said Hunter. "This ring isn't even as good as my high school ring. I hope it's a joke, because the ring looks like a joke.... He promised us last year, standing right here at Rendezvous Park, that if we won again, he'd make the '72 rings look like babies."

Relief ace Rollie Fingers said that Finley sent the rings by mail "because he didn't have the guts to come down here and hand them out himself." Jackson, never at a loss for words, stated simply, "These are trash rings."

At the time, Major League Baseball covered up to $300 of the cost for each ring, with the team picking up anything above that. These rings were rumored to have been appraised at less than $400 each. "At least we don't have to worry about having these rings insured," said coach Irv Noren. "I'll take $300 right now or I'll use it as a fishing weight, quipped pitcher Ken Holzman.

William Leggett, writing in *Sports Illustrated*, captured the vibe. "The A's resembled a soap-opera troupe, and Charles O. Finley, the jolly green gewgaw who owns them, exhibited all his familiar charm and grace. At one stage an Oakland player was asked if he had talked to Finley recently. 'No, not at all,' he said. 'Every time I call him, he's out walking his pet rat.'"

Finley waved off the criticism, saying that the price of gold and diamonds had shot up in the past year. *Me, cheap or vindictive? Never.* "If the players don't like them, they can always send them back," he said. Jackson had the final word when he told Ron Bergman of the *Oakland Tribune*, "I predict a third world championship. We've got the turmoil going, the undercurrent." He was, of course, clairvoyant. The A's won their third consecutive World Series title in October, defeating the Los Angeles Dodgers in five games. The 1974 rings proved to be as disappointing as the 1973 versions. A's captain Sal Bando said, "No one expected much better." In remarks to Ross Newhan in the *Los Angeles Times*, Fingers noted, "I'm waiting for Finley to send us some more Cracker Jack boxes so I can find another ring."

1972
LUXE RING

1973
TRASH RING

A MUSTACHE GROWS IN BROOKLYN

On March 6, 1936, Brooklyn Dodgers outfielder Stanley "Frenchy" Bordagaray reported to the team's spring training camp in Clearwater, Florida. According to the Associated Press, he "created a panic" when he showed up sporting a mustache. Contemporary readers might find this puzzling, but the fact is that facial hair was a notable oddity in America at this moment in time, a quaint relic of the Gilded Age. As such, Bordagaray's 'stache got a great deal of attention.

Baseball history is full of great mustaches, but they bookend our man Frenchy. The late nineteenth century begat whiskered wonders such as Old Hoss Radbourn, Sam Thompson, and Jim O'Rourke, and the 1970s gave us Hall of Famers Dennis Eckersley, Goose Gossage, and Rollie Fingers. But baseball in the 1930s? Well, it was strictly a mustache-free zone. So just who was this pioneer, and how and why did he decide to buck decades of trends and traditions?

Stanley George "Frenchy" Bordagaray was born in 1910, a California native of Basque and French ancestry. A speedy, talented athlete, he played both baseball and football at Fresno State, and enjoyed a standout career in the Pacific Coast League before being called up to the majors by the Chicago White Sox in 1934. Bordagaray was also renowned for his flakiness. He was a master of self-promotion, a free spirit who actively courted publicity, and a reliable quote machine for the media. When he was traded to the Dodgers in 1935, he introduced himself to fans in the *Brooklyn Eagle* with a lengthy article that included such tidbits as, "my favorite indoor activity is eating … I like 1) the color blue; 2) chocolate ice cream; 3) Greta Garbo; 4) Walt Disney's *Silly Symphonies*; and 5) salted peanuts." He fit right in with the Dodgers of this era, a colorful crew nicknamed "The Daffiness Boys" who, in the words of Florida sportswriter Ed Ray, "Stole bases when teammates already occupied them, let fly balls hit them on the nose, [and] kicked grounders into the grandstand, but the next minute would come back with home runs and shoestring catches." When the club acquired Bordagaray in 1935, the manager of this outfit was the irreverent Casey Stengel, then entering the second year of a managerial career that would wrap up three decades later with the New York Mets. Stengel pronounced Bordagaray's mustache to be "very pretty," but when he asked, "don't you think it will have a tendency to slow you up?" Bordagaray reportedly responded that, no, to the contrary—that the mustache would give him strength.

Newspapers provided daily mustache updates. Bordagaray told reporters that he grew it in the offseason while working in Hollywood, where he took bit parts in two movies. He played a Confederate orderly in *The Prisoner of Shark Island*, a film about the imprisonment of Dr. Samuel Mudd in the aftermath of the Lincoln assassination, and a Hawaiian sheepherder in *Sutter's Gold*, a docudrama about the 1849 California Gold Rush.

To say that his mustache captivated the media would be an understatement. Writer John Lardner noted, "It is the wholesome ambition of Mr. Bordagaray to develop his fa-

cial shrubbery to the handlebar stage, made popular in baseball 50 and 60 years ago." Bordagaray told him, "I'm growing it for the good of the game. It will be a lustrous black. My coiffeur tells me I should wax the tips, but I think it will look more dignified if I let the ends curl upon blossom straight out." Photographers seized the moment, and when they objected to the modest size of his mustache, Frenchy "let the foliage run wild." "Hair helped Samson," he said, "and the mustache may help me hit 'em over the fences." He added a goatee and, off the field, completed the look with a monocle, reportedly given to him by a retired Brooklyn physician.

By the end of April, the mustache grew thick, but the whole act grew thin on Stengel. Bordagaray eventually shaved, and when Stengel was asked why, he cited Frenchy's .160 batting average, stating, "No hits, no runs, no mustache." In his obituary, published in *The New York Times* in 2000, Bordagaray was quoted as saying, "I was making $3,000 a year playing baseball, so I figured I could at least have fun while I was not getting rich. But after I had it about two months, Casey called me into the clubhouse and said, 'If anyone's going to be a clown on this club, it's going to be me.'" By the time the season was over, the Dodgers had fired Stengel and traded Bordagaray to St. Louis.

WE ARE THE CHAMPIONS

Baseball's first modern World Series took place in 1903. Take a look at images of past championship celebrations and you'll see players shaking hands, hugging, smiling, and speaking with reporters. At some point—probably in the 1940s—alcohol entered the picture, and by 1955, happy Brooklyn Dodgers players were whooping it up and pouring cans of Schaefer ("the one beer to have when you're having more than one") over one another's heads. Two years later, Milwaukee Braves players were toasting victory with champagne, served in paper cups, and, in 1960, the euphoric Pittsburgh Pirates dumped bottles of bubbly all over the head of Bill Mazeroski, who had just hit a walk-off homer to win the fall classic. There's lots of joy and liquid, but until 1967, there was one thing missing: a World Series trophy, which seems really weird.

Despite the odd absence of an official trophy for so many years, the idea of one was nothing new. Baseball's first interleague championship playoff tournament took place way back in 1884, when the National League's Providence Grays swept the champs of the American Association, the New York Metropolitans (no relation to today's Mets) in a three-game World Series. This was the first of seven postseason matchups between the winners from the rival leagues. The last four Series champs of this era were awarded the Dauvray Cup, an ornate solid silver urn which was fabricated by New York's Gorham Silverware Company. The trophy was commissioned and paid for by actress Helen Dauvray, who later married John Montgomery Ward, a future Baseball Hall of Famer who pitched the second perfect game in MLB history.

The Dauvray Cup was akin to hockey's Stanley Cup—one of a kind, passed annually from winner to winner, and then returned. In 1888, it was joined by the

Hall Championship Cup, a trophy which was intended to become the permanent property of the winning club. The Hall Cup, another elaborately decorated Gilded Age urn, was manufactured by Tiffany & Co. It was made of exactly 106 1/2 ounces of sterling silver and mounted on an ebony base. The New York Giants took home *both* trophies following their 10-game victory over the St. Louis Browns (today's Cardinals) that October. While the Dauvray Cup disappeared well more than a century ago, the Hall Cup currently resides at the Hall of Fame in Cooperstown.

When the American Association folded after the 1891 season, the two organizations effectively merged into a single circuit, which was formally called the National League and American Association of Professional Baseball Clubs—the same National League that began play in 1876 and exists to this day. A postseason championship series was played between the league's first- and second-place finishers from 1894 to 1897, with the victors taking home the Temple Cup—yet another fancily adorned silver trophy, which was donated by Pittsburgh Pirates team president William Chase Temple. This series, however, was never particularly popular. Fans and participating teams alike were largely indifferent and, after the conclusion of the 1897 edition, NL owners voted to discontinue the series and return the trophy to Temple. In 1951, Temple's daughter, Dorothy Temple Mason, donated the cup to the Baseball Hall of Fame.

Sixty-four World Series were contested between 1903 and 1966, a stretch during which not a single one of the winning teams was awarded a trophy. This finally changed in 1967, after the St. Louis Cardinals' Game Seven

World Series win over the Boston Red Sox. Commissioner William D. "Spike" Eckert, a man whose three-year term yielded few achievements to speak of, is credited with the idea. That first trophy included twenty flags, which represented the number of MLB clubs at the time. This number grew to twenty-four in 1969, twenty-six in 1977, twenty-eight in 1993 and, finally, thirty in 1998, when the Tampa Bay Devil Rays and Arizona Diamondbacks joined the fold. Those flags contained the names of each of the clubs, which means that the very first trophy is the only one to reference the Kansas City Athletics, who moved to Oakland in 1968. Team locations were haphazardly spelt out in a strange mix of upper- and lower-case characters that called out both the "Minnesota TWINS" and the "BALTIMORE ORIOLES." The original 1967 trophy was produced by the L. G. Balfour Company, based in Attleboro, Massachusetts, and cost a reported $2,500.

Similar to the Hall Cup, today's Commissioner's Trophy is made by Tiffany & Co. Whereas the old version was a visage in gold, this one is mostly silver—198.12 troy ounces of sterling silver, to be precise. It was unveiled on June 27, 2000, by Commissioner Bud Selig, who said that the time was right for something new, given the dawning of a new century and a new millennium. Since then, the crowning of a World Series champion has become a familiar ritual; the decisive final pitch, a dogpile in the infield, the donning of commemorative shirts and hats, and a joyous explosion of confetti, followed by the presentation of the Commissioner's Trophy, the shiny two foot tall, thirty-pound symbol of a championship season.

THE NATIONAL LEAGUE THROWS A PARTY

The National League celebrated its golden jubilee in 1925, a year-long salute to honor the fiftieth anniversary of the loop's founding. That season, each of the league's eight teams sported a commemorative uniform patch to mark the occasion—the first time in baseball history that a unified patch was worn by all member clubs of a particular league.

On Wednesday, February 2, 1876, representatives from six professional baseball teams gathered at New York's Grand Central Hotel to form the National League. The clubs were previously members of the National Association, baseball's first fully professional league, founded in 1871. The NA was ultimately doomed by its lack of strong central governance, which resulted in erratic scheduling, roster instability, competitive imbalance, and a tolerance toward gambling and game fixing. Led by Chicago White Stockings owner William Hulbert, the group adopted their Articles of the Constitution and Playing Rules that day, thus setting the tone for what we now know as Major League Baseball and all of American professional sports. The new entity restored order to the sport, establishing a strong central authority, defining franchise territories and standards, and codifying the relationship between ownership (aka capital) and labor. A key point was, "To make base ball playing respectable and honorable," a tacit effort to eradicate the rampant gambling and corruption that helped sink the National Association. A few months later, eight teams took the field: Chicago (now known as the Cubs), Boston (which are today's Braves), Cincinnati, Hartford, Louisville, New York, Philadelphia, and St. Louis.

The hotel where they met enjoyed a rich, interesting history and a tragic final act. Built in the ornate Second Empire style, complete with elaborate mansard roofs and dormers, the hotel was the largest in the nation when it opened in 1870. It was a favored stamping ground for the movers and shakers of the Gilded Age, and the site of one of the most notorious scandals of the era, when famed corporate mogul and robber baron Jim Fisk was shot dead by his former business partner in a lover's quarrel over the affections of former showgirl Josie Mansfield. By the 1950s, the place had started to fray, and in the late 1960s it had become one of the city's largest welfare hotels. On the afternoon of August 3, 1973, residents reported ominous rumbling noises. Soon thereafter the building collapsed, killing four people trapped inside. *The New York Times* reported, "In a century of life in downtown Manhattan, the Broadway Central went from a gathering place for the famous and wealthy to a cesspool of squalor and crime." The remains of the once grand structure were demolished, and the neighborhood—along with the city—experienced a rebirth in the decades that followed.

As for the NL's 1925 Golden Jubilee celebration, baseball commissioner Judge Kenesaw Mountain Landis and NL president John Heydler traveled to each of the league's eight ballparks—Braves Field in Boston, Brooklyn's

Ebbets Field, Cubs Park in Chicago, Cincinnati's Redland Field, New York's Polo Grounds, Forbes Field in Pittsburgh, Philadelphia's Baker Bowl, and Sportsman's Park in St. Louis—to help commemorate the anniversary. Things kicked off with a league meeting on February 2, 1925, held in the same hotel room where the league's founding fathers elected Hartford's Morgan Bulkeley as their first president forty-nine years earlier. On May 8 in Boston, the Braves and Cubs, the circuit's two oldest clubs, became the first to celebrate. Three Boston players from the 1876 team were on hand: future Hall of Famer George Wright, outfielder Jack Manning, and infielder John Morrill. They were joined by eighty-nine-year-old Billy McLean, who umpired the first National League game ever played, on April 22, 1876.

Next up was a day of festivities at the Polo Grounds in New York, prior to the May 14 Giants-Reds game. Jim Mutrie, New York's first manager, was in attendance, along with early stars Roger Connor and Dan Brouthers. Pittsburgh's Forbes Field hosted the 1901 Pirates, including Fred Clarke, Deacon Phillippe, and Honus Wagner, who entered the ballpark via an old-fashioned horse-drawn coach. They faced off against the current Bucs in an abbreviated game, losing 5–3. Brooklyn, Chicago, Philadelphia, and Cincinnati followed. Finally, a crowd of 17,500 witnessed the last party, which was held on June 18 at Sportsman's Park in St. Louis. George Washington Bradley, who threw the first no-hitter in NL history (on July 15, 1876), was on hand for the ceremony.

The uniform patches were criticized for their large proportions, which some players thought inhibited movement. Prior to Opening Day, Pirates manager Bill McKechnie told the *Pittsburgh Post* that the emblems, which were placed on the left sleeves of his club's jerseys, would interfere with the effectiveness of his left-handed pitchers. The patches had migrated to the left chest of the uniforms by the time the Bucs won the World Series six months later.

All in all, however, the Golden Jubilee was deemed a rousing success, full of parades, old-time players, and fifty years' worth of memories.

SATCHEL PAIGE'S SAGE ADVICE

Leroy "Satchel" Paige's "six rules for a long life" are so closely associated with the great pitcher that they are etched into the monument that marks his final resting place at Forest Hill Cemetery in Kansas City, Missouri. The rules are pure Satchel—idiosyncratic, unquestionably wise, and more than a little bit humorous.

HOW TO STAY YOUNG

1. *Avoid fried meats, which angry up the blood.*
2. *If your stomach disputes you, lie down and pacify it with cool thoughts.*
3. *Keep the juices flowing by jangling around gently as you move.*
4. *Go very light on the vices, such as carrying on in society. The social ramble ain't restful.*
5. *Avoid running at all times.*
6. *Don't look back. Something might be gaining on you.*

Paige conveyed this sage advice in the June 13, 1953 issue of *Collier's* magazine, included as a sidebar to an article entitled "Time Ain't Gonna Mess with Me," written by Richard Donovan. At the time, Paige was a few weeks away from celebrating his forty-seventh birthday and pitching for the St. Louis Browns in the middle of the final year of his three-season run there. That July, he became the oldest player to ever participate in the All-Star Game. Despite his age, Paige was sill among the best relievers in baseball, so much so that Yankees manager Casey Stengel, who selected him for the American League All-Star squad, was said to have warned his hitters to score early in games against the woeful Browns, saying "Get the runs now! Father Time is coming!"

Satchel Paige's career in professional baseball began at the age of nineteen when, on May 1, 1926, he made his debut with the Chattanooga White Sox of the Negro Southern League. The following day, the *Chattanooga Daily Times* extolled, "the airtight pitching of a long, lanky black boy by the name of Satchell." No last name was given and, eventually, no last name was necessary to identify the man who carved out a career like no other in baseball history. Paige wrapped things up four decades later, just shy of his sixtieth birthday, with a two-inning stint in an exhibition game for the Carolina League's Peninsula Grays, on June 19, 1966. His final major-league game took place the previous September 25, when he threw three shutout frames for the Kansas City Athletics in a game against the Boston Red Sox. In between, he pitched in something like 2,500 games for teams from KC to Cuba, displaying a unique mix of skill and showmanship, the vast majority of which took place in the face of institutional segregation.

Paige's storied assortment of pitches included his blazing fastball, which he called "Long Tom," a forkball, which he called the "whipsy-dipsy-do," and his famous "hesitation pitch," during which he deliberately paused in the middle of his windup before releasing the ball. He once described his pitching arsenal by saying, "I got bloopers, loopers and droopers. I got a jump ball, a be ball, a screwball, a wobbly

HOW TO STAY
YOUNG
Leroy Satchel Paige
KC
ONARCH
K

1 AVOID FRIED MEATS
WHICH ANGRY UP THE BLOOD

2 IF YOUR STOMACH DISPUTES YOU
LIE DOWN AND PACIFY IT
WITH COOL THOUGHTS

3 KEEP THE JUICES FLOWING
BY JANGLING AROUND GENTLY AS YOU MOVE

4 GO VERY LIGHT ON THE VICES
SUCH AS CARRYING ON IN SOCIETY
THE SOCIAL RAMBLE AIN'T RESTFUL

5 AVOID RUNNING AT ALL TIMES

6 DON'T LOOK BACK
SOMETHING MIGHT BE GAINING ON YOU

ball, a whipsy-dipsy-do, a hurry-up ball, a nothin' ball and a bat dodger. My be ball is a be ball 'cause it 'be' right where I want it, high and inside. It wiggles like a worm." He delivered all of these with a high leg kick and a powerful torqued delivery. As if that wasn't enough, Paige possessed an uncanny ability to locate his pitches. Tales of him being able to consistently throw his fastball over gum wrappers, matchbooks, and cigarettes are legendry. His flair for the theatrical involved scenarios where he would call in his outfielders, intentionally load the bases, and then strike out the side.

He was Black baseball's greatest gate attraction, with an estimated 10 million people having seen him pitch over the decades. During his prime years, Paige barnstormed against some of baseball's greatest White players, including Dizzy Dean, a frequent opponent who held him in enormously high regard. Prior to his rookie season in 1936, Joe DiMaggio faced Paige in an exhibition game and called him the greatest pitcher he had yet faced, telling the *New York Daily News*, "Satch has a curve with so many bends it looks like a wiggle in a cyclone; it gave me optical indigestion. And his fastball? Say when he fires it the catcher gets nothing but ashes!"

Paige's travels included stints in the Negro Leagues, the American League, a semipro league in North Dakota, and the California Winter League. He toured with the famous House of David club and even the Harlem Globetrotters. Along the way, Paige pitched in the Mexican League and headlined a team that was sponsored by Dominican dictator Rafael Trujillo. A 1948 article in *Time* magazine provides some additional flavor: "Playing summers in the U.S. and winters in Central and South America, Satchel Paige earned $36,000 one year and spent it in handfuls (he has a white Lincoln, a red Cadillac, a red jeep, a pallid station wagon and an arsenal of over 20 shotguns."

One of Paige's six rules contradicted his once well-documented affection for fried food. In a 1942 *Brooklyn Eagle* profile, Paige was asked about his training regimen and how he kept in shape at such an advanced age (ironically, he would pitch in a major-league game a quarter century after this was written). "Trainin'," he said. "I build up my strength with a hot bath every morning and every night, adding that he ate "Absolutely nothin' but fried foods."

Did Paige lay down these rules verbatim? We may never know. Paige himself, however, threw some cold water on it in his 1962 memoir, *Maybe I'll Pitch Forever*, when he said, "Some sports guy on the East Coast heard me talking about them once and then he went and turned them into a bunch of rules for me to stay young." After Paige's death in 1982, *Sports Illustrated* noted, "Several lively quotes from Paige lay unused in writer Richard Donovan's notes, and rather than lose them, the editors decided to bring them—and perhaps a couple of rules of their own devising—together in a box under the heading 'How to Stay Young.'"

The passing of time only seems to have amplified the mystique and legend of Satchel Paige. Toward the end of his life, Paige told *New York Times* writer Dave Anderson, "Lots of people dispute me, but they can't pinpoint me. My mother told me 'If you tell a lie, always rehearse it. If it don't sound good to you, it won't sound good to anyone else.'" While the recent release of statistical data from his years in the Negro Leagues has brought his on-field accomplishments into sharper focus, Paige's own words continue to sink and dart and flummox, much like his pitches did to opposing batters.

STENGELESE

Casey Stengel's bronze Hall of Fame plaque cites the fact that he won an impressive ten pennants and seven World Series while managing the New York Yankees from 1949 to 1960, including an unprecedented five straight fall classic victories. Stengel's 54-year baseball career began when William Howard Taft occupied the White House and ended when he retired as manager of the New York Mets on August 30, 1965, two weeks after the Beatles first played Shea Stadium. Among Stengel's many accomplishments is his own unique contribution to the English language: "Stengelese," a colorful, confusing, and idiosyncratic syntax which *The New York Times* described as, "a kind of circuitous doubletalk laced with ambiguous antecedents, dangling participles, a lack of proper names and a liberal use of adjectives like 'amazing' and 'terrific.'" He deployed this to great effect, alternately charming and mystifying the media. Columnist Red Smith once said that when Stengel signed on to manage the Yankees, he "learned to use the spoken word to spread confusion and bewilderment," something he utilized to great effect for the rest of his life.

The affable Stengel provided reporters with abundant content for decades. Writing in *Life* magazine in 1952, Clay Felker and Ernest Havemann observed, "At the left side of his mouth, running almost to his chin, is a line as deep as a canyon. It has been worn there through the years by the restless rumble and roar of words pouring out of the side of his mouth like an eternal waterfall." Years after having covered the expansion Mets for *Newsday*, George Vecsey, writing on his personal blog, recalled, "The Old Man also tried to teach 'my writers,' in murky soliloquys very late at night. Just when you were about to give up (or doze off) he would grab you with a stubborn paw and say, 'Look, you asshole, I'm trying to tell you something.'"

One could fill a multi-volume set of books with examples of Charles Dillon Stengel's linguistic quirks. His flair for the comedic arts extended beyond the grammar, predating his managerial career. Famously, there was the 1919 incident when Stengel, playing right field for the Pirates, stepped to the plate at Brooklyn's Ebbets Field and countered the boo birds there with an actual bird. As he stepped up to bat in the top of the sixth inning, Stengel tipped his cap to the crowd and a sparrow flew out from under his chapeau. Shortly before his death fifty-six years later, Stengel, dressed up in a toga and a gladiator's helmet, was delivered to Old Timers Day at Shea Stadium in a Roman chariot.

There are countless examples of Stengelese, but several of Casey's iconic witticisms rise above the others. While managing the woefully inept expansion Mets, Stengel pointed to one of his players. "See that fella over there? He's 20 years old. In 10 years, he's got a chance to be a star. Now that other fella over there, he's 20 years old. In 10 years, he's got a chance to be 30." Years earlier, his advice to Yankees ace Whitey Ford was "Don't drink in the hotel bar, that's where I do my drinking." And speaking to his players' off-field activities, Stengel once said, "Being with a woman all night never hurt no professional baseball player. It's staying up all night looking for a woman that does him in."

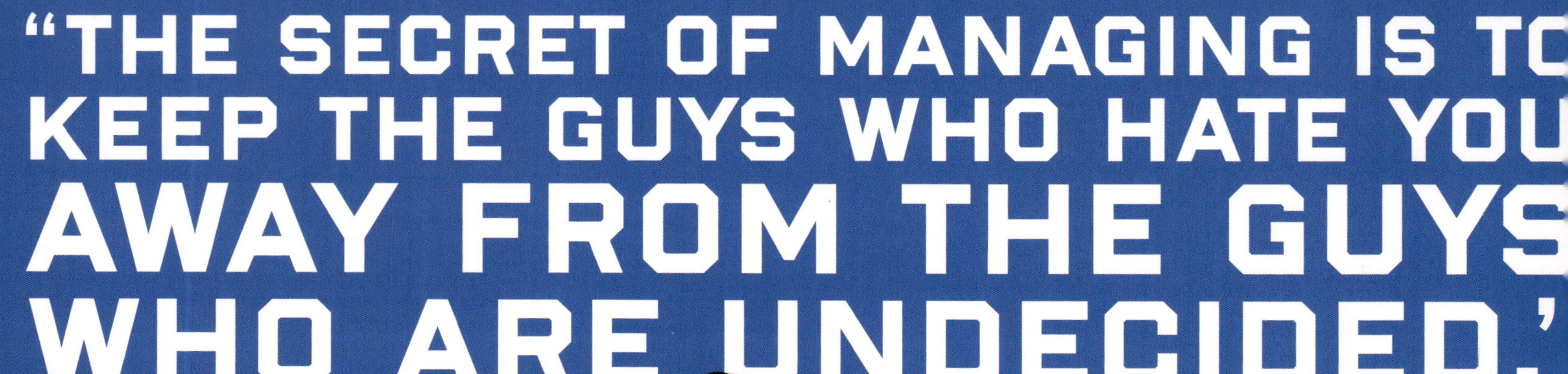
"THE SECRET OF MANAGING IS TO
KEEP THE GUYS WHO HATE YOU
AWAY FROM THE GUYS
WHO ARE UNDECIDED."
"Well, I started in profes 1910. I have been in professiona
ball, I would say, for for . I have been employed by numerou
ball clubs in the majors a leagues. I started in the mino
leagues with Kansas City. ow as class D ball, which was a
Shelbyville, Ky., and also and class A ball, and I have advanced in baseball as a ba many years that I was not so successful as a ballplayer, a of skill. And then I was no doub
discharged by baseball in go back to the minor leagues as
manager, and after being in t ues as a manager, I became a majo
league manager in several c discharged, we call it discharged, because there is n ve. (Laughter). And I returned to the minor leag and Oakland, California, and then returne ten years, natural-
ly, in major league he New York Yankee
have had tremendou layer who does th
work, I have no d ry capable in th
office. I must ha pable men who ar
in radio and tel have mentione
the three names wonderful pres
that follows u have so man
million people ve it, and w
have the Spir you are no
capable of bec as a manager
in ten years, y the ball field
the salary that to play and giv

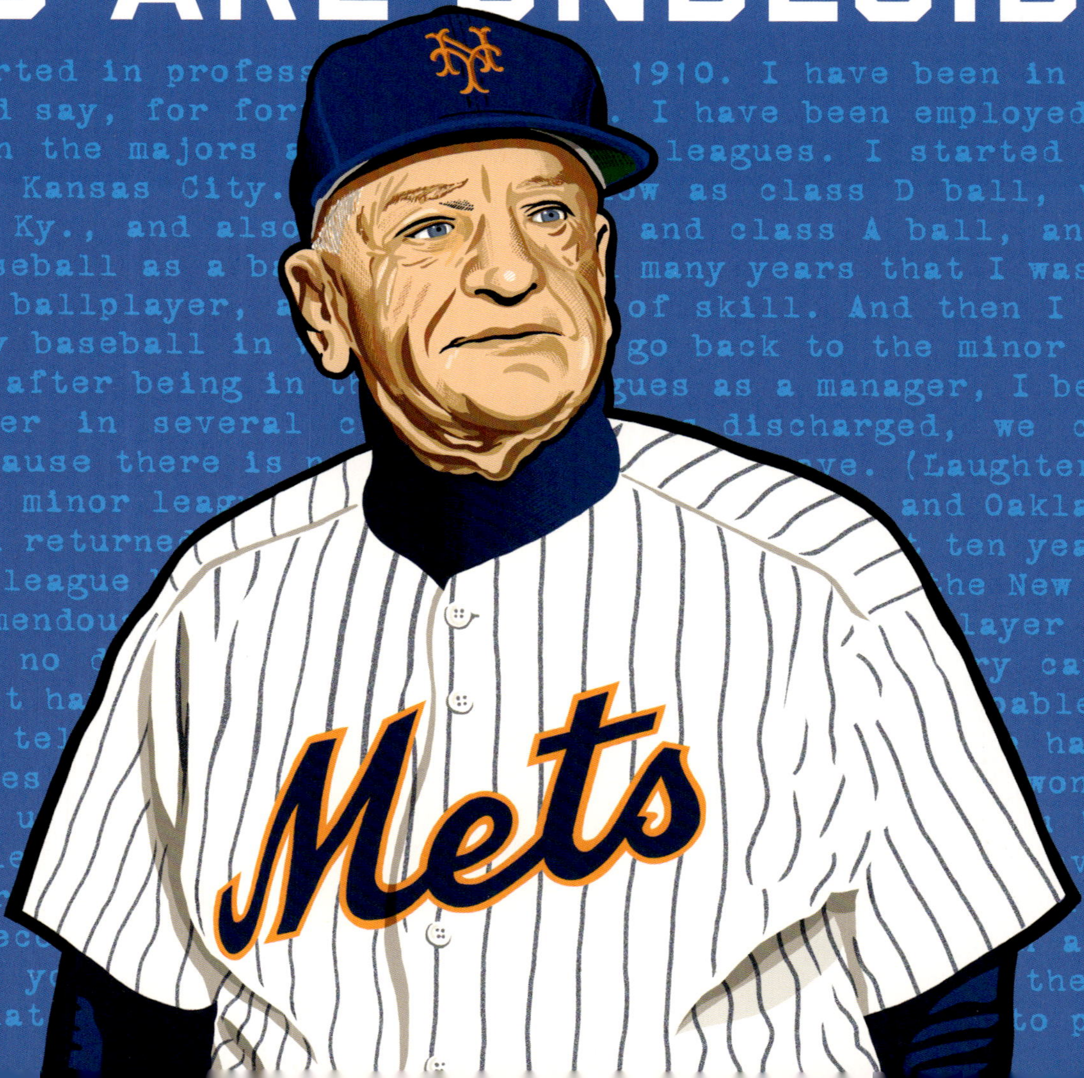

On July 9, 1958, Stengel traveled to Washington to appear in front of the US Senate's Anti-Trust and Monopoly Subcommittee. His testimony that day provided a masterful lesson in Stengelese from the master himself. Tennessee Senator Estes Kefauver, the subcommittee chairman, began the hearing by asking Stengel about his background and his views on the topic at hand, the "applicability of antitrust laws to organized team sports." His response began with, "Well, I started in professional ball in 1910," and caromed wildly onward from there. He spoke of his time as a minor-league player and added, "I had many years that I was not so successful as a ballplayer, as it is a game of skill. And then I was no doubt discharged by baseball in which I had to go back to the minor-leagues as a manager, and after being in the minor-leagues as a manager, I became a major-league manager in several cities and was discharged, we call it discharged because there is no question I had to leave." This drew laughter from the assembled lawmakers and spectators.

North Dakota Senator William Langer attempted to box Stengel in on his views of baseball's monopoly status. He eventually gave up and threw him a fat fastball, right down the middle of the plate, asking, "I want to know whether you intend to keep on monopolizing the world's championship in New York City." Stengel replied, "Well, I will tell you, I got a little concerned yesterday in the first three innings when I say the three players I had gotten rid of and I said when I lost nine what am I going to do and when I had a couple of my players. I thought so great of that did not do so good up to the sixth inning I was more confused but I finally had to go and call on a young man in Baltimore that we don't own and the Yankees don't own him, and he is going pretty good, and I would actually have to tell you that I think we are more the Greta Garbo type now from success. We are being hated I mean, from the ownership and all, we are being hated. Every sport that gets too great or one individual, but if we made 27 cents and it pays to have a winner at home why would you not have a good winner in your own park if you were an owner. That is the result of baseball. An owner gets most of the money at home and it is up to him and his staff to do better or they ought to be discharged."

Senator Joseph C. O'Mahoney of Wyoming said, "This is the best entertainment we have had around here for a long time." Afterward, Yankees coach Ralph Houk told his manager that he heard that the subcommittee adjourned for two weeks following Stengel's testimony, noting, "It'll take 'em that long to figure out just what you said."

Two years later, Stengel was fired as Yankees manager after his team lost an epic seven-game World Series to Pittsburgh. The club held what was, by all accounts, an uncomfortable press conference at New York's Savoy-Hilton Hotel. Yankees co-owner Dan Topping praised Stengel, but said that the franchise had to move on, adding, "I'm just sorry Casey isn't 50 years old, but all business comes to a point when it's best for the future to make a change." Stengel later said, "I'll never make the mistake of being 70 again."

Stengel was back in the same room at the Savoy-Hilton 349 days later for another press conference, formally introducing him as the first manager of the New York Mets. *The New York Times* described him as, "effervescent and confusingly articulate as ever." Silencing a gaggle of assembled reporters, he approached the microphone and said, "Attention: We're going to give away a diamond ring to get this thing started."

THE TRIPLE CROWN

It is one of baseball's most elusive offensive accomplishments, a statistical feat that only a handful of players have ever achieved. Even as advanced statistical measures have firmly taken hold of today's game, the Triple Crown—leading the league in home runs, runs batted in, and batting average in the same season—remains an impressive and historic achievement.

In 2012, Detroit Tigers third baseman Miguel Cabrera paced the American League with a .330 batting average, 44 homers, and 139 RBIs, becoming the first player to attain this rare feat since Boston Red Sox left fielder Carl Yastrzemski took home the honors in 1967. The National League's last Triple Crown winner is Joe Medwick, who did it way back in 1937 (.374/31/154).

The winners' circle is an elite club indeed, and while some of its members are quite famous, others are far more obscure. The first batter to be credited with winning the Triple Crown was Paul Hines of the 1878 Providence Grays. He didn't celebrate, however, because runs batted in were not recognized as an official statistic until 1920, which is two years before he was arrested on pickpocketing charges in Washington, DC. Hines, then sixty-nine years old, had three pocketbooks on his person when he was taken in. A search of his residence revealed twelve more pocketbooks and nineteen pairs of eyeglasses.

The next winner was Tip O'Neill, a Canadian outfielder playing for the American Association's St. Louis Browns, who accomplished the feat in 1887 (.435/14/123). Hines and O'Neill were joined by Hugh Duffy of the Boston Beaneaters in 1894 (.440/18/145). Duffy's expansive baseball career included a long stint with the Boston Red Sox, where he coached and mentored a young Ted Williams. After the 1941 season, when the twenty-two-year-old Williams hit .406, Duffy called him the "greatest hitter it has been my pleasure to look at," adding, "and don't forget I have been looking at Hugh Duffy in the shaving mirror for many a year."

In 1901—the American League's inaugural campaign—Napoleon Lajoie of the Philadelphia Athletics became the next to add his name to this very special group (.426/14/125). Detroit's Ty Cobb slashed .377/9/107 in 1909 to win the AL's Triple Crown—that season he also led the Tigers to an American League pennant. Three years later, Chicago Cubs infielder Heinie Zimmerman paced the National League when he hit for a.372 batting average, slammed 14 homers, and drove in 104 runs. He also led the NL with a .571 slugging percentage, 207 hits, 41 doubles, and 318 total bases. Rogers Hornsby of the St. Louis Cardinals won NL Triple Crowns in 1922 (.401/42/152) and 1925 (.403/39/143.) In 1932 the city of Philadelphia produced *two* Triple Crown winners in the same season, when the A's Jimmie Foxx (.356/48/163) and the Phillies' Chuck Klein (.368/20/120) managed to pull off the feat.

The Triple Crown club gained a few new members when Negro Leagues statistics were added to the historical record, shining a light on a group that includes Oscar "Heavy" Johnson (1923, Kansas City Monarchs:

2012
TRIPLE CROWN
Miguel Cabrera

THE TRIPLE CROWN

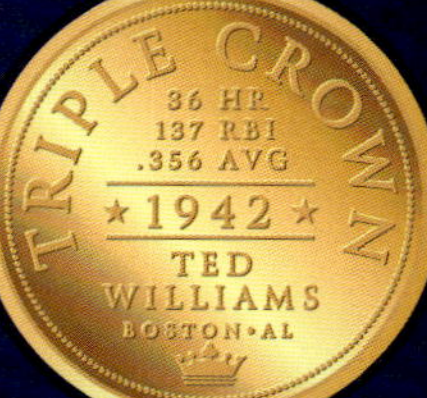

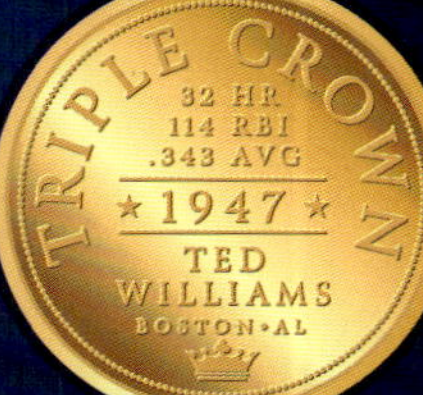

.406/20/120), Ted Strong (1942, Kansas City Monarchs: .364/6/32), Lennie Pearson (1942, Newark Eagles and Homestead Grays: .347/11/56), and Lester Lockett (1948, Baltimore Elite Giants: .362/6/53).

As of today, only four players have won the Triple Crown on multiple occasions and, unsurprisingly, all of them are enshrined in Cooperstown. Rogers Hornsby, cited above, is part of this crew. Oscar Charleston, the legendary Negro Leagues center fielder, did it three times in five years in the 1920s. The great Buck O'Neil, who saw a lot of baseball over the course of his long life, once said, "The greatest MLB player I ever saw was Willie Mays, but the greatest player I ever saw was Oscar Charleston." The mighty Negro Leagues catcher Josh Gibson won back-to back trifectas in 1936 and 1937, and Red Sox great Ted Williams won Triple Crowns in both 1942 and 1947. The Splendid Splinter came within a whisker of joining Charleston as a three-timer when he came up two ten thousandths of a percentage point (.0002) short (behind George Kell) in the 1949 American League batting race.

Yankees slugger Lou Gehrig put up a monster season when he took home AL Triple Crown honors in 1934 (.363/49/166.) Three years later, in 1937, twenty-five-year-old St. Louis Cardinals leftfielder Joe "Ducky" Medwick slashed .374/31/154 to win the NL Triple Crown. Counting Cabrera, only five Triple Crowns have occurred in MLB's post-integration era, from 1947 to the present day. Williams, as noted above, won it in Jackie Robinson's groundbreaking rookie season of 1947 (.343/32/114). Mickey Mantle pulled off the feat in 1956 (.353/52/130), and Frank Robinson did it a decade later in 1966 (.316/49/122). The previous offseason, the Cincinnati Reds had traded Robinson—a perennial National League All-Star—to the Baltimore Orioles. When he made the trade, Cincinnati owner Bill Dewitt called Robinson "an old thirty" and a fading talent.* Robinson exacted revenge in the sweetest way imaginable, winning the Triple Crown and leading the Orioles to their first-ever World Series victory, a four-game sweep over Sandy Koufax and the Los Angeles Dodgers. That year he also became the first player in major-league history to win MVP Awards in both leagues.

Yastrzemski secured the AL Triple Crown the following season (.326/44/121) with a legendary campaign that included an unexpected "Impossible Dream" pennant—Boston's first in three decades—when he seemingly willed his club to a World Series berth after a ninth-place finish the year before. Yaz was magnificent down the stretch, going 27-for-55 and knocking in 18 runs over the final two weeks. His 1967 total of 12.4 Wins Above Replacement (WAR) is fourth all-time, behind only Babe Ruth's 1923, 1921, and 1927 seasons.

After Yaz, it was crickets . . . until Cabrera came along in 2012 (.330/44/139). While many have come close over the years, whoever achieves the feat next will join a long and diverse line of players who powered their way to immortality in regal fashion.

* In exchange for Robinson, the Reds received three players: pitchers Jack Baldschun and Milt Pappas, and outfielder Dick Simpson. A relief pitcher, Baldschun would pitch two years in Cincy, going 1–5 with a 5.25 ERA. Pappas would start 75 games over two and a half seasons as a Red, going 4–11 with a 4.04 ERA. Simpson played two seasons in the red and white, appearing in just 136 total games and hitting .246.

Seattle
83

POSEIDON'S WRATH

The Seattle Mariners were still a young franchise in 1983. As they embarked upon their seventh season, the team was still looking for their first winning campaign. The 1982 club made a spirited run before eventually coming up short. They were four games out of first place at the All-Star break and were playing .500 ball as late as August 17 before losing their next seven games, finishing the season in fourth, with a franchise-record 76 wins. So while expectations were not exactly sky high for a successful 1983 season, there was at least a hint of optimism in the Pacific Northwest air that spring. Seattle owner George Argyros, citing his team's depth, said that the Mariners might even be a playoff contender. They won the first two games of the 1983 season, both against the New York Yankees. This, however, proved, to be the high point.

Things immediately began skidding out of control, and on April 26—just 21 games into the young season—drastic measures were clearly required. The slumping Mariners had lost ten of their last twelve games and Richie Zisk, their cleanup hitter, was hitting .138, fresh off 0-for-20 stretch. Zisk and reliever Bill Caudill were inspired to act. Caudill, abetted by fellow relief pitcher Mike "Gator" Stanton, stacked up fifteen bats outside the clubhouse door and set them on fire. Caudill appealed to "the Great Mariner in the sky," and placed a batting helmet atop the pyre for good measure as smoke poured into the home clubhouse . . . and it worked . . . at least for one night. The Mariners then went out and defeated the Boston Red Sox, 7–6, behind pitcher Gaylord Perry's 309th career victory. Unfortunately, Seattle resumed its losing ways the following day, Zisk was placed on the disabled list a week later, and the club sputtered its way through May, an inconsistent and unentertaining mess.

Coming off the Memorial Day weekend, the Mariners mustered just five runs during a three-game series in Cleveland, and Zisk once again sprang into action. This time, he asked the Mariners' equipment manager to turn the logo decal on his helmet upside down. The Mariners' insignia, an inverted trident which formed the letter M, was bad karma, said Zisk, akin to an upside down horseshoe whose luck was constantly cascading out of the open end. Some of Zisk's teammates joined him, including Julio Cruz, and Argyros encouraged the rest of the team to do likewise. Even so, the club continued their downward slide. On June 25, Argyros fired popular manager Rene Lachemann, replacing him with Del Crandall. That same day, the team cut the forty-four-year old Perry, who told the Associated Press, "There's no fight in them ... they've got to get rid of guys who laugh when they strike out four times like it was something funny." Apparently, the trident emblem wasn't the problem here, and the experiment soon ended.

The Mariners finished the season in last place, more than 40 games under .500, the third 100-loss season in the franchise's short history. As the club retooled after another disappointing season, Argyros took aim at the logo, which clearly stuck in his craw.

In the spring of 1984, the Mariners were reported to be looking at overhauling their identity, starting with the trident. As team president Chuck Armstrong later told journalist Maury Brown, "George Argyros is Greek and his mother told us that in Greek mythology, Poseidon never held the trident pointing down, he always held the trident pointing up." He went on to say that the club considered flipping the trident around, thus securing all the good luck within and having the resulting W stand as the symbol of a newly christened (state of) Washington Mariners team.

None of it came to pass, and the Mariners won 74 games in 1984, which was good for fifth-place in the AL West. The trident and all the attendant bad luck were finally excised in 1987, the same year that the team selected seventeen-year-old Ken Griffey Jr. as the top pick in baseball's free agent amateur draft. Finally, after a decade of losing baseball, things were pointing up.

Three decades later, Seattle foolishly decided to tempt the gods yet again. The team brought back their original upside-down trident logo on their spring training caps that year, and those who knew, knew. Former Mariners catcher Rick Sweet, who played on the ill-fated 1983 club, spoke to the Spokane *Spokesman-Review* about the old/new logo, saying, "I believe in the baseball gods." And, sure enough, Seattle ended up dealing with a spate of injuries that season, which included tying a major league record for most pitchers used in a single season (40). The Mariners challenged the baseball gods yet again by bringing the caps back in 2018, much to the chagrin of skipper Scott Servais. He told 710 ESPN Seattle, "Being a baseball guy and you get so into routine, the superstition becomes part of it. When you get a hot streak going, you're wearing the same socks all the time and eating at the same restaurants. When you have a bad streak going you look to what you need to change up. This might be one of those things we need to change up."

The team's 2018 spring training camp was accompanied by a proliferation of injuries for the second straight year, and Servais, noting the fact that the club was slated to wear the caps during batting practice all season long, said that he'd reserve judgment on whether or not they'd ever again see the light of day. The Mariners wore their regular game day caps in lieu of the unlucky trident lids, but the gods must have still been angry. Seattle finished with a very respectable 89–73 record, but stumbled badly in the second half of the season and missed the postseason for the seventeenth consecutive year.

PICTURE ME ROLLIN'

On May 17, 1950, Cleveland Indians righty Marino Pieretti became the Neil Armstrong of relief pitchers. A hometown crowd of 12,471 fans watched as Pieretti entered the game in the seventh inning against the Philadelphia Athletics to replace starter Bob Feller. Pieretti stepped into a red jeep and was whisked off toward the pitcher's mound, thus becoming the first pitcher to ride a bullpen vehicle in a major-league game. Indians groundskeeper Harold Bossard was the driver, which makes him the Buzz Aldrin of this tale. Since then, the fortunes of bullpen transportation have waxed and waned, but this is where it all began: with one small ride for man, and one giant leap for baseball-kind.

It was all part of an initiative by Cleveland general manager Hank Greenberg to speed up the length of games. The Indians' "jeep service" was his inspired response to the fact that the club's contests were dragging on that spring, averaging a then-long two and a half hours each. Greenberg told the *Cleveland Plain Dealer*, "I figure we will save at least seven minutes every time we bring in a relief pitcher." A little more than a year later, on June 8, 1951, the Chicago White Sox dispatched a station wagon from the center field bullpen to transport lefty reliever Marv Rotblatt to the mound in a game against the Yankees. The following game, when ChiSox hurler Randy Gumpert entered the game to pitch the ninth, the Bombers dugout responded by standing at attention in mock salute, with each player doffing his cap and holding it at arm's length. New York manager Casey Stengel told the media that his team was accustomed to riding in Cadillacs, and the Indians had a cream-colored Caddy convertible limousine waiting for them for their next visit to Cleveland. The stunt backfired, however, when Yankee pitcher Allie Reynolds tossed a no-hitter and the relief corps got the night off.

Other teams soon picked up on the bullpen car idea. In 1959, the Milwaukee Braves rolled out a Harley-Davidson Topper motor scooter to transport pitchers to the mound. Three years later, in 1962, the Los Angeles Angels—playing their home games at the Dodgers' new stadium at Chavez Ravine—used a motorized Turf Rider golf cart that was presented to the club by the city of Palm Springs, the club's spring-training home. Manager Bill Rigney changed pitchers so often that the press joked that the bullpen cart had almost as many miles on it as the team plane.

Boston was also an early adapter. Red Sox groundskeeper Al Forester drove a red, white, and blue electrically propelled cart at Fenway starting in the early '60s (one news report relayed the fact that he called it the "caht"). Forester enjoyed an especially close relationship with Red Sox great Ted Williams, who he drove to the pitcher's mound for the epic ceremony and first pitch that proceeded the 1999 All-Star Game. The New York Mets began to employ an uncovered orange cart in the late '60s—it transported Nolan Ryan in from the Shea Stadium bullpen for the only World Series appearance of his long career, during Game Three of the 1969 fall classic. The Yankees had a pinstriped golf cart which the home fans pelted with a range of objects, some of which were quite dangerous. The Bombers eventually shifted to a Datsun 1200 sedan, a compact passenger car that was decked out in Yankees logos and pinstripes. Toyota later became the automotive sponsor of the ballclub; one could purchase the actual 1979 bullpen Celica for $8,349.75, which included $89.25 for shipping. When Orioles pitcher Mike Flanagan was asked if he'd like to play for the Yanks, he quipped, "I could never play in New York. The first time I came into a game there, I got into the bullpen car and they told me to lock the doors."

The apotheosis of the bullpen cart was definitively achieved in October 1971, when the Baltimore Orioles and Pittsburgh Pirates squared off in the World Series. That fall, each club's bullpen was equipped with a fiberglass vehicle that resembled a large baseball, with oversized team-specific headwear situated squarely on top. The brim of the cap was supported by baseball-bat columns, there were bases for seats, and the front headlights were encased in authentic baseball gloves. The design of the vehicle is credited to Harry Bentley Bradley, who began his career as a member of the General Motors design team and later went on to work for Mattel, where he created the original line of Hot Wheels cars. In addition, he was also responsible for the 1995 redesign of the Oscar-Mayer Weinermobile.

The bullpen carts were manufactured by Universal Electro Motive Corp of North Hollywood, California, and were commissioned and owned by the Major League Baseball Promotions Corp, which was just then beginning to roll out a series of innovative marketing initiatives to help sell the sport. The buggies, which cost about $5,000 each, featured 20 horsepower motors and could pull up to a thousand pounds. MLB viewed the World Series introduction as an experiment, with the hopes that the carts would be "standard equipment" for every club the following season, in 1972.

The carts were a hit, and teams began to take delivery of their bespoke buggies the following spring. The newly formed Texas Rangers got one. The Mets were the only team to order two of them. The Detroit Tigers' bullpen buggy was exclusively reserved for promotional purposes, as the bullpens at Tiger Stadium were so close to the infield that they weren't needed. The Atlanta Braves' buggy featured their brand-new cap design, and the San Diego Padres' version highlighted their unique brown and gold paneled hat.

Unfortunately, we can't have nice things, and the bullpen buggy soon fell out of favor. It was a very 1970s construct and, in retrospect, perhaps it was just another fad of the era (like streaking, waterbeds, and pet rocks). Pitchers began to eschew them. Mike Marshall, the Dodgers' taciturn closer, preferred to jog in from the bullpen, and truth be told, it's hard to envision Trevor Hoffman entering a game to AC/DC's "Hells Bells" while being zipped out to the infield in a tricked-out golf cart.

At the dawn of the 1980s, the White Sox deployed a Chrysler LeBaron and the Seattle Mariners employed a tugboat-themed cart that they christened the *M. S. Relief*. In 1994, the Milwaukee Brewers introduced a Harley-Davidson motorcycle with a sidecar. When Kansas City reliever Hipolito Pichardo became the first to use it, he received a standing ovation.

Bullpen vehicles disappeared completely until 2018, when the Arizona Diamondbacks revived the capped baseball buggy. On May 5, 2018, Houston pitcher Colin McHugh became the first player in nearly a quarter century to hitch a ride, saying, "it was there, they provided it for us, so I decided to give it a shot." The Tigers and the Washington Nationals soon followed suit and, in May 2024, Minnesota Twins lefty Steven Okert made history when he rode in from the bullpen and tipped his driver with a crisp $5 bill before heading to the mound. "If there was an app, I would give them five stars," Okert told MLB.com. "It was a great ride in."

WWW.MARINERS.ORG

Difficult as it is to believe, there was once a time before people had electricity in their homes. Motorized vehicles were once new, and although some citizens of ancient Rome enjoyed the benefits of indoor plumbing, only about a third of all dwellings in America in 1940 had running water. So it was with the internet, which was in its infancy in 1994, the year that Major League Baseball earned the dubious distinction of becoming the first American pro sports league to lose its postseason due to a labor dispute.

As the strike dragged on into the offseason, a spark of light emerged from Seattle, which was fast emerging as a tech epicenter, home to newly formed Amazon and software giant Microsoft. Starbucks was up to 470 stores by the end of the year, with plans for further expansion. Millions of television viewers tuned in every week to watch fastidious Seattle psychiatrist Frasier Crane on NBC. Seattle's grunge music had already reverberated globally by 1994, and that summer, *Sports Illustrated* wrote that the Mariners' Ken Griffey Jr. had "confirmed his standing as the new Image of Baseball."

By year's end, there were only 10,000 websites and approximately 20 million internet users in the entire world. But on November 30, 1994, the Seattle Mariners, in conjunction with the Semaphore Corporation, became the first professional sports team to host their own website: www.mariners.org. The club said that they expected between five and ten thousand people to "tap in" once the season got going, and that they were considering extending its email system to players, so that fans could communicate directly with their favorite Mariners. Technically advanced folks who had sound cards in their computers could hear highlights from M's broadcaster Dave Niehaus. The Associated Press quoted team financial analyst Kevin Mason, who said, "If this thing gets hot and going, it's only a matter of time before all the teams join." A piece in the *Seattle Times* noted, "The M's are encouraged by the visual capabilities of the World Wide Web, which allows Internet users a graphic interface similar to a Macintosh or a PC using Microsoft Windows."

The players' strike officially ended on April 2, 1995, and a couple of weeks later, on April 21, 1995, Major League Baseball launched its own website, appropriately entitled www.MajorLeagueBaseball.com, which was created and maintained in conjunction with MCI, then America's second-biggest long-distance company.*

A feature article in the 1995 World Series program read, "The Internet, a vast network linking computers around the world, allows organizations and individuals to share information and communicate with each other. A part of the Internet known as the World Wide Web allows the delivery of information in multimedia form-words, pic-

* Interestingly, "mlb.com" was claimed by Morgan Lewis and Bockius LLP, the nation's fourth-largest law firm, which represented MLB in its negations with the players' association during the strike. They refused to relinquish the name until 2000, when a deal was finally reached.

tures, audio, and video. Major League Baseball @BAT is what is known as a 'Home Page' on the Web." The site included a trivia contest where fans could win tickets to the All-Star Game and World Series, a daily update of Cal Ripken's progress toward his eventual breaking of Lou Gehrig's longest consecutive games played streak, and reports on Dodgers pitcher Hideo Nomo's first MLB season. Team press releases, statistics, and schedules were included as well, and by August of that year, more than a thousand people were accessing the site every day, The following year, more than 33,000 fans, representing thirty countries, cast All-Star ballots online for the first time. By 1997, that number had risen to 260,000.

As the new millennium dawned, the internet definitively entered the American mainstream. History was made on August 26, 2002, when the 30,000 viewers in sixty-four countries watched MLB.TV's first-ever live-streamed game, between the New York Yankees and Texas Rangers at Yankee Stadium. The contest, which was streamed in 300k broadband video, was blacked out in the two teams' home markets.

Since then, of course, technology has sped forward in ways that would have seemed unfathomable back in the early '90s. Yet once upon a time in Seattle, Mariners fans fired up their 28.8k dial-up modems and connected with their team via the newfound magic of the information superhighway known as the internet.

ONE MILLION TOOTSIE ROLLS

Can you count to a million? Major League Baseball did so back in 1975.

That year, MLB teamed up with the folks at Tootsie Roll Industries to promote a contest in which fans could predict who would score the one millionth run in the history of the National and American Leagues. The promotion originated when Mark Sackler, a twenty-four-year-old baseball fanatic in Westport, Connecticut, received a pocket calculator for his birthday. For those too young to remember, pocket calculators were an expensive standalone tool back in the '70s. Sackler later reckoned that his cost $80, which would be the equivalent of something like $550 in today's dollars. At any rate, Sackler, armed with his fancy machine and a copy of the Macmillan's 1,664-page *The Baseball Encyclopedia*, figured out that someone was going to plate the one millionth run in NL and AL history, likely in early May 1975. The way he figured it, a total of 997,869 runs had been scored through the end of the 1974 season, which meant that MLB was 2,131 runs shy of the magic number.

Armed with this information, Sackler tapped into a family connection and approached Ted Worner Associates, a New York public relations firm, who in turn pitched the idea to MLB. The promotion was launched in Oakland during the 1974 World Series, and Stan Musial, Ernie Banks, and Ralph Branca were enlisted to help sell the contest, which featured a total of 496 prizes, including bicycles, portable television sets, binoculars, and cameras. Whoever named the correct player, team, and date of the big event would walk away with the grand prize: a total of one million pennies, or $10,000. An additional $10,000 would go to the Association of Professional Baseball Players of America, an organization which assisted ex-major leaguers who played too early to have qualified for inclusion in baseball's pension fund.

A nationwide publicity tour was conducted, and on April 29, 1975, what was described as a "computer-type center" was opened in Midtown Manhattan, equipped with state-of-the-art timing equipment intended to pinpoint the exact moment when the milestone occurred. Veteran broadcaster Mel Allen was brought in to officiate, and phone lines were connected to fourteen major league ballparks.

Two high-scoring games took place on Thursday, May 1 (with the Kansas City Royals defeating the California Angels, 11–10, and the Milwaukee Brewers pounding the Detroit Tigers, 17–3), accelerating the countdown, and the media predicted that the big moment would occur in either a night game on Saturday, May 3 or during a day game in the Eastern Time Zone on Sunday, May 4. They were wrong.

Going into Sunday's games, 31 runs were needed to break the mark. Oakland's Claudell Washington scored number 999,999 at 3:26 ET. Scoreboards across the nation lit up with the news that the milestone was nigh. Minnesota's Rod Carew and the Yankees' Chris Chambliss were each 90 feet away from immortality, but both were thrown out at home plate. Milwaukee first baseman

Tootsie Roll
Astros
27

George Scott nailed Chambliss at home on a grounder, and said, "I did that to Chambliss? Poor Chambliss ... If I knew that maybe I wouldn't have thrown him out ... yes, I would have, too."

Meanwhile, in Cincinnati, 51,030 fans at Riverfront Stadium thought they had witnessed history when Reds shortstop Dave Concepción hit a home run and tore around the bases at breakneck speed. He was mobbed by teammates at home plate and the scoreboard light up with the number "1,000,000." In reality, it was run number 1,000,001. The ballpark soon filled with boos when an announcement was made, relaying the news from San Francisco where, at precisely 12:32 and 30 seconds PT, Houston Astros first baseman Bob Watson sprinted home from second on a Milt May homer and plated the history-making run. Incredibly, Watson scored approximately four seconds before Concepción's toe hit home plate. Watson was rounding second and jogging at a leisurely clip toward third when he heard his teammates yelling from the bullpen, urging him to run hard. It turned out to be good advice. Afterward, he said, "It feels good to contribute something to baseball. I ran hard." As for Concepción, he told the *Dayton Daily News*, "I ran as fast as I could. Could I have run faster? Never in my life." Ninety-nine years and twelve days after the Boston Red Stockings catcher Tim McGinley scored the first run in National League history, Watson was credited with number one million.

The Astros-Giants game was halted and home plate was removed, slated for Cooperstown, along with Watson's jersey and spikes. Watson received a $1,000 Seiko watch and a million Tootsie Roll candies, which he donated to the Boys & Girls Clubs of America. The winner of the contest was announced at a press conference on May 22 in Chicago, and it was ten-year-old Arthur Schmidt of Lorain, Ohio, whose winning entry was selected from among fifty-one correct candidates. When young Arthur arrived at the Ford City Bank, there were only 150,000 pennies on hand due to a nationwide penny shortage, so alternative funds were obtained. He posed for a photo op with Watson, who was clad in his rainbow Astros uniform, Melvin J. Gordon, Tootsie Roll's chairman and CEO, and the deficient pile of pennies, which was buttressed by bags of quarters.

Watson earned a berth on the National League All-Star squad that summer and finished the season with a stellar .324 batting average. In 1977, he was featured in a cameo role in the film *The Bad News Bears in Breaking Training*, shouting, "Hey, c'mon, let the kids play!" from the Astrodome dugout. He went on to play for the Red Sox, Yankees, and Braves, where he wrapped up his 19-year playing career in 1984. Watson was back in Houston nine years later, where he was named Astros general manager on October 5, 1993. In 1996, Watson became the first Black GM to win a World Series when he helped guide the New York Yankees to the franchise's first title in eighteen years. After leaving the Bronx, he worked for the Commissioner's Office as vice president of on-field operations, and served as general manager of USA Baseball, helping to put together the 2000 United States Olympic Baseball Team, which won the gold medal in Sydney, Australia, that September. When Watson passed away in 2020, his unique contribution to baseball history was referenced in just about every published obituary, one fleeting moment in an expansive forty-five-year baseball career.

THE WHITE SOX TURN BACK THE CLOCK

When it opened its gates on July 1, 1910, Chicago's Comiskey Park was called the "Baseball Palace of the World." Comiskey hosted the first All-Star Game, Disco Demolition Night, the Beatles, and the first exploding scoreboard in major league history, along with some 6,247 major-league games over its eighty-year lifespan. Designed by Zachary Taylor Davis, an architect who later went on to design Wrigley Field, the place was built on fourteen acres purchased from the family of former Chicago mayor John Wentworth for $150,000. Its cornerstone was laid on St. Patrick's Day, March 17, 1910—a lone green brick that served as a reminder of the fact that White Sox owner Charles Comiskey—a Chicago native and the son of an Irish immigrant—was putting down roots in the Irish American Bridgeport neighborhood. Comiskey Park was a modern marvel. Built entirely of steel and concrete—twelve hundred tons of steel, to be precise—it seated 32,000 spectators when first opened, and its facade was lined with a series of elegant brick arches, offering up views of the surrounding neighborhood and the city beyond.

Eighty summers later it was showing its age, and a replacement was going up across the street. For White Sox fans, 1990 was a season for nostalgia, along with all of the conflicted feelings that accompany it. Paul Goldberger, writing in *The New York Times*, noted that Wrigley Field got all the attention, but "Comiskey is more real, a glorious, raunchy old place that has nothing picturesque about it at all. Over the years, Comiskey Park has been pushed and pulled and altered and expanded every which way, and it is so tough it never loses an ounce of its character. Wrigley is the field of dreams, but Comiskey is Chicago."

The White Sox, an organization with a colorful past and a tradition of innovative promotions, decided to throw a party on the afternoon of July 11, 1990. "Yesteryear is here," read newspaper ads. That day, the Sox rolled out baseball's first "Turn Back the Clock Day," a moment for time travel complete with nickel popcorn, 50 cent general admission tickets, and a manually operated scoreboard. Public address announcer Gene Honda announced the starting lineups with a megaphone, the rounds crew was nattily attired in knickers and suspenders, and legendary Sox organist Nancy Faust roamed the stands, playing an accordion. The star component of the day, however, was the White Sox' uniforms, which were inspired by the ones they wore in 1917. The Sox received special permission from the American League to wear the outfits, which were manufactured by Rawlings. Enthusiasm for the throwbacks was undoubtably fueled by the nostalgic baseball-themed film *Field of Dreams*, which had been released the previous year. The most significant difference between the 1917 set and the replica togs involved uniform numbers, a feature which the originals did not sport. Reactions were uniformly positive, especially among the players. Chicago shortstop Ozzie Guillén told a UPI reporter, "I like these uniforms better than

the uniforms we're wearing. Did you see the All-Star Game? The White Sox uniforms were the ugliest uniforms there." The press ate the whole thing up—the All-Star Game had been played at Wrigley Field the previous day, and many national media outlets hung around to witness the festivities on the South Side.

The idea for the promotion was suggested by fifteen-year-old Ken Adams, the son of Sox media relations chief Chuck Adams. Initially, the day was to have embraced 1910, the year the ballpark opened, but the club landed on a celebration of 1917, when they had last won the World Series. The game itself was ugly, as Chicago blew a 9–3 lead in the eighth and fell to the Milwaukee Brewers—who were wearing their standard road uniforms—12 to 9 in 13 innings. Even so, the 40,666 fans in attendance that day witnessed history and went home full of warm memories.

Several clubs jumped on the "Turn Back the Clock" bandwagon the following season. On June 16, 1991, the Phillies hosted the Reds, with both clubs clad in 1950s-era uniforms. The Baltimore Orioles threw things back to 1966 a few days later, and the San Francisco Giants dressed up like their 1925 New York ancestors a few days after that. A generation later, teams regularly do the throwback thing, but the first such day took place at the onetime "Baseball Palace of the World," Comiskey Park, on July 11, 1990.

EDWIN JACKSON, A TEAMMATE FOR ALL

Edwin Jackson Jr. was born on September 9, 1983, in Neu-Ulm, West Germany, where his father was stationed as a cook in the United States Army. The experience of having grown up in a foreign land served Jackson well during a nomadic baseball career, during which he played for a record-tying fourteen big-league clubs over seventeen seasons. It all began on his twentieth birthday, September 9, 2003, when he made his debut with the Los Angeles Dodgers. That night, facing the Arizona Diamondbacks, he stepped into the LA rotation and outdueled future Hall of Famer Randy Johnson, allowing just four hits and one earned run across six innings for his first career win.

After appearing in just 19 games over three seasons with the Dodgers, Jackson was traded to the Tampa Bay Devil Rays on January 14, 2006, and this set the wheels in motion for a head-spinning, coast-to-coast journey through the major leagues. After the trade, he told the *Los Angeles Times*, "I'm not disappointed. I'm not mad at anyone. As far as I'm concerned, it's a new start and a clean slate." Many such "new starts" would follow.

Jackson played three seasons in Tampa, a span during which the Devil Rays became the Rays, transforming themselves from a last place club into an American League pennant winner. After going 14–11 in 2008, the Rays traded him to the Detroit Tigers. He started the 2009 season with a 7–4 record and a 2.52 ERA and made his first All-Star team, eventually finishing the year with a solid 13–9 record. And while that would seem to have afforded him some job security, that clearly was not the case. On December 8, 2009, he was on the move again, this time as part of a three-team deal which involved Detroit, the New York Yankees, and the Arizona Diamondbacks. Jackson's short stay in Arizona was memorable—on June 25, he pitched a 149-pitch no-hitter against his old Tampa Bay teammates. A month later, however, the Diamondbacks shipped him off to the Chicago White Sox at the trade deadline.

If Jackson had hoped to have a permanent home in the Windy City, he obviously hadn't been paying attention. After 19 starts (going 7–7), he was acquired by the St. Louis Cardinals as part of a mammoth eleven player, three-team swap that included the White Sox and Toronto Blue Jays. Jackson was traded to Toronto, who then flipped him to the Cardinals, meaning that he was a member of two bird-themed teams in two different countries within a 24-hour span.

After appearing in 13 regular-season games for St. Louis, Jackson made his first career playoff start that fall, stepping onto the mound in Game Four of the NLDS against the Philadelphia Phillies. With the Cardinals down two games to one and facing elimination, Jackson stepped up, throwing six innings while giving up just two earned runs to notch his first career playoff victory. Even though he lost his only World Series start in Game Four against the Texas Rangers, the Cardinals won the fall classic, earning Jackson his first (and only) Series ring.

Having played for six teams in nine years, Jackson got his first shot at free agency that winter. In February 2012, he spurned a couple of potential long-term deals with American League teams and agreed to a one-year contact with the Washington Nationals. After 31 starts and a 10–11 record, he once again became a free agent. It was back to Chicago in 2013—this time with the Cubs—who signed him to a four year, $52 million deal. His stint there was disappointing (he went 14–33 in his first two seasons), and Chicago designated him for assignment in July 2015. He hooked up with the Atlanta Braves eighteen days later, where he pitched in 24 games. A free agent once again, Jackson signed with the Miami Marlins on January 13, 2016. He pitched in only eight games there before being released that June. He was then picked up by the San Diego Padres a couple of weeks later, threw a total of 13 games for them, and then signed a minor-league deal with Baltimore for 2017.

He joined the Orioles—his twelfth big-league team—on June 7. Baltimore manager Buck Showalter spoke of Jackson's journey and value in comments he made to the Associated Press. "I look at it as, he's had something for a long time that people are in need of, and he's evolved a little bit as a pitcher as he's gotten older." As for Jackson, he said of himself, "Like a wise man told me, it's not about making it, it's about staying. It's great to make it back, but there's still a lot of work to be done." He made only three appearances for the O's before they designated him for assignment a week later, on June 11.

His next stop was less than forty miles down the road, as he reconnected with the Washington Nationals, the following week. Jackson started 13 games for the Nats (going 5–6) and was cut loose the following June, after which he joined the Oakland Athletics five days later. It was in Oakland that he tied the record for most teams played for, matching pitcher Octavio Dotel, who had been a teammate of Jackson's on the 2011 Cardinals.

The 2019 season proved to be the end of Edwin Jackson's long and winding baseball career. He started the season in Oakland's minor-league system and was then traded to Toronto. On May 15, he set the record when he started and pitched five innings in a game against the San Francisco Giants. One final stop awaited. The Blue Jays released Jackson on July 19, and he signed on to pitch for the Tigers, where he had last played a decade earlier. Jackson tossed the final 10 games of his circuitous career in Motown. He inked a minor-league deal with Arizona

the following spring, but the 2020 season was delayed and then cut short by the COVID-19 pandemic.

Jackson wound up pitching in 412 major-league games, throwing 1,960 innings with a 107–133 record and 4.78 ERA. Always a popular and affable teammate, Jackson seemingly embraced the ups and downs and travels of his meandering career. In 2017, he told Syracuse.com, "That's life, man. I'm a military brat, so I'm used to life on the go, living out of the suitcases. It seemed like it was pre-destined for me to be a rolling stone. I get a chance to say I lived in a lot of different cities. More than the average person. I've got a chance to experience a lot of different cultures. I kind of feel like that's my personality anyway. I like to experience different things. I've definitely had a chance to do that."

Edwin Jackson officially announced his retirement via Instagram on September 9, 2022, his thirty-ninth birthday and the nineteenth anniversary of his major-league debut. He was effusive in his thanks to family, teammates, coaches, and trainers, writing, "Today I am happily hanging up my cleats.… I'm super grateful to have had 14 different organizations allow me the opportunity to represent them. I was once told by a mentor that you are only as strong as the team you have around you, and I have an amazing team." Those teams were the Los Angeles Dodgers, Tampa Bay Rays, Detroit Tigers, Arizona Diamondbacks, Chicago White Sox, St. Louis Cardinals, Washington Nationals, Chicago Cubs, Atlanta Braves, Miami Marlins, San Diego Padres, Baltimore Orioles, Oakland Athletics, and Toronto Blue Jays.

Three years later, forty-five-year-old lefty pitcher Rich Hill tied Jackson's record for most teams played for when he joined the Kansas City Royals. Remarkably, even though their careers overlapped for a decade and a half, Hill and Jackson were never teammates.

THE DISCARDED MASCOT HALL OF FAME

Attend a Major League Baseball game at any ballpark not called Dodger Stadium or Yankee Stadium and you are going to see a costumed mascot. The modern era of costumed mascots originated with the San Diego Chicken, played by Ted Giannoulas, who began entertaining Padres fans in 1974 and continued to do so for decades thereafter. The Phillie Phanatic has been cruising around the field terrorizing Phillies opponents since 1978, and Baltimore's Oriole Bird was hatched a year later. The Rockies have a dinosaur named Dinger, Mr. and Mrs. Met hold forth in Queens, and Wally the Green Monster, the Red Sox' furry green mascot, has been doing his thing at Fenway since 1997. But for every Pirate Parrot, Swinging Friar, or Mariner Moose, there have been outcasts, washouts, misfits, and retired or forgotten mascots that warrant a second look. Some of them, in fact, were downright terrifying.

The New York Yankees have a well-earned reputation as an organization that embraces tradition, but in July 1979, the club introduced a mustachioed seven-foot tall, furry character named "Dandy." The mascot was confined to the uppermost reaches of Yankee Stadium, which is one of the reasons that this short-lived departure from all that Yankee seriousness is nearly forgotten. A game program from the era states that Dandy is "a little different than the others . . . during the game he remains in the stands and off the field. . . . [T]he Yankees introduced Dandy to help add to the enjoyment of families and children at the ball game. But they didn't want him to distract the players or umpires or take away from the great game of baseball." Dandy was created by Bonnie Erickson and Wayde Harrison, the husband/wife team that was responsible for the Phillie Phanatic and the Montréal Expos' "Youppi!" The Yankees leased Dandy from Harrison and Erickson for three years at a cost of $10,000 per annum, and, when the contract expired, Dandy expired as well—a brief, uncharacteristic experiment whose conclusion just happen to kickstart a rare down era in team history, during which the Bronx faithful could have used some lightness and levity.

In 1976, the Atlanta Braves rolled out the "Bleacher Creature," a lumpy, green character with bright red eyes and a large, empty mouth. Some observers compared its appearance to that of a gross shag carpet. The *Atlanta Journal* described it as "miserable," "pitiful," and "embarrassingly awful." Created by Atlanta costume designer Kathy Spetz, the mascot was the brainchild of Braves public relations director Bob Hope, who said that it was inspired by his young daughter's love for *Sesame Street*'s Cookie Monster. He originally proposed calling it "The Baseball Monster," but a naming contest was held ("Rozzin Bag" was one of the finalists), and the Bleacher Creature was born. Georgia Tech student Alan Stensland inhabited the costume, which he described as being extremely hot and smelly. A revised version was rolled out in 1980. and the mascot was soon sent down to the minors to entertain fans of the Braves' Class-A affiliate in Anderson, South Carolina.

Some mascots came and went with such brevity that they barely registered before disappearing forever. The 1978 Montréal Expos had Souki, a figure with a large baseball-shaped head and a spacesuit that was described as a "*Star Wars* creature." *Montréal Gazette* writer Tim Burke dubbed him "Monsieur Foul Ball." On Opening Day of the 1992 season, the San Diego Padres introduced "Bluepper," a large dog in a Padres uniform with a backwards hat and a baseball nose who kind of resembled Walt Disney's Goofy character. Lefty and Righty, a pair of large red socks with droopy eyelids, green eyes, and eye black, were the seldom-seen "alternate mascots" for the Boston Red Sox for a handful of seasons in the mid-2000s, and Twinkie the Loon repped the Minnesota Twins at old Metropolitan Stadium in 1980 and 1981.

The Houston Astros' first live mascot was "Chester Charge," a cartoony Texas Cavalry soldier who was accompanied by his trusty sidekick, Charlie the Horse. In 1981, the club rolled out two mascots, Astrojack, a huge jackrabbit, and Astrodillo, an armadillo who wore a large orange cowboy hat. They patrolled the Astrodome's artificial playing surface on ATVs and interacted with fans in the stands.

In 1972, Cincinnati Reds CEO Dick Wagner attended a football game at Davidson University, where his son went to college. Wagner's wife, Gloria, took note of the school's wildcat mascot and suggested that the Reds create one for themselves. The following season, Mr. Red was born. A walking depiction of the club's logo, Mr. Red sported a baseball head that was 28 inches in diameter, in addition to a reputation for a dull image. Team management confined Mr. Red's activities to shaking hands and signing autographs, mostly outside of Riverfront Stadium. *Cincinnati Enquirer* scribe Tim Sullivan proclaimed Mr. Red as baseball's worst mascot: "Doesn't dance, doesn't mime. Doesn't amuse."

The Texas Rangers rolled out "Rootin' Tootin' Ranger" in June 1979. A Yosemite Sam lookalike with a yellow cowboy hat and yellow chaps, the mascot was cut loose after just a season and a half. The 1980 season witnessed the debut of the Cleveland Indians' "Baseball Bug," a rotund insect that the *Cleveland Plain Dealer* described as "a cross between a bird and a flea." The mascot's high point came the following season when Yankees owner George M. Steinbrenner filed a protest with the American League after the bug used the top of the visiting Yankee dugout to lead cheers. In 1990, the Oakland Athletics introduced a pachyderm mascot named Harry Elephante, which later gave way to Stomper.

Decades before the San Francisco Giants rolled out their loveable Lou Seal character, there was the Crazy Crab, an "anti-mascot" that debuted in 1984 and was intended to parody all of those cute, furry characters that were being introduced at that moment. According to Giants executive Pat Gallagher, "We did a phone survey in the offseason and 63 percent of the Giants fans we contacted said that they would boo any mascot that came on the field. We decided to see if they were serious." The crab was designed to be rejected and to get attention—negative attention—antagonizing crabby Giants fans who attended home games at chilly Candlestick Park, notorious for its howling winds and bitterly cold temperatures. The Giants were a bad ballclub in 1984, and Gallagher and the club got exactly what they wanted. Fans booed the crab, a loopy-looking pink/orange crustacean who skittered across the field and pretended to moon the crowd who, in turn, pelted the mascot with trash and showered it with beer. About a million fans braved the elements and showed up at Candlestick in 1984, the Crazy Crab's one and only season.

Pour one out for the late Chief Noc-A-Homa. Lift a toast to Toronto's BJ Birdy, the White Sox' Ribbie and Roobarb, and the Angels' Scoop and Clutch. They live eternally in the Discarded Mascot Hall of Fame, surrounded by dozens of their peers, at least one of which was compared to a gross shag carpet.

FRANCHISES

LOU 1
ATL 2

FLA 0
INDY 5

INNING
5

0 BALL
2 STRIKE
1 OUT

FIRST IN BOOZE, FIRST IN SHOES...

This jersey bears witness to the sad final chapter in a fifty-two-year saga that began in 1902, when the Milwaukee Brewers moved to St. Louis and were transformed into the Browns. Over the course of that long span, the Browns authored the worst cumulative performance in the American League, posting a winning record on just twelve occasions. They played in precisely one World Series (1944), when MLB's talent pool was decimated by World War II, losing to their hometown rivals and tenants, the St. Louis Cardinals in six games, all of which were played in the same ballpark. The Browns played second banana to the Cardinals for the vast majority of their tenure in St. Louis, which should come as no real surprise, considering the timing of the Cardinals' ascendancy to baseball superpower status, beginning in 1926, when they won their first World Series. This was followed by eight more pennants and five more world championships during the years in which the two clubs shared a city and a ballpark.

The Great Depression was not especially kind to any of the sixteen National and American League clubs, but the Browns suffered a particularly cruel fate. This was the moment when the "Gashouse Gang" Cardinals captured the nation's imagination, and it coincided with a typically dreadful stretch for the Browns, whose attendance—which was by far the primary source of club revenue at the time—suffered tremendously. In 1935, the Browns drew a total of 80,922 fans at home, an average of 1,079 customers per game

THE ST. LOUIS BROWNS EMBLEM

DESIGNED BY HELEN SEEVERS OF ST. LOUIS, A PIONEERING ADVERTISING EXECUTIVE, THE WINNING SUBMISSION IN A 1937 CONTEST THAT DREW MORE THAN 2,000 ENTRIES

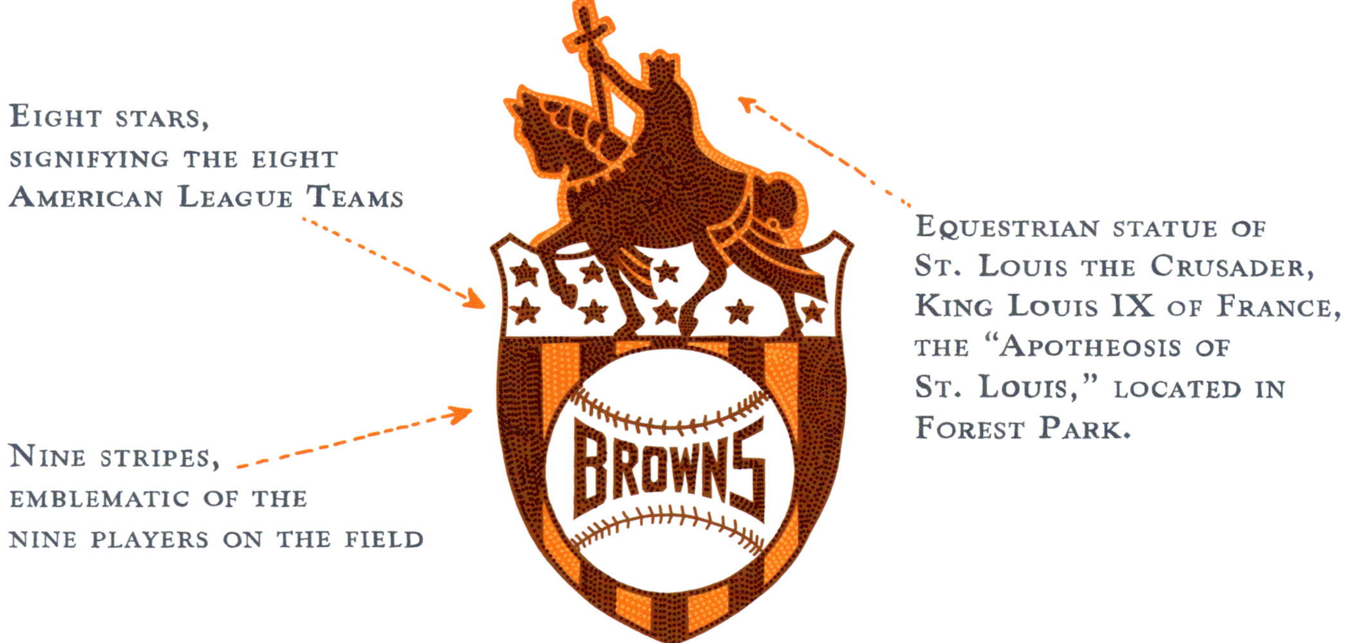

(which was 152,251 less than the last-place Philadelphia A's). While this putrid number no doubt jumps off the page, the fact is that the club struggled to draw throughout its history, with an average game attendance of less than 4,000 fans over the span of their more than half-century in St Louis. Seeking an exit and a fresh start, the Brownies planned a bold and revolutionary move to Los Angeles after the 1941 season—but world events intervened. The club had lined up league approval, a plan for cross-country travel, a schedule, and a home ballpark. American League owners were slated to approve the shift at a meeting on December 8, 1941, but Japan attacked US forces at Pearl Harbor the day prior to the vote, catapulting the United States into World War II. America went to war, and the Brownies stayed put.

By the time that Bill Veeck bought the franchise in June 1951, the Browns were running on fumes. Working his legendary marketing mojo, Veeck immediately set out to improve the club, cleaning and renovating Sportsman's Park, and bringing 3-foot-7 Eddie Gaedel aboard to pinch-hit during an August game against the Detroit Tigers. Forty-five-year-old Satchel Paige (who Veeck had signed to pitch for his Cleveland Indians in 1948), joined the team and, for the first time in a long time, the Browns garnered positive attention, despite losing 102 games.

Prior to the 1952 season, Veeck rolled out new home and road uniforms, and they were praised for their classy, clean, and businesslike appearance. "I know it's a change of pace for me, because I'm sure people probably expect me to trot a ballclub in polka dots," quipped Veeck, but these togs were commended for being downright Yankee-like in their simplicity and elegance. The color brown was in, in a big way, and orange was pretty much eliminated altogether. The 1952 Browns won a dozen more games than they won the previous season, and attendance spiked upward. Even with such an "improvement," this temporary respite did not change the fact that St. Louis could not support two major-league baseball teams. The Cardinals franchise was in the midst of an organization-wide decline at this point. Their vaunted farm system had dried up, and the club's owner, Fred Saigh, was banished from baseball after being sentenced to federal prison for income tax evasion. Amidst this chaotic backdrop, the Cardinals were rumored to be headed for Milwaukee or Houston, and it looked like Veeck would win the battle for St. Louis . . . that was, until local brewing behemoth Anheuser-Busch stepped in and bought the NL club. Veeck, unable to compete with Anheuser-Busch's seemingly endless resources, saw the writing on the wall and sought to transfer his Browns to Milwaukee—the city they started in, way back in 1901. A pair of other cities with both NL and AL clubs, Philadelphia and Boston, eyed new markets, and the Boston Braves struck first when they shook up the baseball map for the first time in a half century, beating Veeck to the punch and shifting the franchise to Wisconsin for the 1953 season. Veeck quickly turned his attention to Baltimore, but ongoing skirmishes with his fellow American League owners did him no favors. Out of options, Veeck sold the Browns to a group headed by Baltimore attorney Clarence Miles, and the team moved to Charm City in 1954, where they still play today as the Baltimore Orioles.

In April 1911, when the Browns were still in their relative infancy, a writer going by the wondrous sobriquet "Bolivar St. Vitus" penned a letter to the *St. Louis Post Dispatch*, terming that city, "first in shoes, first in booze, and last in the American League." The day after the letter was published, the Browns opened up their tenth season in St. Louis with a 12–3 win over Cleveland. By the time October rolled around, the Browns had finished up with a record of 45 wins and 107 losses. The Browns are now mostly forgotten, but at least they looked good when they expired.

ELEPHANTS ON PARADE

It was something akin to a fantasy baseball team come to life. On the afternoon of June 11, 1927, seven future Hall of Famers played in a game for the Philadelphia Athletics: Eddie Collins, Zack Wheat, Ty Cobb, Al Simmons, Jimmie Foxx, Mickey Cochrane, and Lefty Grove. Another future inductee, manager Connie Mack, filled out the lineup card that day. All of them wore this jersey, which featured no wording—just a team symbol that dates back to the earliest days of the franchise.

Why an elephant? Hardly a symbol of athleticism, the Athletics' elephant has a unique origin story attached to it, one that dates back to July 10, 1902. Mack explained it all in his 1950 autobiography, *My 66 Years in the Big Leagues*.

> *The insignia of our Philadelphia Athletics, as you know, is the White Elephant. The story of acquiring it is an interesting one. In 1902, the Baltimore Club forfeited its franchise in the newly formed American League. Its spot was filled by the New York Highlanders, "the acorn from which sprung the mighty Yankee oak." The astute John McGraw took advantage of the opportunity and jumped from the crumbling Orioles to the New York Giants, a leap to fame and fortune. When the sportswriters gathered around McGraw to fire a barrage of questions, one of the questions was, "What do you think of the Philadelphia A's?" "White elephants!" quickly retorted Mr. McGraw. "[Athletics team owner] Mr. B. F. Shibe has a white elephant on his hands."*

The Oxford English Dictionary describes a white elephant as, "A burdensome or costly objective, enterprise, or possession . . . a financial liability."

Within weeks of McGraw's comments, the "white elephant" tag began to take hold in the collective public imagination. Mack turned the tables and adopted the symbol as a badge of honor for his young franchise. It was already being described as "famous" less than three weeks after McGraw made his remarks. The A's and their fans embraced the symbol, and when the team appeared in their first World Series in 1905 against McGraw's Giants, the A's defiantly presented him with a miniature elephant statue.

The club formally adopted the elephant as a part of their visual identity five years later, when they wore sweaters featuring a simple white pachyderm. After the heavily favored Athletics lost the 1914 World Series to the Boston Braves, Mack broke up his perennially contending team, and the A's fortunes immediately plummeted as they finished in last place for the next eight consecutive seasons. Perhaps looking for a change of luck, the team put the elephant on their uniforms for two seasons, in 1918 and 1919, in the form of a sleeve patch. The 1919 club was horrible and finished with a record of 36 wins and 104 losses. As those losses piled up, players began to cut the no longer lucky elephant off of their uniform sleeves.

Mack doubled down for the 1920 season when he decided, for the first time ever, to place the symbol on the *fronts* of his team's jerseys. The uniforms featured a crude-

PHILADELPHIA

KANSAS CITY

OAKLAND

ly drawn elephant in a standing position, rendered in a lucky green color on the home togs and in blue on the road. Robert Maxwell, writing in Philadelphia's *Public Ledger*, quipped, "The sacred elephant will be given another tryout at Shibe Park next season," noting that the symbol would be given "one last chance to show whether he is the goods or only unadulterated hokum."

The 1920 A's lost 106 games.

The 1921–23 version, rendered in blue, was a bit more detailed. Finally, the version worn from 1924–27 depicted the white elephant as a *white* elephant. It could well be that this is what was holding them back all along, as this jersey is connected with a newly prosperous era for the club.

After a decade of insignificance, the Athletics returned to contention, finishing in second place in 1925 and 1927. The traditional Olde English "A" was restored to the fronts of the jerseys in 1928, and the team won two straight World Series in 1929–30, followed by an American League pennant in '31. When the franchise relocated to Kansas City in 1955, it arrived with a refreshed set of uniforms that included an elephant sleeve patch. However, by the dawn of the 1960s, the winds of change began to blow. On January 20, 1961, the day that John F. Kennedy was inaugurated as the thirty-fifth president of the United States, the Athletics announced that they were retiring the elephant logo from their uniforms.

The franchise moved again in 1968, this time to Oakland. A nucleus of talented young players began to emerge, and the A's won three consecutive World Series titles, in 1972, 1973, and '74. The elephant symbol was nowhere to be seen then, but history repeated itself when owner Charles O. Finley, echoing Connie Mack, broke up the team. Difficult years and an ownership change followed, and, by 1987, a change of luck was needed yet again. That season, the Athletics unveiled a new set of traditional uniforms which resembled those worn in Kansas City three decades earlier. One thing, however, was missing. Thankfully, this was rectified the following year, when the team restored the elephant symbol to their jerseys. This move coincided with a new golden era for the A's, culminating in (yet another) three consecutive World Series appearances.

The nomadic A's wandered off yet again in 2025, when they departed Oakland for West Sacramento, an interim shift that will supposedly end with a "permanent" move to Las Vegas in 2028. For the time being, the Athletics have opted to refer to themselves simply as "The Athletics," with no geographic designation as part of their official name. They also dropped the elephant from their uniforms, but one can easily envision it returning at some future point. It's a resilient and defiant symbol, born on a summer day in 1902 when John McGraw dropped an offhanded insult to a group of baseball writers.

CAPITAL CHAOS

Beginning in 1901, two different Washington Senators clubs combined to play seventy-one years of largely uninspired and unspectacular baseball, with but a single World Series title and fifty seasons spent in the second division to show for it. The Senators' final act, however, WAS memorable, though not in a good way. The funeral took place at Robert F. Kennedy Stadium on the night of September 30, 1971, when a crowd of some 18,000 mourners gathered to bid their team adieu before it headed off to Arlington, Texas. While nostalgia and loss unquestionably weighed on people's minds, anger was the principal theme of the night, and the wrath of the crowd was firmly directed at club owner Bob Short.

One week earlier, American League owners had met in Boston to discuss the plight of the Senators, a perennially underfunded operation that suffered from chronic mismanagement and widespread fan apathy. The moguls spent 12 hours and 45 minutes behind closed doors, debating the future of the team. At 11:20 p.m., Oakland A's owner Charles O. Finley escorted Arlington Texas mayor Tom Vandergriff into the conclave. Vandergriff's pitch was Texas-sized—a sweetheart deal that included a guaranteed package of financial incentives to bring the club to the Lone Star State. When a vote was finally taken, only the Chicago White Sox and Baltimore Orioles dissented. Earlier that same evening, a sparse assemblage of 1,311 Senators fans watched their team beat Cleveland by a score of 9 to 1. Within hours, a spokesman for President Richard M. Nixon, an avid Senators fan, said that the chief executive would be shifting his allegiances to the California Angels.

The Senators' final game, against the New York Yankees, provided one final opportunity for fans to vent. Newspapers described the atmosphere as unsentimental. Seventy-four-year-old Bucky Harris, who broke in with the original Senators in 1919 and, as manager, led them to their only world championship five years later, was on hand. He told journalist Jim Ogle, "I'm stunned. I still can't believe it's happening … I never thought I'd see the day when they would leave Washington without a franchise." Fans hung banners throughout RFK Stadium, most of which excoriated Short, but one simply read, "You've been bad, but you're all we've got." Washington pitcher Dick Bosman, who started the game, later told the *Washington Post*, "There were banners everywhere, and I got pretty emotional. They had a Bob Short effigy. It wasn't your typical crowd, because they were there to protest us leaving."

New York staked starter Mike Kekich a to 5–1 lead when DC fan favorite Frank Howard stepped to the plate to lead off the sixth inning. Kekich looked to Yankees manager Ralph Houk in the dugout and threw Howard a cookie, a 2-0 fastball that Howard, nicknamed "the Capital Punisher," catapulted into the upper deck in left field for the final home run in Senators history. He thanked Yankees catcher Thurman Munson, who told him, "You still had to hit it out." Washington fans erupted with uncharacteristic joy, Howard blew

kisses to the crowd, and the Senators scored three more runs to tie the game. Euphoria gave way to darkness an inning later, however, after Washington took the lead. Spectators ran out on to the field in both the seventh and eighth innings, and warnings were issued by the umpires, but the field was cleared after each instance and play resumed. With two outs in the top of the ninth, the dam burst. Hundreds of fans swarmed the field, mobbing the players, stealing bases, attempting to dig up home plate, and dismantling the scoreboard, creating a chaotic and dangerous scene. Scoreboard keeper Norm Hammer was quoted by UPI as saying, "I felt like I was in a castle, looking down on an invading army." Three minutes into the turmoil, chief umpire John Odom declared a forfeit, awarding the game to the Yankees by an automatic 9–0 score, the first time this had happened since 1954.

Exactly 33 years, 6 months, and 15 days later, the Washington Nationals—newly arrived by way of Montréal—played their first home game. The mood at RFK Stadium was joyous and optimistic, and a group of former Senators took in the field during pregame festivities. Frank Howard received the biggest ovation, and President George W. Bush, who was once managing general partner of the Texas Rangers (formerly the Washington Senators) threw out the ceremonial first pitch, welcoming baseball back to the nation's capital.

THE BIRTH OF THE RED SOX

Boston is a charter member of the American League, dating back to 1901. But, as hard as it might seem to believe, they weren't always called the Red Sox, nor have they always played their home games at Fenway Park.

In their inaugural season, the club played their home games at Huntington Avenue Grounds, located across the New York, New Haven and Hartford Railroad tracks from the South End Grounds, which was then home to Boston's National League club (now the Atlanta Braves).

The Red Sox didn't have an official nickname at first and were generally known as the Boston Americans (in recognition of the league in which they played).

The Huntington Avenue Grounds was an intimate facility, primarily made of wood, constructed at a cost of $35,000 on the site of a lot that previously hosted carnivals and traveling circuses. This is where Buffalo Bill's Wild West Show performed when they visited Boston in the late nineteenth century. The site had been known as the Huntington Avenue Chutes, and was described as Boston's favorite pleasure grounds, where patrons could shoot the rapids into an artificial lake, visit an ostrich farm, ride donkeys and ponies, and listen to live music. Throughout its history as a ballpark there were areas in the outfield that were subpar at best, with sandy spots where grass couldn't grow and what were described as "hip-high" weeds. There was a large tool shed located in center field—which was in play—but, surprisingly, that didn't seem to be an issue. The original dimensions were a cavernous 530 feet to center field, but that was changed in 1908—to an even more cavernous 635 feet, or a little more than twice the distance from today's Green Monster in left field to home plate.

On March 7, 1901, a crowd of some three hundred diehards braved a cold west wind to witness the groundbreaking for the new park. Fireworks were set off in the big basin, which was previously used as a skating rink, and a lunch and champagne toasts followed. Construction took only a couple of months, and the new American

League team inaugurated the park on May 8, 1901, with a 12–4 victory over the Philadelphia Athletics. A huge crowd of 11,000 fans filled the place, which included spectators on the diamond behind ropes in both left and right fields. Two years later, in 1903, Huntington Avenue Grounds hosted the first modern World Series. In a best-of-nine tilt, Boston bested the Pittsburgh Pirates (five games to three), winning the championship on October 13, 1903, with Honus Wagner striking out to end the Series. The following season, Young tossed a perfect game there, a 3–0 whitewashing of Philadelphia.

Three years after that, in 1907, the Boston Nationals—who first wore red stockings when they were founded in 1871—abandoned their signature look. Sensing a void, the owner of Boston's American League team, John Irving Taylor, swooped in, announcing that his club—which was coming off a turbulent season (finishing 49–105)—would henceforth be dubbed "Red Sox." The hosiery part was simple, but Taylor took things a step further when he ordered up these jerseys, which conveyed the new moniker in unmistakable fashion. Cy Young pitched the team's opening game on April 14, 1908—a complete-game victory—and Red Sox they have been ever since.

As the 1911 season concluded, the Red Sox had a decision to make. The lease on Huntington Avenue was expiring, and opportunities awaited in Boston's Fenway neighborhood. The team played their final game at Huntington Avenue Grounds on October 7, 1911, an 8 to 1 win over Washington, and the ballpark was razed soon thereafter. Northeastern University later acquired the site and in 1954, built the Cabot Center, an indoor athletic facility, atop where the first modern World Series was contested. There is a statue of Cy Young there, along with a commemorative plaque marking the spot.

Back to 1908. That year, the newly designated Red Sox finished the season in fifth place, 15 1/2 games behind the league champion Detroit Tigers. Shortly before Christmas, club treasurer Hugh McBreen announced that the uniforms were to be eliminated. "'Red Sox' is ugly, indistinguishable, and doesn't carry with it the dignity that should go with a uniform," he said. The name, however, stuck.

GUNS-A-BLAZING

They are the only MLB club ever to have displayed a smoking Colt .45 pistol across the fronts of their uniforms. Named in honor of "the gun that won the West," the Houston Colt .45 made their debut in these jerseys on April 10, 1962, in a 11–2 win against the Chicago Cubs. Houston had been awarded a National League franchise in 1960, with plans in place to construct the world's first domed stadium. The team, however, would need to brave three seasons outdoors at Colt Stadium, a $2 million, 33,000-seat temporary ballpark that was described as "a cross between Disneyland and the Wild West."

Constructed in a mere five months, Colt Stadium was a bare-bones affair, consisting of a one-level uncovered grandstand that stretched from foul pole to foul pole, with small bleacher sections in right and left field. There was no roofline or canopy—nothing to offer protection from the relentless Texas sun or rain. The makeshift structure was reportedly built on a marsh, and the mosquitoes there were the stuff of legend. Rusty Staub, who broke in with the Colts during their second season, later told *The New York Times*, "We kept mosquito repellent in the dugout, and we'd spray ourselves before we went on the field," Ron Swoboda never played there, but said that, as a visiting rookie playing in the Astrodome in 1965, "They told us we were lucky. They said the mosquitoes in the old ballpark used to pick cats right off the ground and fly away with them."

During one doubleheader in June 1962, seventy-eight fans and an umpire received medical attention due to the extreme conditions. The same month, Colt Stadium became the first major-league park to sell insect repellent at its concession stands. All that aside, the ballpark was, in many ways, colorful. The exterior of the stadium was painted aqua and white, and the colors of the seats corresponded to the colors of a fan's tickets—chartreuse, turquoise, burnt orange, and pink. A team of 150 female ushers, dubbed "Triggerettes," helped patrons find their seats—they were outfitted in customized pinstriped baseball jerseys, pleated skirts, and orange patent leather shoes. Parking attendants wore orange ten-gallon hats. They directed cars into areas named for legendary figures of the Old West, such as "Wyatt Earp Territory." The Fast Draw Club, a members-only restaurant and bar, cost $150 a season to join. Servers there were garbed in saloon-style attire, and because Texas law prohibited the sale of liquor by the glass (except in private clubs), members could purchase what was described as "a Texas sized schooner of beer" for 50 cents, while booze was a dollar a shot.

No tears were shed when the Colts played their final game there, on September 27, 1964. A gathering of 6,246 diehards watched Don Drysdale of the Los Angeles Dodgers pitch 10 innings of shutout baseball—but the Colts' Bob Bruce bested that, tossing a 12-inning complete-game shutout, as the home team won, 1–0.

As for the ballpark, it quickly fell into disrepair and became populated by rattlesnakes. In 1971, it was sold for $100,000 to a minor-league team in Mexico, disas-

COLTS

sembled, combined with pieces of the ballpark that the Texas Rangers' Arlington Stadium had recently replaced, and shipped south of the border, where it was given the nickname "El Mecanico"—Spanish for "erector set." This took four years. The reconstituted park was taken apart and moved again in 1982, this time to Tampico, Mexico. A section of the stadium now sits in a playground there, and the original site in Houston is a parking lot, just north of where NRG Stadium (home of the NFL's Houston Texans) now sits.

The team shifted across the parking lot to "the Eighth Wonder of the World" in 1965: the Houston Astrodome. With the move, they also transformed their identity, changing their name to Astros—a symbolic move toward the future, leaving the Wild West behind. This played out just as the good folks at NASA, located just down the road, were making plans to put a man on the moon by the end of the decade. The Dome debuted during an exhibition game with the Yankees, on April 9, 1965. President Lyndon B. Johnson nibbled on hors d'oeuvres and ate chicken and ice cream and Mickey Mantle hit the first indoor home run, but none of that would have been possible without the Colt .45s and their austere, mosquito-plagued stadium having led the way.

THE ANGELS TAKE FLIGHT

At 2:25 on the afternoon of Wednesday, December 7, 1960, a gaggle of reporters gathered in the Tiara Room of the Park Plaza Hotel, twenty-seven floors high above the Central West End of St. Louis. The American and National Leagues had convened there for several days for their annual winter meetings, and Commissioner Ford Frick was on hand to convey some momentous news: the American League had been granted permission to expand into Los Angeles for the 1961 season. The agreement between the rival leagues amounted to what many called "The Missouri Compromise," with New York scheduled to return to the National League fold in 1962. As for LA, Opening Day was around the corner, a mere 125 days away. Those eighteen weeks represented the shortest runway between the granting of an expansion club and its first game in MLB history. A franchise would need to be built, from the ground up, in just over four months: a front office would need to be hired, a roster constructed, and a spring training home secured. How about a farm system? And marketing and ticket sales and a manager and coaching staff?

A useful, more modern comparison would involve the Tampa Bay Devil Rays and Arizona Diamondbacks franchises, who were added on March 9, 1995. Their first games took place more than three years later, 1,118 days after the teams were officially welcomed into the MLB family. The newborn Los Angeles Angels, on the other hand, had no time to waste.

The franchise ownership group was headed up by Gene Autry, Hollywood's "Singing Cowboy," and Bob Reynolds, a radio station executive and former Stanford football star. They immediately announced that the team would play its home games at 21,000-seat Wrigley Field, the former home of the minor-league Pacific Coast League Angels. The compromise agreement that opened the doors for their new entry involved a significant payment to Walter O'Malley and the Dodgers for the right to join them in their territory, which O'Malley had strenuously defended from the moment he shifted his franchise west from Brooklyn. The Angels also inked a four-year lease to play at the Dodgers' luxurious new ballpark, which was slated to open in 1962.

Autry and Reynolds immediately tabbed former Milwaukee Braves general manager Fred Haney to build the club, and his first task (of many) was to find a field manager. Casey Stengel, who had been dismissed by the New York Yankees at the conclusion of the 1960 World Series, was the front-runner. He interviewed for the position but declined it, citing the fact that he had just signed a $400,000 deal to serialize his life story for the *Saturday Evening Post*, an arrangement which stipulated that he not manage in 1961. The job instead went to Bill Rigney, the former Giants skipper. This was announced on Monday, December 12, which provided "ample time" to prepare for the team's expansion draft, which was scheduled to take place the following day. The weather gods provided a brief respite in the form of a blizzard, which postponed the draft twenty-four hours.

L
A

The Angels and their expansion partners, the new Washington Senators, took turns selecting twenty-eight players each from the rosters of the existing eight American League franchises: a group of castoffs, discards, and leftovers, forking over a cool $75,000 per man. Twenty-six-year-old Yankees pitcher Eli Grba was selected first by Los Angeles, a newly minted trivia answer in search of a vowel.

The weeks ahead were frenetic, to say the least. On Friday, the club appointed its first publicity director, Irv Kaze. More importantly, they announced the site of their spring training camp: Palm Springs, California, where players would report to some seventy-two days later. The week prior to Christmas brought forth a series of front office appointments, and the week between Christmas and New Year's involved community outreach, marketing, and the unveiling of a spring training schedule.

After a short break to start the new year, the Angels named thirty-four-year-old Roland Hemond as their farm director on January 3. He immediately got busy planting a brand-new farm with nothing but soil. With just about all the minor-league clubs already affiliated with big-league partners, Hemond was left with few options. The Triple-A Dallas-Fort Worth Rangers soon joined the fold, and Class D Statesville (North Carolina) of the Western Carolina League was added on February 17.

On February 6, a total of 272 candidates attended an open tryout that was held at the Veterans Hospital baseball field in West LA. Multitasking was the order of the day, so the Angels used the opportunity to unveil their new uniforms, with Rigney modeling the team's new white home togs and his coaches Marv Grissom, Red Kress, and Bob Elliott showing off the road grays.

Equipment manager Tommy Ferguson and trainer A. J. "Freddie" Frederico arrived in Palm Springs on February 15, followed by Rigney and his staff a few days later. The club announced the signing of its first Black American player, the outstandingly named pitcher Morris Cigar. Former president Dwight D. Eisenhower showed up to training camp on March 1, donning a halo-topped Angels cap and chatting amiably with members of the new club, cracking jokes, and demonstrating a keen knowledge of the players. He autographed first baseman Steve Bilko's glove, posed for pictures, and watched the franchise's first intrasquad game from the first-base dugout, staying for all five innings.

The Angels' first spring training game took place on March 11, against a Chicago Cubs split-squad team. Entertainer Dinah Shore threw out the ceremonial first pitch, an errant toss that wound up striking a photographer. Finally, a month later, on April 11, the club played its first regular-season game, a convincing 7–2 road win over the Orioles during which slugger Ted Kluszewski slammed homers in his first two at bats. Just 125 days after they were created out of thin air, the mighty Los Angeles Angels were not only alive, but undefeated.

ONE AND DONE

The Seattle Pilots were a one-year wonder, an expansion club that moved to Milwaukee just days before what would have been their second season in the Pacific Northwest. More than a half-century removed from their lone campaign, the Pilots are perhaps best remembered for two things: their innovative uniforms—which included caps with embroidered oak leaves, or "scrambled eggs" across their visors—and their role in Jim Bouton's seminal book, *Ball Four*. Those trivial facts, along with the 162 games that they played in 1969, give them a unique place in modern baseball history.

Seattle, a city with a storied minor-league past, was officially admitted to the American League on October 18, 1967, along with a new team in Kansas City. This hastily arranged scheme was conceived in conjunction with the approval of the Kansas City Athletics' move to Oakland. Both new franchises were to join the league "as soon as practicable," but no later than 1971. Seattle's team was conveyed on a contingency basis, dependent upon local voters' approval of a new $40 million domed stadium, which would later become The Kingdome. The league's timeline was accelerated, however, when Missouri Senator Stuart Symington, stung by the A's departure, threatened to attack baseball's antitrust exemption. Chaos ensued—the National League made noises about grabbing Seattle for themselves, but AL owners decided to fast track things, and both Kansas City and Seattle began play in 1969. This exceptionally short runway was not a problem in Kansas City, where deep-pocketed Ewing Kaufmann was tapped as owner of the Royals. Seattle's situation, on the other hand, was entirely different.

The Seattle franchise was awarded to a consortium that included Pacific Coast League president Dewey Soriano and his brother Max, with former Cleveland owner William Daley coming aboard as the club's biggest shareholder. The group was highly leveraged and severely undercapitalized, and was saddled with antiquated, undersized Sick's Stadium as its home park. Sick's, built in 1938, underwent a crash renovation, which immediately went awry. Construction was delayed, costs ballooned, subcontractors went unpaid, and more than 200 workers were still toiling away to get the place ready the night before the April 11 home opener. The ballpark's total capacity for the first half of the season hovered at somewhere around 20,000, and the slapdash renovations did nothing to improve the park's water pressure, which was reputed to have been virtually nonexistent when crowds exceeded 10,000, forcing players to return to their hotels or homes to shower up after games. Meanwhile, attendance was hindered by the fact that the Pilots' ticket prices were the highest in baseball, which was necessitated by the fact that they were playing in the smallest stadium in all of MLB.

Expectations for on-field success were low, but the Pilots hung tough through the first half. Summer proved to be their undoing, however, as the club went 15–42 in July and August, en route to a 64–98 record at season's end. In August, the club and the city of Seattle locked horns, with the Pilots accusing the city of failing to deliver a major-league

S
attle

quality facility. The city, in turn, threatened to evict the team unless they posted a reported $600,000 letter of credit and a $150,000 performance bond. Rumors flew of a move to either Dallas-Fort Worth or Milwaukee, and the Pilots limped to the finish line, drawing only 680,495 paying customers, an average of just 9,451 fans per game.

The Pilots' sad one-year journey ended with a series of court injunctions, aborted attempts to keep the club in the Pacific Northwest, and, ultimately, the decision of a federal bankruptcy court referee named Sidney Volinn, who ruled that the club was insolvent. At precisely 10:21 p.m., on March 31, 1970, Volinn approved the sale of the Pilots to Milwaukee Brewers, Inc, a group led by Allen H."Bud" Selig, for $10.8 million. With Opening Day just a week away, the Pilots' equipment truck was stuck in Las Vegas, awaiting word on whether it would head west to Seattle or east to Milwaukee. "It's obvious that the club cannot pay its debts and may well be insolvent, wrote Volinn. "The unique character of a major league baseball team has been considered, and its importance to the community has been considered, but it's obvious the debtors (Pilots) are incapable of carrying on. That is beyond question."

The Pilots' demise resulted in yet more legal drama when local officials sued the American League, claiming antitrust violations, fraud, and breach of contracts. The case meandered its way through the court system and was suspended when the league voted to place a new franchise in Seattle—the Mariners—for the 1977 season. The Pilots' tenure was brief, but their legacy lives on two cities: Milwaukee and Seattle.

NEW BEGINNINGS IN THE VALLEY OF ASHES

The New York Mets entered the world as an expansion franchise in 1962—a National League replacement for the Giants and Dodgers, who both departed the Big Apple for California five years earlier. The Mets, along with their expansion brethren, the Houston Colt .45s, were disadvantaged right from the start. The draft to stock the new clubs' rosters was held the day after the 1961 World Series concluded, and the group of available players consisted of a motley assortment of unheralded prospects and veteran castoffs in a process that *The New York Times* likened to "a rummage sale." The existing National League clubs devised a draft system that was heavily stacked against the new entries, offering up what author Jimmy Breslin termed "mostly old guys" on the cusp of being released anyway. As expected, the Mets' first two seasons were abysmal. They went 91–231 over the course of those campaigns, resulting in a .283 winning percentage and back-to-back last-place finishes.

The club sprung to life at the decrepit Polo Grounds, which had begun to fall into disrepair two decades earlier when the Giants played there (by the end of the Giants' tenure, *Sports Illustrated* called it "an antiquated museum"). The Mets spiffed up the old place, sinking $350,000 into renovations, which included a coat of blue and orange paint, but when they left after the 1963 season, the demolition crew arrived, using the same wrecking ball that brought down Ebbets Field in 1960.

Bigger things and a brighter future awaited in Queens, where the state-of-the-art Shea Stadium would usher in a new era for the ballclub and for the city of New York. In 1964 and 1965, the Mets wore a sleeve patch commemorating the New York World's Fair. The patch depicted the Unisphere, the 140-foot tall stainless-steel globe that served as the theme symbol of the Fair, which took place at Flushing Meadows–Corona Park (right next to Shea). All of this was constructed atop F. Scott Fitzgerald's "valley of ashes," the former Corona Ash Dumps.

The stadium was named for William Shea, the powerful New York lawyer who was instrumental in delivering National League baseball back to Gotham. On April 16, 1964, he consecrated the new structure by pouring out the contents of two small champagne bottles at first base. One contained water from the Harlem River at the exact location where it passed the old Polo Grounds, the other from Brooklyn's Gowanus Canal. Shea said, "You couldn't see the Gowanus from Ebbets Field, but you could always smell it."

Shea Stadium opened to the public on April 17, when the Mets lost to the Pittsburgh Pirates, 4–3—Mets manager Casey Stengel quipped, "the park is lovelier than my team."

Expectations for the Mets were tempered, but the promise of a new, ultramodern stadium—combined with the big party taking place next door—brought 1.7 million spectators through the turnstiles. Those fans saw their share of history in 1964. This was Stengel's final full season as manager, the beginning of the end of a long career that began in Brooklyn back in 1934. Six weeks into the season, on May 31, the Mets and Giants gathered at

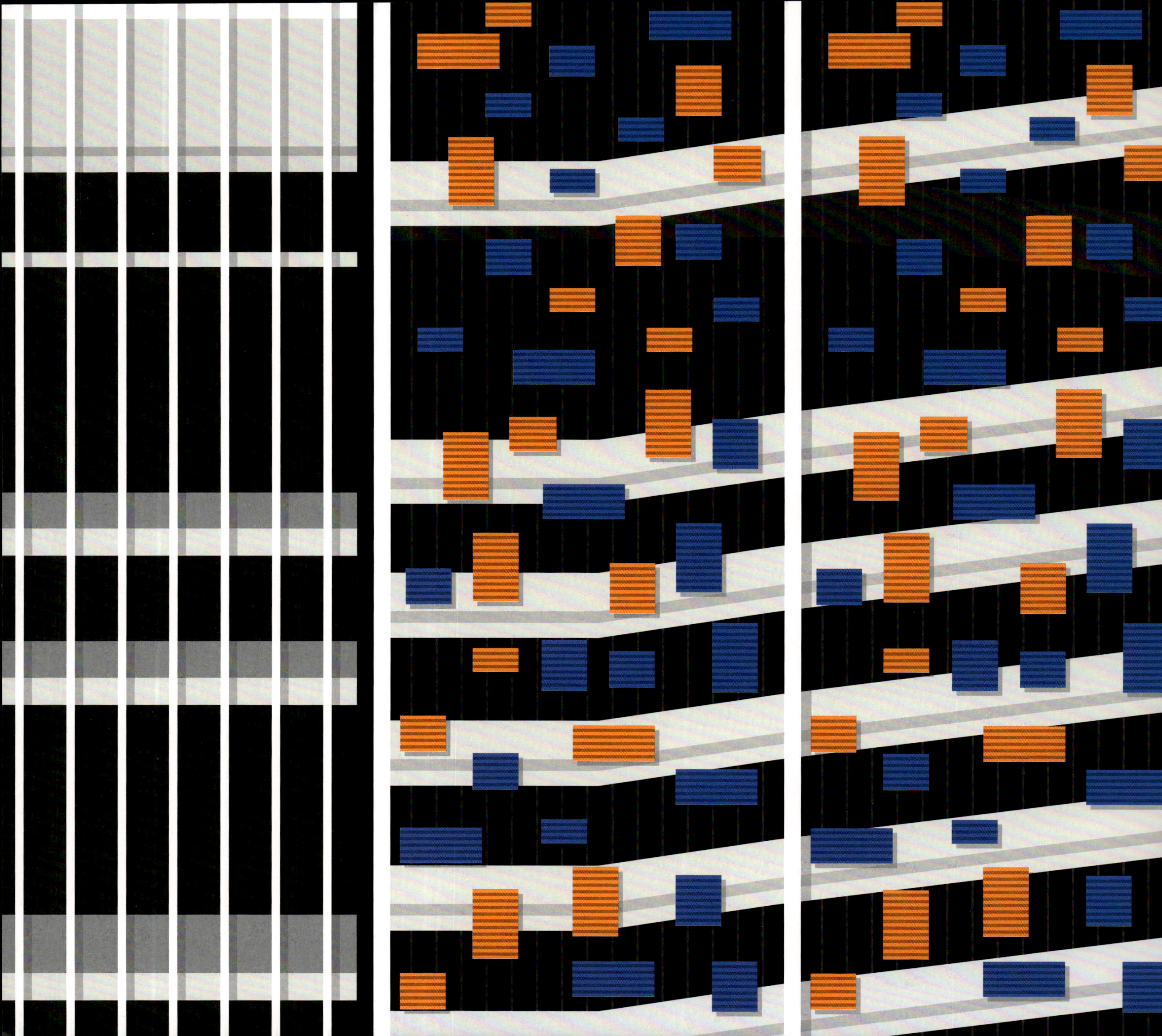

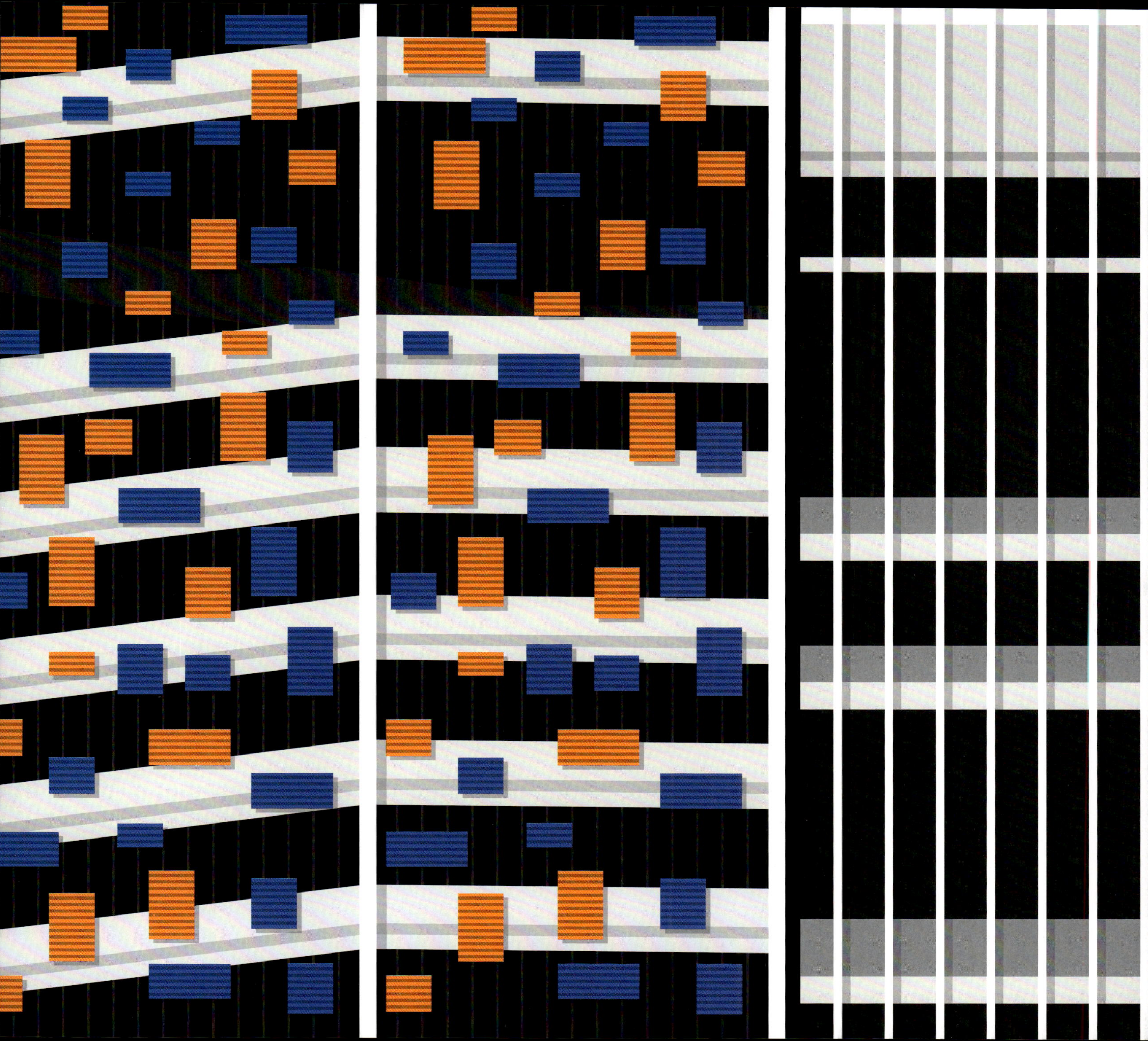

Shea for what would be an epic and exhausting day for players and fans alike. A huge Memorial Day weekend crowd of 57,037 braved windy, drizzly conditions and came out to see a scheduled doubleheader. The two teams completed the first game in a snappy two and a half hours, with San Francisco emerging victorious, 5 to 3, powered by a complete game thrown by Juan Marichal.

The second game, on the other hand, was a 23-inning marathon, which lasted 7 hours and 23 minutes. With the final pitch thrown close to 11 o'clock at night—nearly ten and a half hours after the initial first pitch—an estimated 8,000 to 10,000 fans stayed until the whole thing was over And, of course, the Mets came up short again, this time by a score of 8 to 6. Future Hall of Famer Gaylord Perry got the win in relief, throwing 10 (!) innings, and the game also included a triple play, which the Mets pulled off way back in the 14th inning.

On Father's Day, June 21, Philadelphia's Jim Bunning threw a perfect game, the National League's first perfecto since John Montgomery Ward of the Providence Grays tossed one way back in 1880. A little more than two weeks later, Shea was the site of the All-Star Game, a 7–4 victory for the NL. The Phillies' Johnny Callison ended the game with a walk-off home run, and did so while wearing a blue Mets batting helmet (as he had neglected to bring his own to New York with him).

But there were green shoots available for the optimists who were following along that summer. On July 12, the Mets swept a doubleheader from the Reds, the first time they had won two games in one day since June 23, 1963, when they swept the Phillies at the Polo Grounds. As *The New York Times* pointed out, "That was so long ago that the site no longer exists." Between those two sweeps, the Mets played in an amazing twenty-one doubleheaders without sweeping one, or, as *The Times* put it, "In the 2 1/2 years of their existence, they have achieved two successes in one day just seven times in 62 opportunities." The faithful were rewarded just five years later when the Amazin' Mets won the 1969 World Series—at Shea—proof, as Tug McGraw would later say, that "ya gotta believe."

BALLPARKS

TROY	6	INNING	2	BALL
KC	0	6	1	STRIKE
STL	2		0	OUT
TB	3			

THE GREAT
CONFLAGRATION
SOUTH END GROUNDS
BOSTON, MASS.
MAY 15, 1894

A FANCIFUL TURRETED BASEBALL CASTLE

The Atlanta Braves were founded in Boston, where they played for their first eight decades. For seven seasons, their home ballpark was a remarkable structure that some have called the most beautiful stadium in the history of major-league baseball. The South End Grounds, constructed on the same parcel of land as a previous ballpark, first opened its gates on May 25, 1888. Its appearance was magnificent—an ornate, elegant castle which included a series of medieval-style spires and turrets. Pennants flew atop the grandstand, which suggested an arena from the days of King Arthur, or maybe a jousting tournament at a modern-day renaissance faire.

Designed in what was described as "modernized form of Romanesque style," the park's exterior was clad in brick and terra cotta, and was flanked by a pair of 100 foot tall staircase towers at either end. It also included what the *Boston Evening Transcript* described as a "base ball register," invented by the Parker brothers of Waltham, which was erected on the center-field fence. "By means of electric wires, which run from the board along the fence to a position in the pavilion, an operator sitting there, by touching a knob, registers on the board the decisions of the umpire as to balls and strikes, giving the number of each, and also whether a batter or a runner is out."

Built at a cost of some $70,000, the South End Grounds remains the first and only double-decked stadium ever constructed in the city of Boston. (Fenway Park's rooftop seating was added decades after it opened in 1912.) This revolutionary setup meant that fans in the bleachers and grandstand were separated, a precursor to assigned seating at modern ballparks. The inclusion of an upper deck also inspired one unfortunate spectator to pen a letter to the *Boston Globe* shortly after the place opened, which read, in part, "Is there no way in which spitting tobacco juice from the balcony of the new grandstand on the South End grounds down on the clothing of the spectators below can be stopped? At the afternoon game on Memorial Day, myself and a friend were greatly annoyed by the ungentlemanly and filthy conduct of those above our heads."

The elaborate two-tiered, curved grandstand, which sat a total of 2,800 fans, was rightfully referred to as "the Grand Pavilion." It was designed by Philadelphia architect John Jerome Deery, who also designed the Phillies' Baker Bowl. There was a press box directly behind home plate, and every reporter was assigned what was described as "a hinged desk." The team, known in those days as the Boston Beaneaters, finished in fourth place in 1888 but drew well, with a reported 300,000 paying customers having passed through the turnstiles by season's end.

The story of this stylish stadium, however, ended in a violent conflagration. On May 15, 1894, the Beaneaters were playing the Baltimore Orioles when, in the middle of the third inning, a fire began underneath the right-field bleachers. Boston outfielder James "Foxy Grandpa" Bannon attempted to stomp it out with his feet, but high winds conspired to propel the embers, and the flames quickly spread to left field. At 4:22, a general alarm brought out the city's entire fire department, along with departments from all neighboring towns within twenty miles. However, when grounds superintendent John Haggerty urged the fire marshal to ring in a second alarm, the marshal balked. As the *Boston Globe* reported, "District Chief Sayer told Haggerty to go to a place reputed much warmer than even the ball grounds." Beaneaters co-owner William Conant raced to the nearest available telephone and called it in, but by then it was too late. At 4:40, the blaze "kissed the handsome tower of the $70,000 pavilion" and, ten minutes later, "shot across the roof as if by electricity." The entire ballpark ignited. Within an hour, twelve acres were laid to waste, including 200 structures. Nearly 2,000 people were left homeless in what became known as the Great Roxbury Fire.

After the fire, the team relocated to Congress Street Grounds in what is now Boston's Seaport District. That ballpark's first tenant was the Boston Reds of the Players' League, which disbanded after its lone season in 1890. The Beaneaters' stay there was even more brief, just 27 games over two months, and it featured an inordinate number of home runs due to its offense-friendly proportions. The *Baltimore Sun* noted that "the great number of home runs which are daily made in Boston might induce some to believe that the Boston players are terrific batters," but "The left field fence in Boston is so short that any long fly to left field sails over it." On May 30, 1894, Boston second baseman Bobby Lowe went yard four times there, becoming the first major leaguer to hit four home runs in a single game.

As spring gave way to summer, Boston management constructed a new, single-decked park, but it paled in comparison to the majestic structure that had previously stood there. The old ballpark was insured for only 60 cents on the dollar, and its replacement was modest by comparison. Built in ten weeks, the new South End Grounds served as home to the club until 1914, by which time they had become known as the Braves. A visit to the site today offers up few if any hints of what stood there from 1888 until 1894. Northeastern University's ultramodern $225 million, 234,000 square foot Interdisciplinary Science and Engineering building opened on the site in 2017. This cutting-edge science facility has won multiple architectural awards, hosting labs, classrooms, offices, and the like, and it features a glazed curtain wall that's been described as a "glowing, textural envelope." Even so, it's no fanciful and elegant medieval baseball castle.

ONE DOZEN CONCRETE DONUTS

They were bland, gray, and symmetrical, and they popped up all across the land in the 1960s and '70s, from Cincinnati to Seattle. Multi-purpose stadiums were once all the rage—practical, convenient, and usually carpeted with synthetic turf. These "concrete donuts" symbolized the future for many cities . . . and it worked for a while, even if the sightlines were less than optimal and the fan experience was often forgettable.

New York's Shea Stadium housed the champion Mets and Jets, the Oakland Coliseum hosted the dynastic A's and the Super Bowl–winning Raiders, and in Pittsburgh, Three Rivers Stadium was home to the Pirates and Steelers, who won a combined six championships there.

Baseball's resurgence in the late 1980s signaled the death knell for the cookie-cutter stadium as team owners wanted greater control over stadium revenues and fans wanted more amenities and greater charm. Baseball's stadium boom of the '90s and early 2000s ensured that its future would look much like its past, but concrete and AstroTurf once reigned supreme, from sea to shining sea.

YANKEE STADIUM'S MAJESTIC CROWN

For fifty years it sat perched high atop Yankee Stadium: an elegant, signature design element that served as the backdrop for generations of glorious New York Octobers. It appears in countless images, unmistakable and graceful, oozing pure Yankee gravitas. Yankee Stadium's majestic ornamental frieze—which crowned its upper deck—embodied the grandeur of the original stadium from 1923 until 1973, when it was disassembled and discarded for scrap.

Often referred to as the "façade," the frieze was created by an unknown architect employed at Cleveland's Osborn Engineering Company. At first it was said to have been as shiny as a copper penny. Even before the Stadium opened its doors, however, the frieze began to oxidize to a verdigris hue, which was the intended effect all along. A December 1922 article in the *Binghamton Press* and *Sun Bulletin* stated, "The frieze is already taking on a greenish "patina" over 100 feet above the level of the lower boxes." Initial plans called for it to be fabricated out of galvanized metal, which was to have been painted a "soft green color," meant to harmonize with the color of the field. Maintenance costs were projected to be prohibitive, however, so the Osborn Engineering folks turned to copper—a lot of copper. The numbers were staggering: the frieze weighed fifteen tons and covered some 900 linear feet. Its stately arches and keyholes were topped by a series of flagpoles, which imparted an even greater sense of celebration and majesty.

Some have speculated that the design was influenced by Pennsylvania's Tunkhannock Creek Viaduct, also known as the Nicholson Bridge, which was the world's largest concrete railroad bridge when it was completed in 1915. There are also similarities to the High Bridge, the 1848 steel arch structure that spans the Harlem River, connecting the Bronx and Manhattan, located just north of the stadium.

The Yankees, their stadium, and its surrounding neighborhood were in steep decline in the mid-1960s. Just prior to the 1967 season, the club embarked upon a $1.3 million "modernization program" for the ballpark

that was most visibly embodied by a new coat of paint, both inside and out. A total of ninety tons of white paint were used to resurface the stadium's 3.7 million square feet, which included the copper frieze. This all-white look, with blue seats—as opposed to the original green—defined the stadium over the course of its last seven seasons.

The old ballpark underwent a massive structural renovation that began shortly after the Yankees played their final game of the 1973 season, and one of the first items of business was the dismantling of the iconic frieze, which was cast aside and sold for scrap—presumably melted down and recycled. A couple of small fragments survived, including one that's displayed in the museum at the current Yankee Stadium.

While the capacity of the newly renovated park was downsized by more than ten thousand seats, the upper deck of the grandstand was expanded upward. The tall steel pillars that obstructed views for half a century were eliminated and replaced by a cantilever system that added ten very steep new rows, which were topped off by a sleek and modern bank of lights that spanned the structure where the frieze might otherwise have been. The initial "conceptual" renderings for the refurbished stadium appeared in the 1972 Yankees yearbook, and there was no trace of the frieze to be found. However, a diminished concrete replica was included when the new/old ballpark opened its doors in 1976, built atop the state-of-the-art bleacher-length scoreboards.

Yankee Stadium was, of course, replaced by another Yankee Stadium, which made its debut in 2009. This one is ringed with a new generation frieze built for the twenty-first century, made of steel and coated with zinc to prevent it from rusting, protected by two layers of clean white paint on top. It represents a reverent nod to the real thing, but it's decidedly flat and unidimensional, a little dumbed down, and kind of flimsy-looking—a "fauxback," a pastiche.

Two sections of the 1976-era concrete frieze were eventually incorporated into Heritage Park, the public ballfield that occupies the site of the original Yankee Stadium. Go there, watch the neighborhood residents play softball, and imagine the dignified splendor of the 1923 ballpark and the patinaed copper frieze which once ringed its apex, a silent witness to all the history and memories that once played out on the vast green field below.

TIGER
STADIUM

LAST CALL AT THE CORNER

The ghosts of Detroit's Tiger Stadium gathered for one last game on September 27, 1999—a sunny, unseasonably warm day that rekindled memories of summers past for those in attendance.

A crowd of 43,356 fans came out to celebrate the venerable ballpark and its long history that day, and Detroit's starting lineup wore the uniform numbers of Tigers legends. Center fielder Gabe Kapler wore no number at all, a tribute to Ty Cobb, whose career predated digits on jerseys. Karim Garcia wore Al Kaline's number 6, first baseman Tony Clark wore Hank Greenberg's number 5, and catcher Brad Ausmus wore Bill Freehan's 11. All of them were united by the Tigers' Olde English D, a Detroit mainstay that was first worn by the Western League's Detroit Tigers in 1896.

The Tigers beat the Kansas City Royals that day, 8–2, and the final hit was an eighth-inning grand slam off the bat of Detroit's Robert Fick, who wore Norm Cash's number 25. After the game was completed, the grounds crew dug up the seventy-five-pound home plate and transported it to the club's future home, Comerica Park, located one mile east.

Longtime Tiger broadcaster Ernie Harwell presided over the postgame ceremonies, which featured a range of Tigers legends, suited up in full uniform. Mark "The Bird" Fidrych headed out to the pitcher's mound, where he dropped to his knees and tidied things up to his liking, just as he did during his magical summer of 1976 (he also took a little baggie of the dirt for himself). Alan Trammell and Lou Whitaker took the field together, as always. Trammell told the *Detroit Free Press*, "We said we were just going to run out there and do what was natural." Michigan native and fan favorite Kirk Gibson hopped out onto the field from behind the center field fence to the crowd's delight. A ceremonial Tigers flag was lowered and passed down the line of former players, finally landing in the hands of former pitcher Elden Auker, who made his major-league debut with Detroit in 1933. As he prepared to pass the flag to Ausmus, he said,

> *Sixty-six years ago, I threw my first pitch as a Tiger from this very pitcher's mound that we see tonight. It's a great honor to be selected to present this flag to you, Brad. This flag symbolizes eighty-eight years of baseball here at the corner of Michigan and Trumbull. Behind me stands over seventy years of Tiger history. Each of us has touched this flag today, as this ballpark has touched not only the players, but the many millions of fans who have watched a game at Tiger Stadium.*

Baseball was played at the corner of corner of Michigan Avenue and Trumbull Street in Detroit's Corktown neighborhood for 103 summers. The first park there was secured in November 1895 by George Vanderbeck, owner of the minor-league Tigers, who signed a five-year lease for what was previously the site of a haymarket. He built a 5,000-seat wooden park and named it Bennett Field. The Western League was renamed the American League in 1900, and the AL declared itself a major league the following year. As Detroit's nascent auto industry prospered and the city's population boomed, Bennett Park was razed after the 1911

season, replaced with a steel and concrete ballpark that would eventually play host to 6,873 regular-season games, 35 postseason games, and three All-Star Games. A total of 11,111 home runs were hit here, including Babe Ruth's 700th career homer. Reggie Jackson hit a titanic shot in the 1971 All-Star Game that caromed off a transformer on the roof in right field. The stadium was called Navin Field, then Briggs Stadium, and finally, from 1961 until it closed in 1999, Tiger Stadium.

The 23,000-seat Navin Field opened on April 20, 1912, the same day as Boston's Fenway Park made its debut and the very same day that the RMS *Titanic* sank after hitting an iceberg in the North Atlantic. Ty Cobb stole home in the first inning of play there, thus scoring the very first run at the new venue. The park was expanded in the middle of the Great Depression, a leap of faith for a community that suffered from an unemployment rate of approximately 35 percent. The renovated ballpark, now called Briggs Stadium, ballooned to a mammoth 53,000 seats. It hosted World Series–winning clubs in 1935 and 1945, and lights were added in 1948, making it the final American League ballpark to be illuminated for night games.

New ownership rechristened the place Tiger Stadium in 1961, with $3,000 allocated to amend the ballpark's four large electric signs, a cost that was contained by the fact that only two new letters were required to swap BRIGGS for TIGER in neon tubing. On the other hand, 4,300 scorecard pencils needed to be replaced, along with what was described as 4,675 souvenir buttons and 2,370 pennants.

The Tigers won the 1968 World Series, just as the city was in the midst of a precipitous decline. Tiger Stadium was aging, and the area around it had become dangerous. A series of potential replacement venues was floated, including a triple-decked 110,000-seat behemoth that would have hosted the 1968 Summer Olympics, along with the Tigers and the NFL's Lions. In 1972, the club signed a forty-year lease to play at a new $126 million domed stadium on Detroit's downtown riverfront, scheduled to open up in 1975. This fell through. The club won the 1984 World Series for the final world championship at the fabled Corner. In October 1997, ground was broken in downtown Detroit for what would become Comerica Park, which opened in 2000.

The hulking abandoned old ballpark remained standing for years after the Tigers moved; demolition finally began in 2008. Ten years later, it was reimagined and rededicated as the Detroit Police Athletic League's Willie Horton Field of Dreams, complete with a nine-acre diamond, situated atop Tiger Stadium's old footprint. The ghosts presumably stuck around. But on that evening in 1999, after all the fanfare and with the stadium lights dimmed, the last words spoken—most appropriately—were by the great Ernie Harwell.

> *It's been 88 moving years at Michigan and Trumbull. The tradition built here shall endure, along with the permanence of the Olde English D. But tonight, we must say goodbye. Farewell, old friend. Tiger Stadium, we will remember.*

SAVE FENWAY PARK!

Fenway Park has served as home of the Boston Red Sox since William Howard Taft was president. It is a Boston institution on par with the Freedom Trail, Beacon Hill, and the Boston Common, a living landmark that has welcomed more than 175 million fans through its turnstiles over the generations. Today, Fenway is revered and marketed by the club as "America's Most Beloved Ballpark"—but that wasn't always in case.

Back in 1999, Fenway was targeted for extinction, slated to be replaced by a $545 million successor that was scheduled to open in 2003.

The opening of Baltimore's revolutionary, retro-styled Oriole Park at Camden Yards in 1992 ushered in a golden age of ballpark construction, and the writing was seemingly on the wall for the game's oldest parks. The promise of thoughtfully designed, baseball-only stadiums—complete with comfortable seats, improved access, and better sightlines, dripping with evocative nostalgic ambiance—appealed to a lot of fans. Team owners salivated at the potential for increased revenues. And while few tears were shed when San Francisco's Candlestick Park bit the dust in 1999, the potential loss of Fenway inspired a robust public debate. Rick Reilly, writing in *Sports Illustrated*, summed one side of the discussion up perfectly when he wrote, "Let me get this straight: We're bulldozing real vintage ballparks like Tiger Stadium and Fenway Park to put up fake vintage ballparks?"

On May 15, 1999, the Red Sox unveiled a plan for what was supposed to have become Fenway II, a 44,130-seat brick-and-steel pastiche version of the real thing, replete with ornamental arches, keystones, replica old-timey decorative tapestry brickwork, and a healthy dollop of Fenway's signature green paint. It was to have included 5,000 club seats, ninety-five luxury suites, and two parking garages—all of which were designed to goose revenues in order for the Red Sox to be able to compete with their baseball brethren, especially the despised New York Yankees. An emotional chief operating officer John Harrington told the *Boston Globe*, "In the long run, it's just not feasible to compete in Fenway." And, of course, it goes without saying that all of this was to have involved a significant public subsidy.

The new Fenway was to have been built adjacent to the existing ballpark, between Brookline Avenue and Boylston Street. Plans involved sinking the new park twenty feet below street level grade—an accommodation to the modest scale of the old park and its surrounding neighborhood. The original Green Monster was to have been preserved in place as part of a public park, with a shiny new version replacing it in the new stadium. There were discussions about the inclusion of a ladder on the new wall (just like the old one!) and a new Pesky's Pole in right, as well as a single red seat in the right field bleachers, marking where Ted Williams's mammoth 502-foot home run landed in 1946, even if *that* ball actually landed in a spot that was to be demolished in favor of new development.

Two months after the announcement, the Red Sox hosted the 1999 All-Star Game, which was envisioned as a grand farewell to the old place. The various events that surrounded the game itself unfolded in electric fashion,

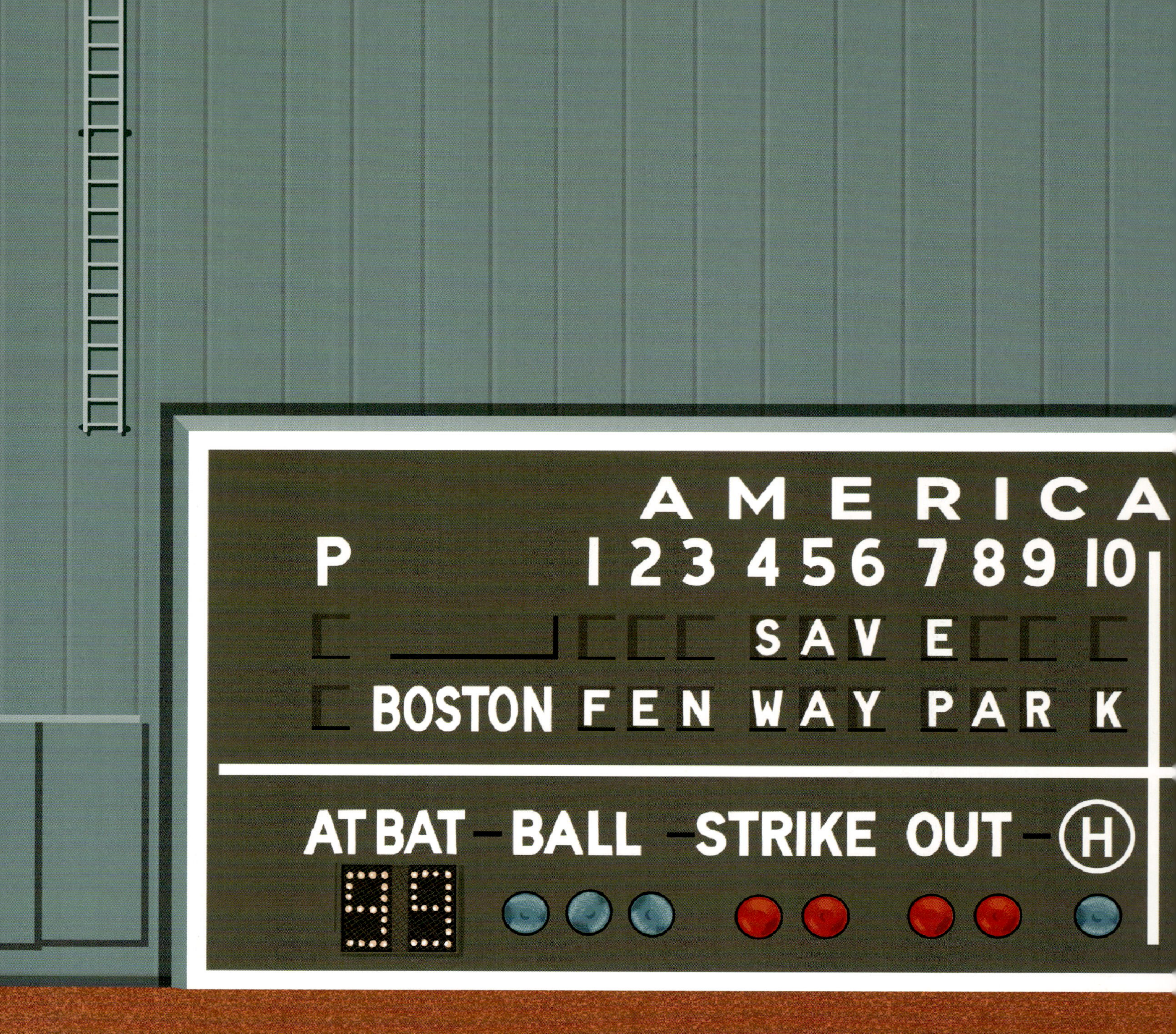
AMERICA
P
1 2 3 4 5 6 7 8 9 10
SAVE
BOSTON FENWAY PARK
AT BAT — BALL — STRIKE OUT — H
99

LEAGUE
H E P IN R P IN R
CWS 12
NYY 4
BAL 1
TEX 8
CLE 12
DET 7
KC 11
SEA 10
MIN 5
OAK 6
TB 3
ANA 1
E

including an epic Home Run Derby and a stirring celebration of MLB's All-Century Team, which featured what was quite likely the greatest assemblage of talent ever assembled on a diamond. Eighty-year-old Boston legend Ted Williams stole the show that night, abetted by a group of starry-eyed contemporary All-Star players, many of whom would later take their place in Cooperstown alongside The Splendid Splinter. Red Sox ace Pedro Martínez punctuated the festivities by striking out five of the six batters he faced and earning MVP honors. It has been said that the events of this week effectively saved Fenway Park from its intended oblivion.

Opposition to the plan quickly coalesced, with a group calling itself "Save Fenway Park!" leading the charge. The coalition engaged the public and the media and met with lawmakers, releasing a detailed proposal to renovate and expand the old ballpark. The complexities of financing the project were fast becoming clear as well, even as a team spokeswoman told the Associated Press, "We understand the emotion that pushes people to renovate Fenway Park. No one loves Fenway Park more than the Red Sox. We looked at renovation for a long time but it clearly is just not feasible," adding that the ballpark could not be remade into a modern facility without razing it entirely.

In October 2000, Harrington announced that the Red Sox franchise was for sale, and speculation immediately centered on the pronounced lack of progress toward securing the funding for the project. Meanwhile, state and local politicians sparred over a host of issues surrounding the controversial plan, not the least of which involved the hundreds of millions of dollars of public investment that the ballclub was seeking.

Finally, In December 2001, the club was sold to a group headed up by Florida Marlins owner John Henry and former San Diego Padres owner Tom Werner for $660 million. New team president Larry Lucchino brought in Janet Marie Smith, the visionary ballpark architect and designer. A decade earlier, this dynamic duo collaborated to build Camden Yards. Now they teamed up to embark upon what would eventually become a massive ten-year renovation and improvement program that saved Fenway from the wrecking ball, extending its lifespan well into the twenty-first century.

The renovations leaned into the quirks and character that Fenway had long been famed for. In 2003, 273 seats were added atop the Green Monster in left field. Premium-priced seats were installed at field level, new auxiliary scoreboards were built, and the right field concourse was dramatically expanded, adding restrooms and concessions stands, enhancing and improving the fan experience. In April 2005, the Red Sox confirmed that they were staying put at Fenway—"no strings attached"—while committing to maintaining and preserving the historic feel of the old park. They applied to the National Park Service to make Fenway a designated landmark, and the ballpark was placed on the National Register of Historic Places in 2012, its centennial season. Historic preservation organizations and fans alike embraced all of the changes. All of this coincided with a golden era of on-field success, which included a string of once-unimaginable World Series championships.

Venerable old Fenway Park was saved, and a new generation of fans have been able to enjoy all of the history and authenticity that comes with it, which, in some cases, includes narrow seats build for 1912 posteriors and close-up views of girders. It's all part of the Fenway experience.

ON THE FIELD

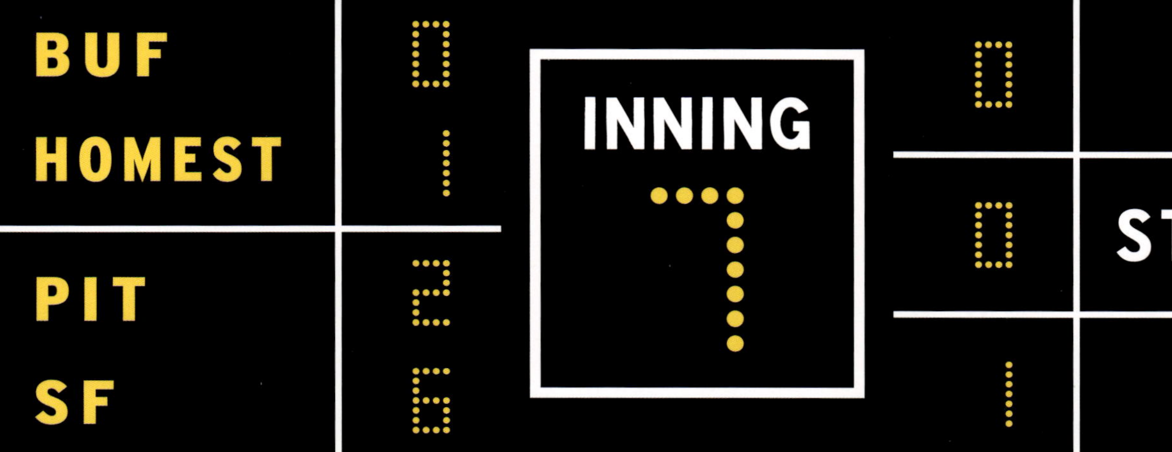

DIVISIONS, PLAYOFFS, AND A MIRACLE

For six decades, the structure of the National and American Leagues was rigid and often highly predictable. There were eight teams in each circuit and only the first-place team advanced to the World Series, which began days after the regular season concluded. If you were the 1909 Chicago Cubs, a team that went 104–49, you were out of luck, because the Pittsburgh Pirates won 110 games that year. Ditto for the 1942 Dodgers, who also won 104 games but came up short to the St. Louis Cardinals and went home empty handed. The Yankees won about half the American League pennants over that stretch, and teams like the St. Louis Browns and Washington Senators often found themselves out of contention before the summer heated up. From 1904 until 1960, both leagues played a 154-game regular-season schedule where each club played each other twenty-two times. That all changed in 1961, when the AL expanded to ten clubs and a 162-game schedule, with the NL following suit the following season.

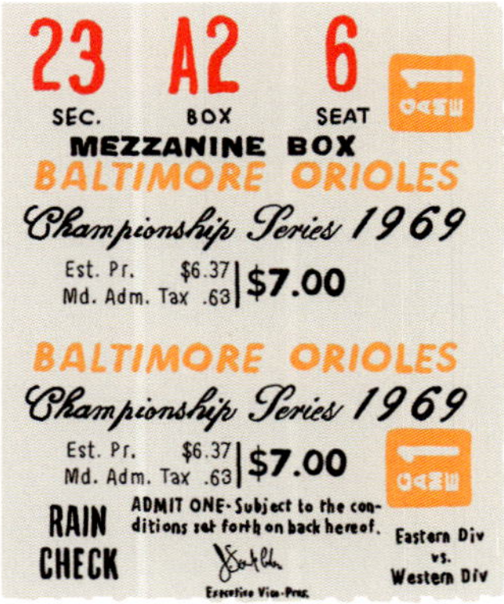

A ten-team scrum to get to the World Series was not a pretty prospect for many clubs. The challenge of selling tickets and keeping sponsors happy was a big challenge for teams like the Senators and the Kansas City Athletics, not to mention the expansion 1962 New York Mets, who were eliminated from pennant contention on August 7. They ended the year a whopping 60 1/2 games behind the Los Angeles Dodgers. The American League embarked upon another round of expansion for 1969, and something clearly had to give.

The two leagues were still highly independent, standalone entities at this point, and often had differing priorities and strategies. Their leaders were, however, united in their belief in tradition and autonomy, and they zealously guarded the status quo. These were the years when National League president Warren Giles would gather his players before the All-Star Game to give them a spirited pep talk. Pete Rose later told AP writer Hal Bock that Giles "would come in and the veins in his neck would be popping out" as he implored his troops to beat the supposedly inferior American League.

As was the case in 1961, the AL moved quickly and unilaterally when they decided to add new franchises in Kansas City and Seattle, who were slated to begin play in 1969. The National League took a decidedly more cautious approach, despite the widely held perception that the AL would be getting a leg up on territory, potential revenue, and player talent. Giles advocated for "a slow and orderly expansion." At first, the NL said that they would commit to expand no later than 1971, but things accelerated when league owners voted to expand to twelve clubs for the 1969 season.

On May 28, 1968, the American League announced that they would be going with a two-division setup the following year, which would include a 156-game regular season schedule and a best-of-five playoff series to determine a pennant winner. Giles said that the National League would continue to preserve the longstanding tradition of having its best club participate in the World Series. He told *The Sporting News*, "Under the American League's plan, you might have a team with the fourth-best record playing in the World Series. I don't think the public will accept this." AL president Joe Cronin shot back, "You can't sell a twelfth place club."

On June 26, 1968, MLB's executive council heeded Commissioner William Eckert's call and recommended a uniform scheduling and divisional setup for both leagues. The two circuits met separately the morning after the All-Star Game in Houston and reached a compromise: the National would follow the American's lead in establishing two six-team divisions, and both leagues would play a 162-game schedule. Individual clubs jockeyed for placement. The Mets, for example, wanted to be included in the same grouping as the Dodgers and Giants, who were still lucrative draws in New York. The White Sox and Twins resisted being placed in the AL West, and the Cardinals and Cubs wanted to be paired together in the NL East. The Reds agreed to go to the western division, even though Cincinnati was (and remains) farther east than either St. Louis or Chicago, and Atlanta, located about 300 miles from the Atlantic Ocean, was placed in the west.

As the 1969 season neared, prognosticators looked at the American League East and saw the previous year's top five clubs all bunched up in the same division: Detroit, Baltimore, Boston, Cleveland, and New York. Meanwhile, the expansion Kansas City Royals and Seattle Pilots were placed in the AL West, which was seen as an advantage for

the Oakland A's. The Cardinals, coming off two consecutive World Series appearances, were thought to be the class of the NL East, and the Giants were highly regarded in the West. By the time September rolled around, ten teams—three in the American League and seven in the National League—were given permission to print playoff tickets.

At season's end, some things went exactly as expected: The National League's newest clubs, the Montréal Expos and San Diego Padres, were woeful; each club lost 110 games. In the AL, the Royals won a very respectable 69 games, good for fourth place. The Pilots hung tough for the first half of the season and wound up winning 64 games and finishing last in their only season in Seattle. The Baltimore Orioles coasted to the inaugural AL East title, winning an impressive 109 regular-season games. On April 16, the O's defeated Boston, 11–8, in a rain-shortened game at Fenway Park and took over first place, where they remained for the rest of the season. They clinched the division on September 13 and finished with a whopping 19-game lead over the second place Tigers. In the AL West, Minnesota, led by rookie manager Billy Martin, took over first on July 5 and never looked back. They wound up winning the division by a nine-game margin, with Oakland finishing second. Atlanta won ten straight games down the

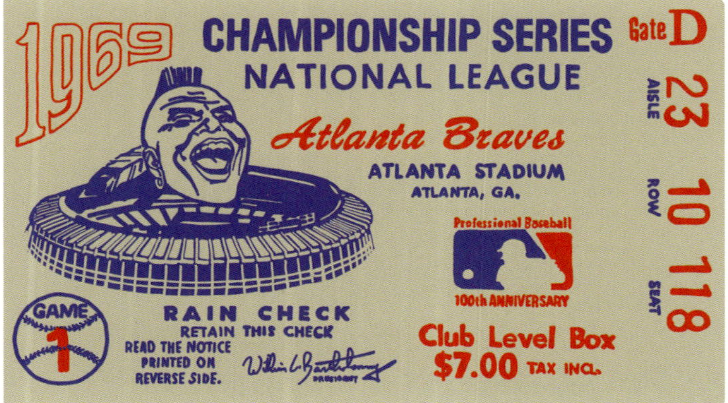

stretch and took the National League West, finishing three games up on San Francisco. In the NL East, the most improbable of longshots emerged victorious. The previously hapless New York Mets caught fire when it counted, going 23–7 in the month of September. The Chicago Cubs spent 155 straight games in first, but the Mets overtook them on September 10, moving into first place for the first time in club history. When New York clinched the division on September 24, a 6–0 whitewashing of the St. Louis Cardinals, Phil Pepe of the *New York Daily News*, wrote, "At precisely 9:07 last night, the Mets stopped being a joke."

There was an air of mystery heading into the postseason. A best-of-five series was something entirely new, and the pundits gave the Braves and Orioles the edge. Atlanta was listed as 11/10 favorites in the NL, despite the fact that the Mets had won 8 of 12 against them in the regular season, and Baltimore was favored in the AL, a nod to their 109 wins and deep starting pitching. Mets manager Gil Hodges told the AP, "Any manager with a Tom Seaver and a Jerry Koosman has a good chance to beat anybody," noting the fact that they'd need to pitch around Atlanta's Henry Aaron. The AL opponents, having won their respective divisions in blowout fashion, knew they'd be facing each other for a month. This was a star-studded matchup featuring several future Hall of Famers—Baltimore's Brooks Robinson, Frank Robinson, and Jim Palmer against Minnesota's Rod Carew, Harmon Killebrew, and Tony Oliva (the Twins' Jim Kaat did not pitch in the series).

The two inaugural League Championship Series were played over the course of three consecutive days, October 4, 5, and 6. Minnesota and the O's kicked things off first at Baltimore's Memorial Stadium, which was decked out in orange and black bunting for the occasion. Despite blue skies and a pleasant 71-degree day, attendance was poor—only 39,324 fans, well short of capacity, showed up, and the *Baltimore Sun* described the atmosphere as lacking in "World Series flavor." The fans who did attend were treated to a marquee pitching matchup featuring two 20-game winners, Baltimore's Mike Cuellar (23–11), who'd be named the AL Cy Young Award winner, and the Twins' Jim Perry, who'd gone 20–6. The Orioles' Frank Robinson, Mark Belanger, and Boog Powell each hit solo homers, but outfielder Paul Blair was the hero of the day. His surprise two-out 12th-inning suicide squeeze bunt traveled only thirty feet, but it brought Belanger home with the winning run to give Baltimore a 4–3 win and a 1–0 series lead. The Braves and Mets countered with two starting aces of their own, Atlanta's Phil Niekro, who had gone 23–13 during the regular season, and New York's Tom Seaver, whose 25–7 record would later net him the NL Cy Young Award. A total of 50,122 fans were on hand at Atlanta Stadium for Game One, and they saw the red-hot Mets rally for five runs in the eighth inning to top the Braves, 9–5.

Baltimore and New York each went up two games to none the following day. In Baltimore, O's starter Dave McNally pitched a gem, allowing only three hits while striking out twelve over 11 innings. The Twins' Dave Boswell tossed 10 2/3 innings in a losing effort as Baltimore scratched out a 1–0 victory on the back of pinch hitter Curt Motton's two out single, which drove home Boog Powell for the win. Back in Atlanta, the Mets' remarkable momentum continued forward unabated as they pummeled the Braves, winning 11–6.

Both series shifted locations for the third and ultimately decisive games. In Bloomington, Minnesota, Baltimore's offense exploded, lashing seven Twins' pitchers for 18 hits in an 11–2 blowout victory to sweep the series. A sparse crowd of 32,735, some 13,000 short of a sellout, witnessed the carnage. Many began to head for the exits by the fourth inning. In New York, 53,195 fans packed Shea Stadium and witnessed the unimaginable as the Mets, a 100/1 longshot heading into the season, rode the strong right arm of young flamethrower Nolan Ryan, who came out of the bullpen and threw seven quality innings, giving up only three hits, to secure a 7–4 victory. *The New York Times'* Joseph Durso wrote, "the impossible dream came true at 3:34 o'clock on a cool and sunny afternoon," after which delirious Mets fans swarmed the field, stripping large pieces of the sod bare and pillaging all three bases and home plate.

The Mets completed the miracle a week and a half later when they upset the Orioles to win the World Series in five games, a fitting conclusion to a remarkable season in which Major League Baseball welcomed four new teams and broke with six decades of tradition, realigning both leagues into divisions and expanding postseason play. MLB next realigned in 1994, when both leagues went to a three-division setup, and the postseason expanded the following year, when wild card teams joined the playoffs. The ensuing seasons have brought forth additional postseason participants and formats, an evolution of the revolution that forever changed baseball back in 1969.

CONNIE MACK'S LAST HURRAH

Cornelius McGillicuddy was born on December 22, 1862—smack in the middle of the Civil War and less than two weeks after Robert E. Lee's victory over the Union Army of the Potomac at the Battle of Fredericksburg. He died on February 8, 1956, less than two weeks after Elvis Presley released "Heartbreak Hotel." In between, he became familiarly known as Connie Mack, while setting the records for the most games managed in major-league history (7,755), most wins (3,731), losses (3,948), and ties (76). In 1950, he celebrated his fiftieth and final year at the helm of the Philadelphia Athletics, and his club wore commemorative jerseys all season long, featuring a golden anniversary sleeve patch and festive gold trim. This represents an ironic tribute, as Mack was famous for his choice of managerial attire: a somber business suit, as opposed to a uniform.

Long before any of that, Mack began his major-league career in 1886 as a catcher for the National League's Washington club. He later jumped to the Players' National League of Professional Base Ball Clubs—popularly known as the Player's League—for that circuit's only season, 1890, catching for the woeful Buffalo Bisons. The twenty-seven year old Mack invested $500—his entire life savings—in the club, and was wiped out when the league went bust. He glossed over the Buffalo experience in his 1950 memoir, *My 66 Years in the Big Leagues*, devoting just a dozen words to the ill-fated venture. Following that, Mack shifted back to the NL, where he closed out his playing career with six seasons in Pittsburgh. On September 3, 1894 he was named manager of the Pirates, and the club won his first game at the helm in blowout fashion, defeating Washington, 22–1. Mack's next stop was Milwaukee, where he managed and held an ownership stake in the Western League's Brewers for four seasons, from 1897 through 1900. When Western League president Ban Johnson transformed his circuit into the American League in 1901, he tapped Mack to run Philadelphia's new entry, the Athletics.

Mack recruited and signed players, identified a playing field for the club, and piloted the Athletics for the first time on April 26, 1901, in a 5 to 1 loss to Washington. His final game as skipper took place more than 18,000 days later, on October 1, 1950, a 5 to 3 win over those same Senators. During his long tenure, Mack led the Athletics to nine American League pennants and five World Series titles, while shrewdly transforming his 25 percent ownership share into a controlling majority in 1937, which afforded him job security of the highest order. He was also elected to the recently established Hall of Fame that very same year.

Mack's final stretch was a slog, featuring a string of last or next to last place finishes. He dismantled the Athletics' second dynasty, a club that won back-to-back World Series in 1929–30, and the club cratered, averaging less than 57 wins a year between 1934 and 1946. The A's climbed as high as fourth place in the eight-team AL in 1948, but this represented the last successful moment for the franchise in the City of Brotherly Love. Mack's Shibe Park tenants, the Phillies, were coming on strong, and in 1950 they won their first National League pennant in thirty-five years. The hearts and minds of Philadelphians were clearly focused on the "Whiz Kids," and the Athletics' prospects as a viable franchise were bleak at best, nearly two decades removed from their most recent pennant and drawing an anemic 4,000 fans per home game. Dysfunctional Mack family dynamics contributed mightily to the dismal situation, and the then-eighty-seven-year-old Mack announced his retirement at a hastily convened luncheon press conference at Philadelphia's Benjamin Franklin Hotel on October 18. "I'm not quitting because I'm too old," he said, "but because I think the people want me to."

After a dramatic series of twists and turns, the club was sold and transferred to Kansas City at the conclusion of the 1954 season. Ninety-two-year-old Connie Mack, now "honorary president," attended the Athletics' home opener in KC on April 12, 1955. He received a standing ovation and a kiss on the forehead from an adoring fan, Mrs. James Irwin, who told him, "Honey, we love you for helping bring the Athletics to Kansas City." Mack is reported to have broken into a wide grin. When he passed away the following February, the *Philadelphia Inquirer* noted, "This was the first winter Connie had spent in the north since 1888," when as a player he participated in baseball's first spring training in Florida with Washington.

A MONUMENTAL BASEBALL LIFE

Charles Evard "Gabby" Street's baseball odyssey spanned nearly half a century, and it involved one of the most monumental catches ever made. Born in Huntsville, Alabama, in 1882, Street was a player, coach, manager, and broadcaster. He was known as "Old Sarge," a tribute to his service during World War I, when he took a machine gun bullet from a German airplane in his right leg. He was later awarded the Purple Heart.

Street's big-league playing career began with the Cincinnati Reds in 1904. He was jettisoned to the Pacific Coast League's San Francisco Seals just prior to the 1906 season, and it was there, less than two weeks after Opening Day, that he survived the deadliest earthquake in American history. In 1908, Street began a four-year stint with the Washington Nationals (Senators) that defined his career, catching twenty-year-old fireballer Walter Johnson as he blazed his way across the American League, including three complete-game shutouts in four days against the New York Highlanders over Labor Day weekend—all caught by Street.

His Washington years earned him a reputation as a skilled defensive receiver, a solid game tactician, and a popular and affable clubhouse presence. He joined the Highlanders in 1912, but his stay there was short lived, as he was released in July, seemingly the final act in a solid major-league playing career. Street kicked around the minors both before and after World War I, and eventually found himself managing, which was not really too much of a reach for a catcher and a former army sergeant. In 1930, Street was named skipper of the St. Louis Cardinals and, on September 20, 1931, with his team having already clinched the National League pennant, he inserted himself into the lineup in a meaningless game against the Brooklyn Robins, thus resuming his big-league catching career nineteen years after he last left off. That day, Street, who was approaching his forty-ninth birthday, donned the tools of ignorance and caught three innings. He got one at-bat, launching a fly ball to deep right field in the third. In his four years at the Cardinals' helm, he led the club to two National League pennants and one World Series title.

All of this brings us to what was arguably Street's most noteworthy achievement . . . and it didn't even take place on the field of play. On the morning of August 21, 1908, Street snagged a baseball that was dropped from the top of the Washington Monument, thus settling a $500 bet between Washington journalist and social figure Preston Gibson and DC baseball fan John Biddle. Gibson wagered that Street would be able to secure the sphere. Biddle thought otherwise, and put his money where his mouth was. Gibson secured a permit from the Superintendent of Public Buildings and Grounds, and he invited the press to witness the spectacle. A *Washington Post* photographer was on hand to capture the moment, accompanied by a group of some fifteen to twenty spectators.

Street, dressed in shirtsleeves and a dark tie, stood on the north side of the obelisk, sixty feet away from the

base. More than 500 feet above him stood Gibson, who rolled a series of ten baseballs down a wooden chute and out a small window at the top of the structure. Each of them either drifted away from Street or bounced off the side of the monument.

At this point, Gibson began *throwing* the balls down, and, on the thirteenth try, Street made a clean catch. Spectators compared the sound of ball hitting mitt to that of a rifle shot. Street said that he couldn't see the ball until it was halfway down, and added, "I felt it right down to my heels when it finally hit." News reports indicated that he "quivered from head to foot, as a ship would in a collision." That afternoon, Street caught Johnson, who scattered five hits over nine innings as Washington defeated the Detroit Tigers, 3 to 1. Ironically, five days later, Street broke his finger on a foul tip.

After his managing days were over, Street became a beloved radio broadcaster, calling games for both St. Louis clubs, the Browns and Cardinals. From 1945 to 1950, he was paired with a young broadcaster by the name of Harry Christopher Carabina, aka Harry Caray. In 1945, the sixty-three-year-old Street caught two of three balls dropped by Caray from the top of St. Louis's 387-foot Civil Courts Building, a full-circle moment for a man who survived Walter Johnson's fiery fastball, the San Francisco Earthquake, and a ball tossed from the top of the Washington Monument.

ROAD TO THE RECORD

On July 18, 1921, New York Yankees slugger Babe Ruth stepped up to bat in the eighth inning of a game at Detroit's Navin Field to face Tigers rookie pitcher Bert Cole. Ruth, who had been walked in all four of his previous plate appearances that afternoon, absolutely destroyed Cole's third pitch, hitting it *way* out of the ballpark—an estimated 575 feet from home plate. It's considered by some to be the longest home run ever hit, and, seemingly unbeknownst to all who witnessed it, it broke the all-time record for home runs in a career with 139, which had been held by nineteenth-century slugger Roger Connor. Ruth hit his final three home runs on May 25, 1935, in Pittsburgh, finishing his illustrious career with a total of 714, a mythical record which was long deemed unbreakable. His former Yankee teammate, Lou Gehrig, was a distant second at the time, having slammed his 352nd career shot the very same day. When writer Fred Lieb interviewed Ruth shortly before his death in 1947, the Bambino theorized that his record would stand forever.

Forever ended up equating to 38 years, 10 months, and 15 days, which is when Hank Aaron surpassed Ruth, on April 8, 1974, when he hit number 715 off Los Angeles Dodgers' hurler Al Downing. The road to that record was pretty much unimaginable in the years after Ruth's retirement. Boston Red Sox slugger Jimmie Foxx became the second member of the 500 home run club in 1940 at the age of thirty-two, but he rapidly faded after that and finished with a total of 534 dingers when he hung it up five years later, in 1945. That same season, New York Giants outfielder Mel Ott hit his 500th homer, en route to a total of 511. Ted Williams lost nearly five prime years of his playing career in service to his country and ended up with 521 homers before calling it quits in 1960.

As home run production soared in the 1950s and expansion diluted the pool of pitching talent as the majors went from sixteen to twenty-four clubs in the '60s, the possibility of Ruth's record falling at some point was seen as something very real by a select few observers.

The American League added two teams in 1961, and both the AL and NL expanded their playing schedules from 154 to 162 games. Roger Maris broke Ruth's single-season mark with 61 home runs that season, and a certain amount of chatter commenced on the viability of the Bambino's longstanding record. Going into the 1962 season, the Yankees' Mickey Mantle, with 374 homers, and Milwaukee's Eddie Mathews, with 370, were seen by some as the heirs to the throne. Both players were just thirty years old.

On September 13, 1965, thirty-four-year-old San Francisco Giants' superstar Willie Mays hit his 500th career homer—he eclipsed Foxx for sole possession of second place on the all-time list the following August. Foxx sent him a telegram of congratulations, noting the fact that both he and Mays were right-handed hitters. Foxx told the Associated Press, "For 25 years they thought only left-handers could hit the long ones." "I hope he hits 600," he said, but added that Mays had zero shot at the record. "The only one who had a chance was Ted Williams," he said. That same year, Ralph Kiner, a man who knew something about hitting home runs, told the *Pittsburgh Post-Gazette*'s Al Abrams that Mays would break the record "within the next five or six years." He also predicted that Aaron, who had 405 round trippers at the time, would wind up at number three on the list.

Right around this time, Aaron's name began to enter into the conversation with greater frequency. In 1967, Furman Bisher of the *Atlanta Journal* gave Aaron, then thirty-two years old, "the best chance" of breaking the mark. When Aaron hit the 493rd home run of his career on June 17, 1968, UPI ran a story suggesting that he had a legitimate chance, even if the odds were "heavily against" him. He became the eighth member of the 500 home run club a few weeks later, and his teammates dubbed him "Henry the Eighth." Aaron was three years younger than Mays and aging well, and he also played half his games at Atlanta Stadium, aka "the Launching Pad," while Mays's home field, Candlestick Park, was notorious for its howling winds, which the Giants slugger later claimed cost him over 100 home runs.

Mantle retired after the 1968 season with 536 homers, well shy of Ruth, and called Aaron "the best player of my era." As the '60s concluded, Aaron began to speak openly about the record. In 1970, Aaron, then thirty-six, told *The Sporting News*, "If I can have two more good years

and get close to 650 homers I will hang around and give Ruth's record a shot." "I'm not trying to make anyone forget the Babe, but only to remember Aaron," he added. While Ruth endured a steady decline over the course of his final seasons with the Yankees, Aaron seemingly defied father time, hitting 44 home runs at age thirty-five, 38 homers at age thirty-six, and a career-best 47 homers in 1971 at age thirty-seven. Aaron moved past Mays into second place with his 649th career shot on June 10, 1972, putting him 65 behind Ruth.

Hank Aaron famously endured bigotry and vitriol as he marched toward Ruth's record and told *The Sporting News* that he had been the target of "hatred and resentment" as he neared Ruth's mark. "All I want is to be treated like a human being," he said, adding "The more they push me, the more I want the record."

On July 21, 1973, Aaron connected on a fastball off Philadelphia lefty Ken Brett for number 700. He hit a remarkable 40 homers that year in only 392 at-bats, and when the season ended in October he sat at 713, one behind Ruth's 714. Baseball's most hallowed record was within striking reach. Mays, by then a New York Met, retired after the 1973 World Series, having concluded his career with 660 round-trippers. Aaron launched number 714 on his first swing of the 1974 season in Cincinnati, tying the record, and broke it at home four days later.

Hank Aaron finished his legendary career where it began, in Milwaukee, where he played his final two seasons with the Brewers. He slammed a dozen homers in 1975 and tacked on ten more in 1976—including number 755, which he hit on July 20 off California Angels pitcher Dick Drago at Milwaukee's Country Stadium, depositing a hanging slider well into the left-field bleachers. To the dismay of many, Aaron's record was itself broken by Giants slugger Barry Bonds, who connected for his 756th on August 7, 2007. The Hammer offered a video tribute in honor of Bonds's achievement that night, noting, "throughout the past century, the home run has held a special place in baseball, and I have been privileged to hold this record for thirty-eight years."

In 2022, Albert Pujols of the St. Louis Cardinals became just the fourth player to reach the 700 home run mark, finishing his career with 703. Nearly two decades after having established the record, Bonds's final tally of 762 homers remains the standard. As of this writing there are no current players anywhere near that total. Hitting 500 homers may possibly be an attainable mark for a couple of today's stars, but the distance between that and 762 seems gargantuan. Ruth revolutionized the game with the longball and shattered record after record, while Aaron's march toward the mark was a methodical two-decade-long marathon.

As the twentieth century gave way to the new millennium, the proliferation of performance-enhancing drugs and engineered changes in the ball itself caused home run rates to skyrocket, but scoring began to decrease in the early 2020s, just as a series of rule changes and the use of analytical data and statistical models changed the game. Bonds's record would appear to be safe for right now, at least until the next Babe Ruth or Hank Aaron comes along.

PHILLIES 23, CUBS 22

There have been more than 200,000 regular season Major League Baseball games played over the past century and a half. Most of them are run of the mill 3–2 contests, quickly forgotten and then consigned to history. Some games are pitchers' duels, while others are blowouts. A handful of really unique occurrences stand out: things like unassisted triple plays, 20-strikeout games, perfect games, and cycles, which pepper the record books, rare though they may be. It's fair to say that one of the best things about attending a game is the fact that you never know when you are going to witness something really special, something to tell the grandkids about. On the afternoon of May 17, 1979, a total of 14,952 fans gathered at Chicago's Wrigley Field and got more than their money's worth.

That day, the Philadelphia Phillies defeated the Chicago Cubs in 10 innings, 23–22—a unique score in the long annals of big-league history. This offensive explosion for the ages was wind-driven, with gusts blowing out at 18 mph. Philadelphia's Mike Schmidt told the *Chicago Tribune*, "Ballplayers often will say that you never can get enough runs to win in this park, but they always say it sarcastically. After today, they can forget the sarcasm." Wrigley's reputation for high-scoring games is well earned—just the previous day, the Phillies blew out the Cubs, 13–0.

As Bake McBride stepped to the plate to lead things off for the visitors, Phillies broadcaster Andy Musser presciently noted, "the wind is blowing out, so look out for some explosions here today." He had no idea. Over the course of the next 243 minutes, the Phillies and Cubs combined for 45 runs and 97 total bases. There were 50 hits, including a whopping 11 home runs, 15 walks, 127 plate appearances, and 109 at-bats.

With two men on in the top of the first, Schmidt got under a ball and propelled it into the jet stream, hitting a three-run homer over the head of Cubs leftfielder Dave Kingman, who clearly assumed that it was just a routine fly ball. A few batters later, catcher Bob Boone launched another three-run shot, this one a low line drive to left, to give the Phillies a 6–0 lead, knocking Cubs starter Dennis Lamp out of the ballgame. Lamp recorded just one out. Donnie Moore came in to relieve Lamp and promptly struck out Rudy Meoli before surrendering a solo shot to Philadelphia pitcher Randy Lerch. After McBride popped up to third to end the frame, Lerch took the hill for the visitors, staked to what seemed like a healthy 7–0 lead.

Chicago's first three batters all singled, plating a run, and Philadelphia broadcaster Richie Ashburn quipped, "I've got a feeling that this might wind up about 19 to 12."

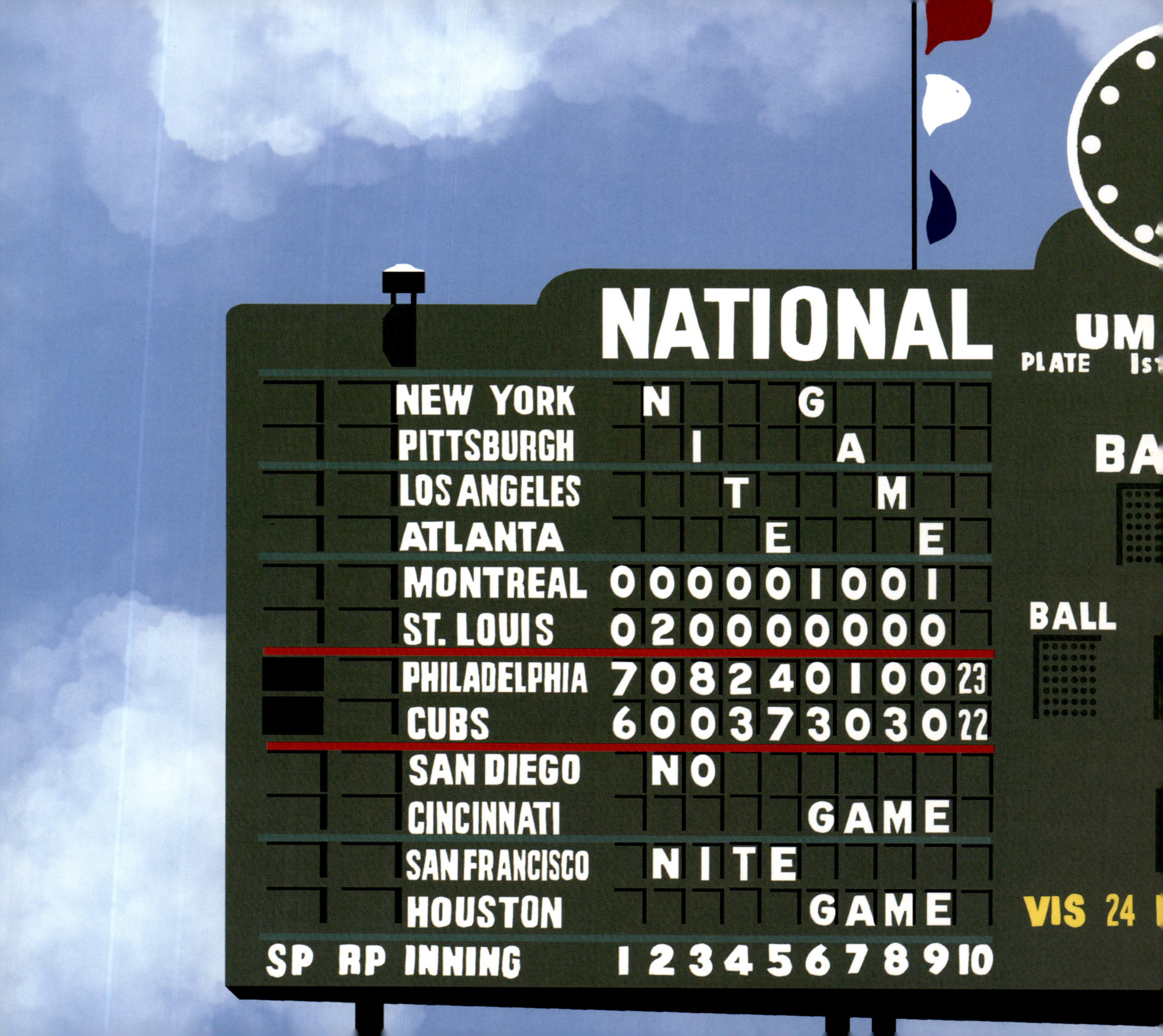

NATIONAL

SP	RP	INNING	1	2	3	4	5	6	7	8	9	10
		NEW YORK	N					G				
		PITTSBURGH		I					A			
		LOS ANGELES			T					M		
		ATLANTA				E					E	
		MONTREAL	0	0	0	0	0	1	0	0	1	
		ST. LOUIS	0	2	0	0	0	0	0	0	0	
		PHILADELPHIA	7	0	8	2	4	0	1	0	0	23
		CUBS	6	0	0	3	7	3	0	3	0	22
		SAN DIEGO	N	O								
		CINCINNATI						G	A	M	E	
		SAN FRANCISCO	N	I	T	E						
		HOUSTON						G	A	M	E	

UM
PLATE 1ST
BA
BALL
VIS 24

AMERICAN
3RD
STRIKE
26 CUBS
MINNESOTA N G
KANSAS CITY I A
BALTIMORE T M
BOSTON E E
TEXAS NO
NEW YORK GAME
SOX 0 0 2 0 0 0 0 3 0
OAKLAND 0 0 0 0 0 0 0 0 0
MILWAUKEE NO
DETROIT GAME
TORONTO 1 0 1 0 1 0 0 0 0
CLEVELAND 0 3 0 0 0 3 0 2
SP RP INNING 1 2 3 4 5 6 7 8 9 10

He was shy by only 14 runs. Kingman, batting cleanup, came up and catapulted a mammoth blast to left—the *third* three-run homer of the game—to make it a 7–4 game. Lerch then retired third baseman Steve Ontiveros, but the next batter, Jerry Martin, hit a line-drive double into the gap in right-center field, ending Lerch's short day, which consisted of having pitched a third of an inning and having hit a home run. Doug Bird came in from the bullpen and allowed two more hits, including a triple off the bat of Moore, the Cubs' pitcher. At the end of one inning of play, the score was Philadelphia 7, Chicago 6.

Both offenses rested for an inning before the Phillies exploded for eight runs in the top of the third. Thirteen Phils came to bat and seven of them recorded hits, including Garry Maddox who started the inning with a looping double to right and then hit a three-run homer into the bleachers in left to make it 15 to 6. Philadelphia tacked on two more runs in the top of the fourth, and then Kingman, batting in the bottom of the inning, launched another moonshot—this time a two-run homer—that bounced off a building on the other side of Waveland Avenue in left to make it 17 to 8. Ontiveros hit next and cleared the right-field fence, cutting the deficit to eight runs.

On to the top of the fifth they went. The Phillies answered with four runs on two hits and an error, and, as Chicago batted in the bottom of the inning, they faced a 12-run deficit. Philadelphia's Larry Bowa later told the *Chicago Tribune*, "When we got up by 12, I figured we could win it if we could hold them under two touchdowns and could block a couple of extra points." Tug McGraw came in to relieve for the Phils and got absolutely torched, facing ten batters and allowing seven runs on four hits and three walks before being replaced by Ron Reed. The inning included a Bill Buckner grand slam, a line shot halfway up the right center field bleachers, which made it 21–14, and a two-run homer off the bat of Martin, which closed the gap to 21–16. Suddenly, the Cubs were down by less than a touchdown.

In the bottom of the sixth, the Cubs scored three more runs, one of which was driven in by Kingman on his third homer of the afternoon, another gargantuan shot that cleared the left-field bleachers (he now had a solo shot, a two-run homer, and a three-run homer). It was now a two-run game.

Top seven. The Phillies responded with another run when Greg Gross tripled and scored on Bob Boone's double, giving Philadelphia a 22–19 lead. Undeterred, the Cubs bounced back yet again in the bottom of the eighth, scoring three runs to tie the game. Incredibly, Chicago had erased a 12-run deficit.

Future Hall of Famer Bruce Sutter entered the game to pitch the top of the ninth and got the Phillies out in undramatic fashion. Rawly Eastwick came in for Philadelphia and mowed the Cubs down 1-2-3. It was just the second time in the game that there was a scoreless inning.

Destiny seemingly willed that the game should go to extra innings, and Sutter retired the first two batters (Larry Bowa and Pete Rose) in the top of the 10th. Up stepped Schmidt, who started all of this scoring with his first-inning homer, which he followed up with four consecutive walks. Schmidt hammered a high pitch, a flat split-fingered fastball, on a full count. It sailed over the left-center field bleachers and gave Philadelphia a 23–22 lead. Eastwick came in for his second inning of relief and retired the Cubs in order once again, securing the victory. At the end of the day, the Phillies had tallied 23 runs on 24 hits, making two errors and leaving 15 men on base. As for Chicago, they scored 22 runs on 26 hits, including six home runs. The media understandably ran out of superlatives and descriptors, leaving the words of the participating players to frame exactly what happened that day. Players spoke of being exhausted and of eschewing confidence as the game unfolded, knowing full well that no lead was safe until the final out was recorded. Schmidt said that when he was taking batting practice, he saw the flags atop the Wrigley scoreboard standing straight up and pointed straight out, a surefire sign that the offenses were going to be busy that day. He looked at Cubs infielder Mick Kelleher who, like Schmidt, wore uniform number 20. Schmidt patted his own back, then pointed toward Kelleher's back: it's going to be a 20–20 game. Like Ashburn, he underestimated the final score. Philadelphia catcher Tim McCarver told the *Philadelphia Daily News*, "It's the only game in my career where I had a jock rash before it started and it was healed by the time it was over."

The full game broadcast is available on YouTube and, as you might expect, it's both entertaining and dramatic. The fans cannot believe what they are witnessing, the announcers are similarly agog, and the players just keep stepping up to the plate, hitting all manner of line drives, bloopers, soft liners, and taters.

Remarkably, this was not the highest scoring game ever. That distinction belongs to an August 25, 1922, game which, *of course*, involved the same two clubs and was also played at Wrigley Field. In that one, the Cubs blew a 19-run lead, but went on to win, 26–23. That game included 19 unearned runs, nine errors, and 21 walks.

The 1979 slugfest seems far more entertaining, populated by a gang of mustachioed All-Stars and colorful fan favorites. Wrigley Field's wild winds have been part of the game there for well more than a century, but the events of May 17, 1979, stand apart. Larry Bowa reportedly said that it was "the craziest game ever, and then the second inning started."

A's

THE MAN OF STEAL

For a quarter century, Rickey Henderson blazed a trail across baseball, the consensus choice for greatest leadoff hitter ever and the game's all-time leader in both runs scored and stolen bases. In 1980, his first full big-league campaign, the twenty-one-year-old Henderson shattered Ty Cobb's American League record for most steals in a season, finishing with an even one hundred. The following February, he told Ralph Wiley of the *Oakland Tribune*, "My main thing ever since I've been playing baseball has been stealing bases. That does it for me. Reggie Jackson says there's no feeling like the feeling of hitting a home run. I feel the same way when I steal a base." He retired a quarter century later, with a total of 1,273 stolen bases, presumably feeling really good.

The breadth and longevity of Henderson's career are arguably as astonishing as his achievements. Starting in Oakland in 1979, he played for nine different clubs. He played against Tommy John, who was a teammate of Early Wynn, a player who broke into the majors in 1939. In 2003—his final season—he played against Miguel Cabrera. Cabrera continued to play until 2023. His teammates included a forty-year-old Joe Morgan, whose final season came in Oakland in 1984, and a nineteen-year-old Edwin Jackson, who was a rookie with the 2003 Dodgers. Others included Pedro Martínez, Álex Rodríguez, Tony Gwynn, Eddie Murray, and both Niekros, Phil and Joe.

Bill James famously said of Henderson, "If you could split him in two, you'd have two Hall of Famers." He finished his career with 3,055 base hits and 2,295 runs scored. Henderson's numbers are ridiculous and warrant no embellishment. His record 1,406 career steals are 468 more than the runner-up, Lou Brock, whose mark he broke at the Oakland Coliseum on May 1, 1991. Henderson hit an astonishing 81 leadoff home runs. He stole four or more bases in a game nineteen times. His July 1983 was especially eye popping: he swiped 33 bases that month and was only thrown out just once. He set a record for stolen base attempts in 1982, when he tried to swipe a base an astounding 172 times. On July 29, 1989, Henderson walked four times, stole five bases, and scored four times.

He stole his first base in his first MLB game, against John Henry Johnson and the Texas Rangers, on June 24, 1979. His final steal took place 24 years, 2 months, and 6 days later, on August 29, 2003, off Colorado Rockies pitcher Cory Vance, who was born four days before Rickey made his professional debut. In between, Rickey Henderson carved out a career like no other, playing the game with joy, swagger, and skill—all of which landed him in Cooperstown, where the inscription on his bronze plaque begins with the words, "Faster than a speeding bullet."

CHICAGO'S COLLEGE OF COACHES

One could attend the Harvard Business School and study management innovation, seeking knowledge on competitive advantages and dramatic, long-lasting shifts in organizational cultures. Alternatively, one could look to the Chicago Cubs' College of Coaches, a strange two-year experiment that dramatically upended a century of baseball tradition.

The wheels for the whole thing were set in motion in October 1960, when the Cubs turned down manager Lou Boudreau's request for a two-year contract. The franchise was in the midst of a prolonged tailspin at this time, with fourteen-straight seasons in the second division. In fact, the Cubs had not enjoyed a winning season since 1946, the year after the club's most recent World Series appearance. With the 1961 season fast approaching, the team held their annual press luncheon at the Wrigley Building restaurant on January 12, where owner Philip K. Wrigley announced that the Cubs were scrapping the role of manager in favor of a rotating system of head coaches who would oversee field operations in various capacities across the entire organization. Acknowledging the obvious, he displayed a small sign for reporters which read, "Anyone who remains calm in the midst of all this confusion simply does not understand the situation."

Wrigley told *The Sporting News*, "This is the day of specialists, and I think it makes good sense to get the best men for each individual job. They do it in football and it works quite well." When asked by a reporter if he ran his gum business this way, he replied in the affirmative. "No man is indispensable." He continued, "I've resigned twice myself. It's like hiring a man to run a bulldozer. If the man gets sick, that doesn't mean the bulldozer has broken down. You simply have another driver step in."

Yet more innovation from the owner involved the use of analytical data, as newfangled IBM electric computers were to be deployed by the club to study both the Cubs and opposing players. The media noted that the machines retailed for $275,000 each (approximately $3 million each in today's dollars), a serious expenditure for a club that reported a $27,411 profit the previous year.

Forty-four-year-old Avitus "Vedie" Himsl, the Cubs' pitching coach in 1960, was the leadoff man. Cubs vice president John Holland said that Himsl's reign would last only two weeks, even if the team went undefeated. On April 11 at Cincinnati, he became the first "head coach" in MLB history when he piloted the Cubs to a 7–1 loss to the Reds. Himsl eventually served three different stints in the head coaching role, posting a 10–21 won-lost record. He was followed by Harry Craft, El Tappe, and Lou Klein. The four men combined for a record of 64–90, 29 games behind the National League champion Reds. Tappe and Klein were joined by Charlie Metro in 1962, but the Cubs cratered, going 59–103, finishing in front of only the legendarily putrid expansion New York Mets. Chicago made history that year when future Hall of Famer Buck O'Neil became the first Black coach in the American or National Leagues. Despite the breakthrough appointment, he was not part of the "College of Coaches" rotation, and was not given the opportunity to coach on the baselines during games.

As the 1963 season dawned, the President of the United States chimed in. In a March 23 speech that concerned automation in the labor force and attendant unemployment issues, President John F. Kennedy quipped, "Chicago, I might add, also provides the exception to this pattern—since it now takes ten men to manage the Cubs instead of one!" A different Kennedy, Bob, took the Cubs' reigns for the 1963 season as Wrigley abandoned his innovative plan, saying, "the aim of standardization of play was not achieved because of the various personalities." Bob Kennedy led his team to a very respectable record of 82–80, their first winning campaign in seventeen years. The organization continued to rotate coaches between the parent club and its minor-league affiliates through 1965, which also marked the end of the "head coach" designation. In a strikingly conventional move, old friend Lou Klein was brought in to replace Kennedy on June 14, making him the final head coach in the history of major-league baseball.

"DO I LOOK LIKE A DOCTOR?"

Rule 3.01 of Major League Baseball's official rules states:

> *No player shall intentionally discolor or damage the ball by rubbing it with soil, rosin, paraffin, licorice, sandpaper, emery-paper or other foreign substance.*
>
> *PENALTY: The umpire shall demand the ball and remove the offender from the game. In addition, the offender shall be suspended automatically for 10 games.*

The great Tony Gwynn once said, "A baseball purist will tell you that it's only cheating if you get caught," and on the night of August 3, 1987, Minnesota Twins pitcher Joe Niekro got caught.

Niekro, a forty-two-year-old knuckleballer, was approaching the tail end of his 22-year major league career when he faced the California Angels in Anaheim. Pitching in the bottom of the fourth inning, he had just thrown a strike on a 2-0 count to the Angels' Brian Downing when home-plate umpire Tim Tschida called time and approached the mound, wanting to inspect the ball that Niekro held in his glove. Niekro tossed him the ball, the two exchanged words, and Tschida inspected the pitcher's glove. Minnesota manager Tom Kelly sprinted out and was joined by the rest of the umpiring crew, including crew chief Dave Phillips, who ordered Niekro to empty his pockets. It was at this moment that comedy ensued.

He proceeded to put his hands in each of his pockets and removed what appeared to be a photo from his left pocket—no big deal—and then Niekro, seemingly feigning innocence, raised his hands above his head. He then pulled out both of his pocket linings, and, in one fluid motion, flung an emery board to the ground with his right hand, as if no one would notice. All 33,983 fans in attendance and the four umpires on the field definitely noticed.

The umpires later claimed that Niekro had thrown a total of six defaced balls, with Phillips adding, "We'd been collecting the evidence for several innings. We had several of them doctored in the same place." Angels manager Gene Mauch said, "Those balls weren't roughed up. Those balls were borderline mutilated." As for Niekro, he fessed up to having brought his manicure set to the mound with him, saying that he filed his nails between innings and that he always carried sandpaper with him, just in case his emery board got wet. Umpire Steve Palermo said, "They can carry a chainsaw as long as they don't use it on the ball." Adding to the drama, a seventeen-year-old Angels batboy accused Twins utility infielder Al Newman of accosting him after the game in an attempt to get the bag of scuffed

baseballs, which were in the process of being delivered to the umpires' locker room. Newman did not necessary deny it, saying, "I may have asked for the balls, but why would I attack a little kid?"

Two days later, American League president Dr. Bobby Brown suspended Niekro, who immediately appealed the verdict. The appeal was swiftly denied, and Niekro made the most of his forced vacation, appearing on *Late Night with David Letterman* on August 15, 1987. He walked onstage sporting a carpenter's apron and a power sander on his right hip. At Letterman's urging, Niekro removed a variety of items that, speaking theoretically, a pitcher might use to doctor a baseball, including a tube of Vaseline, scissors, tweezers, a nail file, and a bunch of emery boards. "So, you're telling me that you did not doctor the ball that night?" asked Letterman, to which Niekro playfully replied, "Do I look like a doctor?"

Niekro served his suspension and returned to his club on August 20, after which the Twins continued their march toward the American League West title. The team won only 85 games during the regular season, but defeated Detroit in six games in the American League Championship Series and then went on to beat the St. Louis Cardinals in a seven game World Series, securing the team's first fall classic win since they moved to Minnesota in 1961.

Niekro made one appearance in the World Series, throwing two scoreless innings in a Game Four loss in St. Louis. That night, he broke a major league record, having waited 20 years, 6 months, and 5 days to make his first Series appearance. The previous month, Joe's brother, Phil, announced his retirement after a 24-season career *without* a World Series appearance, which remains a record. Joe pitched in five games for the Twins the following season and then retired at the age of forty-three, presumably sporting ten very well-trimmed fingernails.

TED TURNER TAKES THE HELM

Robert Edward "Ted" Turner III has led an expansive, colorful, controversial, and consequential life. Best known for founding CNN—the first 24-hour news channel—Turner married actress Jane Fonda, was once named *Time* magazine's "Man of the Year," and was, at one point, the largest private landowner in the entire United States. He purchased the Atlanta Braves prior to the 1976 season for $10 million and, for one day, on May 11, 1977, he served as the club's manager.

With his team sitting at 8–21 to start the season, and buried in a 16-game losing streak, the thirty-eight-year-old Turner dispatched skipper Dave Bristol off on a ten day "special assignment"—ostensibly to go scout Atlanta's farm clubs—and installed himself as acting manager. He donned a gray road jersey with the number 27 that night in Pittsburgh, where he presided over the Braves' 17th consecutive defeat, a 2–1 loss to the Pirates. Prior to the game, Turner signed a coaches contract, a move designed to circumvent major-league rule 20 (e), which stipulated that managers or players could not hold stock or ownership in their club.

That evening, the Three Rivers Stadium scoreboard flashed the following message:

THE PIRATES WELCOME THE ATLANTA
BRAVES' OWNER-PRESIDENT-GENERAL
MANAGER—
AND NOW NEW FIELD MANAGER
TED TURNER-NO. 27

Bristol, the deposed manager, immediately went home to North Carolina. He was reached by reporters at the Pittsburgh airport, where he commented, "it's a strange thing to happen to a man. I'd rather not take questions … I'm taken aback right now." As for Turner, he at least tried to look the part, shoving a wad of Red Man tobacco into his left cheek as he commandeered a seat in the visitor's dugout. "One good thing about being down there on the bench," he told Dan Donovan of the *Pittsburgh Press*, "is that you don't have to use a cup for your chewing tobacco … you can spit on the ground." In his 2008 autobiography, *Call Me Ted*, Turner wrote, "In the dugout, I really didn't do a whole lot other than crack some jokes and yell encouragement. I didn't know the signs, so I had to sit next to one of the other coaches, and when I thought we should steal or bunt, I'd have to tell him so he could relay the signal." When asked by writers about a ninth-inning hit off the bat of Atlanta's Darrel Chaney, Turner said, "Sure, I know what a ground-rule double is. I may be dumb, but I'm not stupid. Only stupid thing I've done is buy the franchise," quickly adding, "I'm just joking about that, fellows."

The only game of Ted Turner's managerial career was witnessed by 6,816 fans. The following day, National League president Charles S. Feeney issued a ruling disqualifying Turner's coaching contract, citing the aforementioned rule prohibiting managers from having a financial interest in their club. Commissioner Bowie Kuhn quickly affirmed the decision, and Bristol was reinstated. With the previous and current field boss on his way back to the club, third-base coach Vern Benson served as skipper on May 12, piloting the Braves to a 6–1 win and breaking the losing streak. Bristol came back for the next game (and lost), the club's 23rd defeat of the young season. The team would go on to lose a grand total of 101 games, which was the first time the franchise had lost 100 games in a season since 1935, when they played their home games in Boston. Bristol was then dismissed (again) as manager, and replaced by Bobby Cox—the first MLB managerial post of Cox's illustrious career.

Turner's tumultuous 1977 took yet another turn on June 3, when commissioner Kuhn reinstituted a one-year suspension that had been tied up in litigation for months, the result of a tampering charge. The Braves' owner took advantage of his forced summer vacation, skippering his yacht *Courageous* to victory in the 1977 America's Cup competition.

Turner's suspension was lifted in December 1977, and his innovative promotional efforts soon began to bear fruit. Attendance increased, and Turner's WTBS "Superstation" beamed Braves games into homes across the nation. By the middle of the 1980s, TBS reached more than 80 percent of American households wired for cable television, delivering more than 140 Braves games a season into every nook and cranny of the country. They were billed as "America's Team," and gained a broad following which included outposts that were far removed from major league markets.

The 1982 Braves started the season with a major-league record 13-game winning streak, and won their division for the first time since 1969. When his club clinched the NL West, the *Atlanta Journal* quoted Turner, who said, "This is just the start of a dynasty. This team is going to win a lot more championships." They fell to the St. Louis Cardinals in the National League Championship Series, but Turner's unlikely prediction came into sharp focus less than a decade later. As he stepped back from club operations, the Braves built a strong front office and a solid farm system. They finished with the worst record in all of baseball in 1990 (65–97), but made an improbable march to the seventh game of the World Series the following season, falling short to the Minnesota Twins in the fall classic. Another pennant followed in 1992, and, finally, in 1995, the Braves broke through with a World Series victory, their first since arriving in Atlanta in 1966. Acting Commissioner Bud Selig presented Turner with the championship trophy, the crowning achievement of his two decades at the helm of the franchise.

When the Braves moved to the repurposed Centennial Olympic Stadium in 1997, the ballpark was christened Turner Field, which soon became known as "The Ted." And although many preferred that the stadium be named for Hank Aaron, the general consensus was that Turner was a fitting choice, a remarkable turnaround for the one-time "Mouth of the South." After the Braves won the 2021 World Series, Turner tweeted out, "How about them @ Braves? I'm on top of the world. As someone who had a front row seat to the World Series win in 1995, I understand the sheer talent & determination required. What a legacy for ATL & the franchise." He also paid tribute to Aaron, who passed away several months earlier.

Never one to shy away from a good quote, Turner once said, "If I only had a little humility I would be perfect."

His all-time managerial record stands at a less-than-perfect 0–1, but his impact on Atlanta and the Braves is both significant and enduring.

NOLAN RYAN HAS NO PITCH COUNT LIMIT

On the night of June 14, 1974, a crowd of 11,083 gathered to watch the California Angels and Boston Red Sox square off at Anaheim Stadium in the opener of a three-game series. To say that everyone in attendance got their money's worth that evening would be an understatement. The home crowd got a win as the Angels triumphed 4–3, in a 15-inning marathon that lasted four hours and two minutes, but they also witnessed one of baseball's most legendary pitching performances.

Those lucky fans enjoyed the privilege of watching Angels ace Nolan Ryan throw 13 innings, during which he faced 58 batters and gave up three runs—all of them earned—while scattering eight hits. Ryan walked 10 batters and struck out 19 Red Sox, but the most astounding stat of the night was his pitch count—235—which was widely reported at the time. Pitch counts were not really a part of the game in those days, but this achievement stood out to contemporary observers. The following day, the *Los Angeles Times* noted, "For someone who had allowed only one hit through four innings, Ryan threw an inordinate number of pitches—84," saying that Ryan "had struck out nine batters during that span, but also issued six walks, including four in the fourth inning." With the score tied at three, he urged manager Bobby Winkles to let him pitch the top of the 13th in an effort to break what he said was his own record for most pitches in a game. On May 2, 1973, Ryan pitched a 12-inning complete game in Detroit, throwing what he claimed to be 242 pitches against the Tigers. (An account of that game in the *Long Beach Press Telegram*, however, noted that Ryan "threw the awesome total of 205 pitches," giving up 10 hits, eight walks, and striking out "a mere seven" batters.) Any way you slice it, that's a lot of pitches—especially given today's standards. Ryan finally exited the game after the 13th inning in favor of reliever Barry Raziano, who pitched two hitless innings of relief to earn his only major-league victory.

An examination of the June 14 box score reveals multitudes. The Red Sox' leadoff man, Cecil Cooper, went 0-for-8 with 6 Ks. Catcher Carlton Fisk went 3-for-7 and didn't strike out at all. Clif Keane, writing in the *Boston Globe*, said that in the first three innings, Fisk "was the only Red Sox player who could get the ball out of the infield" when he singled in the first and flied out in the third. Ryan's pitching opponent, the great Cuban righty Luis Tiant, went all the way—14 and a third innings—marking his ninth consecutive complete game as he threw what has been reported as 163 pitches that night. Tiant faced 56 batters, which would make for a hair less than three pitches thrown per batter faced, a number that seems pretty conservative.

Nolan Ryan's 1974 season is the stuff of legend. He started 41 games and went 22–16. He threw an astonishing 26 complete games and led the majors with 332 2/3 innings pitched. Ryan also led MLB in strikeouts with 367, which was a whopping 118 more than Minnesota's Bert Blyleven, who finished second. How about walks allowed? Ryan led the majors in this category too, with 202,

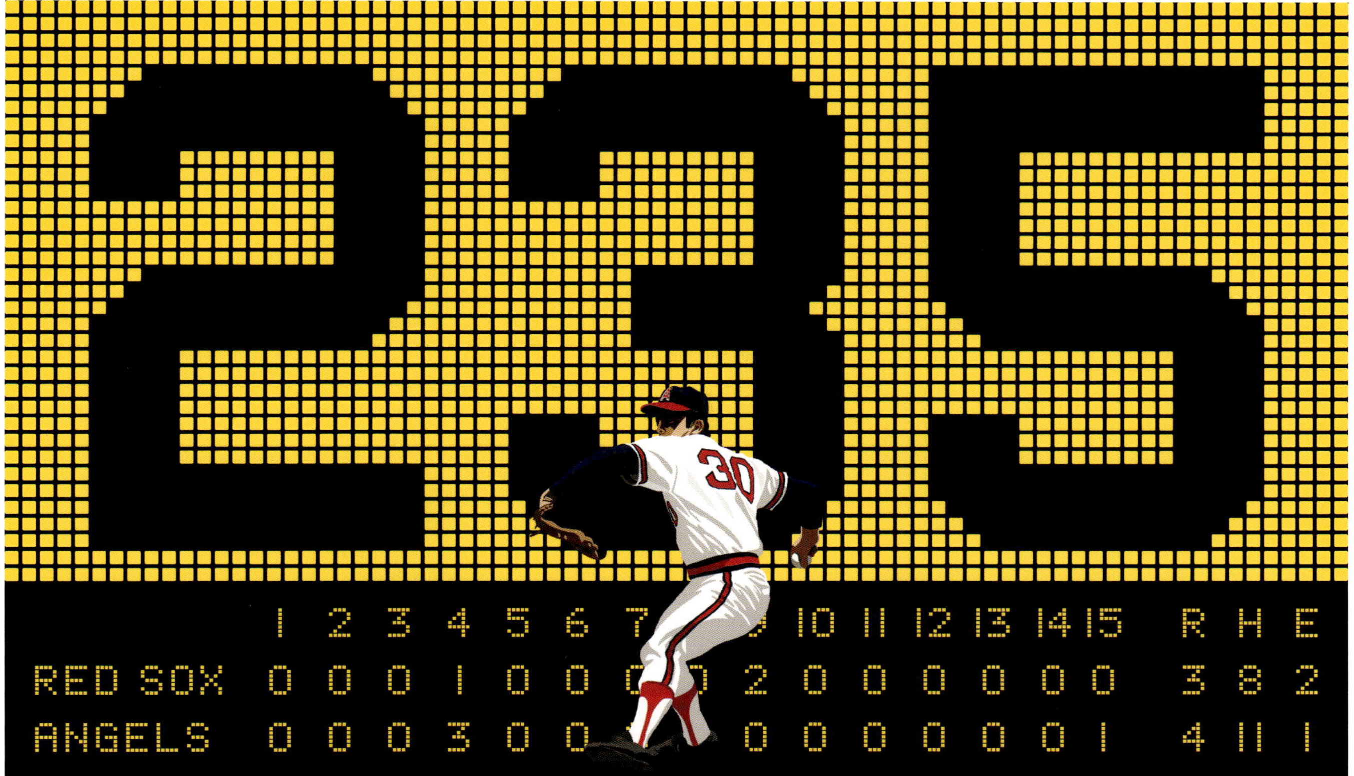

which was 44 more than Detroit's Joe Coleman coughed up. All in all, Ryan faced 1,392 batters in 1974, which also led all of baseball. He concluded his remarkable 1974 campaign with a no-hitter in his final start, on September 28, against the Twins. Despite all of that, Ryan finished third in the American League Cy Young Award voting, behind the winner, Oakland's Catfish Hunter, and the runner-up, Texas' Fergie Jenkins. Amazingly, Ryan, who was later elected to the Hall of Fame with 98.8 percent of the vote, never took home the Cy Young Award over the course of his long and legendary career.

After his marathon effort against the Red Sox, Ryan made his next start on just three days' rest, throwing six shutout innings against the Yankees at Shea Stadium.

Improbably, Ryan continued to throw heat until he finally retired in 1993, at the advanced age of forty-six. When he finally hung up his spikes, he held the all-time records for career strikeouts (5,714) and walks (2,795)—he still holds both records. A 2004 *Los Angeles Times* story about Ryan's 235 pitch effort included a quote by Bill James, who said, "It obviously ruined his arm because he had to retire 19 years later."

FOREIGN UNIFORMS

Mickey Mantle, Derek Jeter, and Lou Gehrig were quintessential Yankees, Cal Ripken Jr., Jim Palmer, and Brooks Robinson were iconic Orioles, and Craig Biggio and Jeff Bagwell are forever Astros. Playing an entire career in a single team's uniform is a rarity, especially in baseball's free agency era. There are plenty of franchise mainstays, Hall of Famers, and notable stars who spent a brief moment in time in an unfamiliar uniform, but some stand out more than others.

Many of these examples involve final acts. Tigers slugger Hank Greenberg finished up with the Pirates while Ty Cobb concluded his lengthy career with the Philadelphia Athletics. Dodgers icon Duke Snider spent his final season with, of all teams, the San Francisco Giants. He spent the previous year with the New York Mets, laying the groundwork for fellow future Hall of Famer Warren Spahn, who similarly ended his career with stops in New York and San Francisco after 20 seasons with the Braves. Giants great Juan Marichal pitched the final two games of his stellar career with the Los Angeles Dodgers in 1975, following an 11-game stint with the Boston Red Sox the year before.

Yogi Berra appeared in 2,116 games in a Yankees uniform, but played his final four games across town with the Mets. Harmon Killebrew finished up with the Kansas City Royals, Hank Aaron was a Milwaukee Brewer at the tail end of his career, Willie Mays was a Met, Manny Ramírez's last MLB stop was Tampa Bay, and Dale Murphy's was Colorado. Christy Mathewson spent his first 17 years with the New York Giants, yet pitched his final game with Cincinnati. Pedro Martínez's last game took place during the 2009 World Series as a member of the Philadelphia Phillies. Frank Robinson played for the Dodgers and Angels before he ended up as player-manager of the Cleveland Indians. John Smoltz excelled as both a starter and a reliever with the Atlanta Braves for two decades, starting in 1988, but closed things out with Boston (eight games) and St. Louis (seven games) in 2009. Steve Carlton spent parts of 22 seasons with the Cardinals and Phillies and then bounced around to San Francisco, the White Sox, Cleveland, and Minnesota for two and a half years before he finally retired in 1988.

The final 28 games of Babe Ruth's illustrious career were spent with the woeful Boston Braves. Club owner Emil Fuchs sought to boost interest in his moribund franchise and acquired the aging Bambino after he was released by the New York Yankees prior to the 1935 season. Ruth hit a mammoth homer off of New York Giants ace Carl Hubbell on Opening Day, but things quickly went downhill from there. By the middle of May he was mired in an 0-for-20 slump, and his retirement appeared to be imminent. The *Dayton Daily News* wrote, "There is nothing more pathetic than a falling idol in sports," adding that Ruth had "become a tremendous handicap to the Braves as a fielder and his batting has been weak and wan." On May 25, Ruth hit the final three runs of his career at Pittsburgh's Forbes Field. He played in five more games and was released by the club on June 2.

BREWERS
BREWERS
HENRY AARON
BABE RUTH
TY COBB
PHILADELPHIA ATHLETICS

Tommy Lasorda famously said, "I bleed Dodger blue and when I die, I'm going to the big Dodger in the sky." He spent 3,692 games in Dodger blue—eight as a player, 644 as a coach, and 3,040 as manager. He also scouted for the organization for five seasons and spent seven years as a manager in their minor-league system ... but in between, in 1956, he spent 18 games as a member of the Kansas City Athletics. Lasorda's brief pitching career began with the Brooklyn Dodgers, where he appeared in four games in both 1954 and 1955. After the club sold him to KC the following spring, he told the *Kansas City Times*, "I guess it was about the happiest day of my life when I heard I had been sold to Kansas City." In July 1956, the A's sold Lasorda to Denver of the American Association, a Yankees farm team. He continued to pitch in the minors until 1960, when the Dodgers' Triple-A Montréal affiliate released him, after which he became a Dodgers scout.

A bunch of Hall of Famers have been traded in the middle of their careers, but Mike Piazza's five-game stint with the Florida Marlins in 1998 is especially noteworthy. It was a brief pit stop, but he did hit one of his eight career triples clad in aqua. Similarly, Pete Rose was once an Expo, George Sisler was a Washington Senator, and Ken Griffey Jr. played a total of 41 games with the Chicago White Sox. Ichiro Suzuki notched his 3,000th MLB hit with the Miami Marlins and Frank Thomas slammed his 500th homer in a Toronto Blue Jays uniform. Willie McCovey played a total of 11 games for the Oakland A's and Greg Maddux had two separate stints with the Dodgers in his forties at the tail end of his career.

Some guys begin their careers in what later become odd uniforms. Nolan Ryan started out with the Mets, Nellie Fox began with the Athletics, and Ryne Sandberg played 13 games with the 1981 Phillies before being traded to the Cubs, where he spent the final 15 years of his Hall of Fame career. Trevor Hoffman began his major-league career with the expansion Florida Marlins in 1993, and Honus Wagner started out with the National League's Louisville Colonels before moving on to Pittsburgh when the National League eliminated the Louisville club after the 1899 season.

Some legends go on to coach or manage in the foreign uniforms. Joe DiMaggio once patrolled center field at Yankee Stadium as a pinstriped god, but he coached for the 1968 Oakland A's garbed in kelly green and Fort Knox gold. Player Ted Williams wore the same Red Sox uniform from 1939 until 1960, but later managed the Washington Senators and Texas Rangers. Duke Snider was a coach for the Montréal Expos, Yogi Berra wore the Houston Astros' rainbow jerseys, and Bob Gibson coached for the Mets and Braves. Walter Johnson managed the Cleveland Indians, Detroit cornerstone Alan Trammell skippered the Arizona Diamondbacks for a mere three games in 2014, and Rogers Hornsby, whose rookie playing season took place in 1915 with the St. Louis Cardinals, concluded his time in uniform as a hitting instructor for the 1962 expansion New York Mets.

All of it serves as proof that the Carl Yastrzemskis and Tony Gwynns of the world are rare birds indeed, franchise lifers with but a single team listed on their impressive resumes.

OFF THE FIELD

BALT 5
PHILA 6
CHI 4
MINN 0

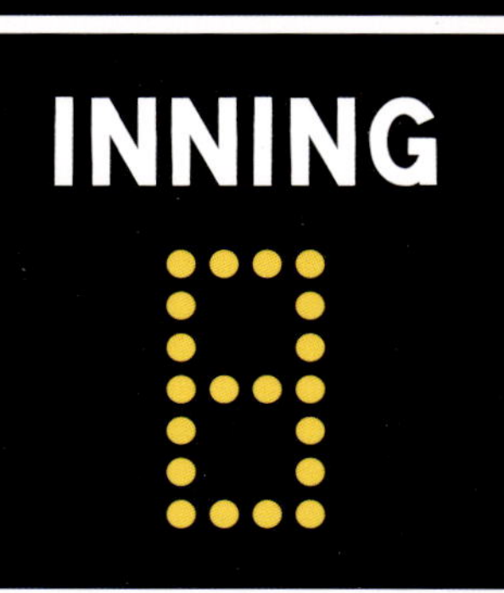

0 BALL
2 STRIKE
0 OUT

SHE'S A BASEBALL BOSS

There's a park in Chicago's Lakeview neighborhood, about a half-mile from Wrigley Field, on West School Street, just west of Racine Avenue. It's got a playground, a rubberized play surface for kids, benches, and walkways. It was dedicated in 2015, partly funded by a $1 million donation from the Chicago Cubs, and is named Margaret Donahue Park.

The name Margaret Donahue may not ring a bell to most fans, but she was a pioneering baseball executive who was inducted into the Cubs' team Hall of Fame in 2021. Her thirty-nine-year tenure with the club coincided with their rise as a business juggernaut. Considered the leading expert on baseball waiver transactions, Donahue is credited with having introduced the practice of selling season tickets, back in 1929 (the first two purchasers were women). She was an ardent advocate for women fans, and was responsible for the then-novel approach of selling game tickets at remote locations—not just at the ballpark. She also came up with the idea of offering discounted tickets for children.

Margaret "Midge" Donahue's baseball journey began in 1919. According to a 1937 *Sporting News* interview, the chemical firm that she was employed at during World War I burned down, prompting her to put an ad in the "situations wanted" section of the *Chicago Tribune*, seeking employment. The Chicago Cubs, looking for a stenographer, responded. While she preferred a job in The Loop and was "annoyed" that the job was not downtown, she reported for work the following morning, on June 23, 1919. A year later, Donahue took over the club's bookkeeping responsibilities, and then, on December 3, 1926, she was elected to the office of secretary by the Cubs' board of directors at their annual meeting, thus becoming the first woman to rise to the level of corporate officer of an MLB club. (At the same meeting, the board voted to rename what was then called Cubs Park as Wrigley Field.) The *Chicago Tribune* ran a short piece about her a few weeks later, accompanied by the headline, "She's a Baseball Boss."

With her promotion, Donahue was now responsible for checking receipts against turnstile counts and paying visiting clubs, in addition to arranging for monetary transfers and the allocation of press passes. She distributed game balls to the umpires before each game which were stored in a cabinet in her office. She managed Wrigley Field's office staff and was a close confidante of team president William Veeck (father of future Hall of Famer Bill Veeck) and owner William Wrigley Jr. Donahue was a familiar presence to Chicago fans, and a valued member of the front office. According to Paul Dickson, author of *Bill Veeck: Baseball's Greatest Maverick*, the younger Veeck later called Donahue, "as astute a baseball operator as ever came down the pike," adding, "She has forgotten more baseball in her forty years with the Cubs than most of the so-called magnates will ever know." Emblematic of her visibility and importance is her appearance in the pennant-winning 1929 Cubs' team photo, where she appears front and center, sandwiched right in between Veeck Sr.

and Wrigley. The following year, she and William Veeck were featured in an ad for Quaker Oats that ran in the *Saturday Evening Post*. In 1950, she was named vice president of the Cubs—she retired eight years later as the team's longest tenured employee. Donahue passed away in 1978 at the age of eighty-five.

The role of women in baseball continues to evolve, both on and off the field, and Margaret "Midge" Donahue helped to lead the way. She is honored with a plaque in the concourse of Wrigley Field's bleachers which reads, "Margaret broke the barrier for women in sports as Major League Baseball's first female officer outside of team ownership." a fitting testament to the enduring impact that she made on her club and on the sport.

DEPICTED IN BRONZE FOR ALL ETERNITY

The Norse sagas tell us of Valhalla, the majestic fortress that was reserved for the souls of slain Viking warriors. Baseball's deities reside at the Hall of Fame in Cooperstown, that idyllic little village in central New York State where the game's foremost figures are immortalized on austere bronze tablets that celebrate the greatest of the great. The dimensions and format of each plaque are identical, but their individual depictions, details, and descriptions contain multitudes.

Let's begin with language. The career of Babe Ruth, one of the Hall's first five inductees, is summed up with but twenty-seven words: "Greatest drawing card in history of baseball. Holder of many home run and other batting records. Gathered 714 home runs in addition to fifteen in World Series." Today's descriptions are far more detailed and verbose, clocking in at right around one hundred words. There's a ton more information now, and the captions have been loaded up with superlatives and statistics. For example, Larry Walker, inducted as part of the class of 2020, was a "Dynamic right fielder with a feared plate presence who brought all-out effort and five-tool skill set to his native Canada's Expos before becoming [a] Rockies superstar." Edgar Martinez won three on-base percentage titles, and Jeff Bagwell "Topped the 30-home run mark nine times and finished with 449 moon shots overall." Moon shots! Reggie Jackson's gargantuan home run in the 1971 All-Star Game, on the other hand, is cited as a "mammoth clout."

Jackie Robinson's original 1962 plaque omitted his historic role in breaking baseball's modern color barrier, a nod to his preference to be considered for election solely on the basis of his merits as a player. Seeking greater context, in 2008 the Hall replaced that original tablet with a new one whose text concludes with the following: "Displayed tremendous courage and poise in 1947 when he integrated the modern major leagues in the face of intense adversity."

A number of plaques have been replaced due to statistical errors or text revisions. Ruth's plaque erroneously marked the first year of his career as 1914. This was amended to the correct 1915 some seventy years after the Babe's induction. Numbers can also get jumbled; Warren Spahn was originally credited with 2,853 strikeouts, as opposed to the correct total of 2,583 (though one can be pretty sure Spahn didn't mind the typo).

The great Roberto Clemente's tablet was recast in 2000, twenty-seven years after his induction. The original version referred to him as "Roberto Walker Clemente," which was replaced with "Roberto Clemente Walker," acknowledging the Latin American custom in which a person's mother's maiden name traditionally follows the given last name. Juan Marichal's plaque underwent a similar revision. It originally read "Juan Antonio (Sanchez) Marichal," but was later amended to read "Juan Antonio Marichal Sanchez."

These bronze plaques also contain a plethora of nicknames, including Amos Rusie, "the Hoosier Thunderbolt." Michael Francis Welch "Smiling Mickey," and Frank Thomas, aka "The Big Hurt." James Thomas Bell is (and should be) "Cool Papa," Gary Carter is "Kid," Willie Mays is "The Say Hey Kid," and George Kenneth Griffey Jr. is cited as "The Kid," in addition to being called "Ken" and "Junior." Derek Jeter is "The Captain." Mariano Rivera's nicknames are both "Mo" and "The Sandman." Paul Waner is "Big Poison" and his brother, Lloyd, is "Little Poison."

Joe McGinnity is "Ironman," with one word, yet Cal Ripken Jr.'s plaque reads "Iron Man." Ozzie Smith is listed as both "Ozzie" and "The Wizard," both of which are rendered in upper and lower case characters—the only examples of such in the plaque gallery. Both Earl Averill and Tim Raines are simply "Rock." Andre Dawson is "The Hawk," Johnny Evers is "The Trojan," Martín Dihigo is "The Maestro," and Phil Rizzuto is "Scooter."

Oddities abound. Wee Willie Keeler is portrayed wearing a cap that the Brooklyn Dodgers wore for a single year, in 1912, when Keeler was a coach, despite the fact that he was inducted as a player. Rollie Fingers wears an Oakland A's cap that contains the unmistakable outlines of the San Diego Padres' signature curved front panels. Slugger Jim Thome's plaque features the Cleveland Indians' "block C" logo, which he wore for just a handful of games during his final season in 2011. Thome spent 13 of his 22 seasons in a Cleveland uniform, and his induction took place in the summer of 2018, shortly after the team announced that it was discontinuing the use of its polarizing Chief Wahoo logo, which Thome wanted no part of. "I know my decision would be to wear the 'C' because I think it's the right thing to do," he told the media after an event in Cleveland that February. "I think I need to have a conversation with the Hall of Fame because of all the history and everything involved. I just think that's the right thing to do."

The depictions of these immortals vary in style as well, a direct reflection of the artist's hand at work. In Cooperstown, Tommy Lasorda beams for all eternity, Todd Helton and Jeff Bagwell sport goatees, and Bruce Sutter's voluminous beard grows wild. Alex Pompez and Jacob Ruppert wear homburg hats, Rube Foster has a

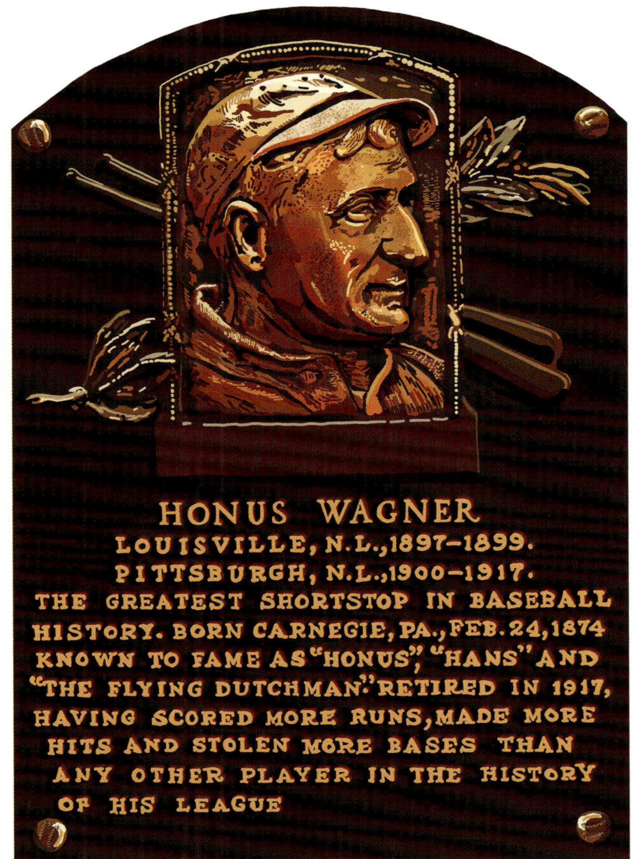

slouched newsboy cap atop his bronzed head, and Branch Rickey sports his signature bow tie. Bronzed hair was critical for the 2015 class; Randy Johnson has a mullet while Pedro Martínez is immortalized in Jheri curls. Charles "Old Hoss" Radbourn looks like a cartoon villain and Pie Traynor exudes determination and grit.

While most players are moved by seeing their plaque, that was not the case for Ted Williams, who reportedly hated his likeness. In fact, there were at least two previous versions depicted on his tablet prior to the current one. Yankees executive Ed Barrow's original plaque depicts a somewhat wizened, disengaged old man, while the current one portrays him with his eyes focused directly on the viewer, square-jawed and knowing, the very picture of sagacity and authority.

All of which brings us to what has become a seemingly annual debate: the robust discussion about what logo should be displayed on the cap of a given inductee. Starting in 2002, the Hall declared, "If any player should earn election to the Hall of Fame, the Museum staff will decide which logo appears on his plaque, though all teams for whom he played will be listed. The National Baseball Hall of Fame and Museum is a nationally renowned history museum and independent from Major League Baseball. To us, the logo selection is important from an historical standpoint. Each candidate will be informed of this." The decision is a collaborative one, but the Hall of Fame has final say, and the choice is "based on where that player makes his most indelible mark."

This wasn't really an issue until the late 1980s, when the Hall began to induct players whose careers took place during baseball's free agency era. Pitcher Catfish Hunter was the first big-name free agent of his time. He left the Oakland A's after a decade in green and gold and signed with the New York Yankees on December 31, 1974, a little more than a dozen years before Cooperstown came calling. The choice of which logo to wear belonged to Hunter alone, and he took as long as he could before deciding on … neither! as he wanted fans of both clubs to remember him as one of their own. Greg Maddux is also shown with a blank cap, as is Fred McGriff, who opted to "equally represent" each of the teams he played for. Pitchers Roy Halladay and Mike Mussina are similarly logo-less. Gary Carter, a 2003 inductee, wanted to go in as a New York Met, but was instead bronzed up as a Montréal Expo, a decision that he agreed with, given the fact that the majority of his career and accomplishments took place in an Expos uniform. Yogi Berra is pictured in profile, with no visible logo. His legendary Yankees tenure spanned 18 years and 2,116 games, as opposed to the four games he played in as a New York Met at the tail end of his career in 1965.*

Baseball's own Valhalla, Cooperstown, is not an easy place to get to, and that sentiment applies to both visitors and the immortals who are commemorated there. A pilgrimage to the Hall of Fame's hallowed plaque gallery is an almost religious experience for baseball fans: a sacred place reserved for contemplation, reflection, and quiet conversation. The several hundred bronze tablets that line its oak walls speak to the history of the sport with often surprising facts, details, and artistry.

* In his induction speech, Yogi thanked both teams, "the only two organizations I ever worked for."

THE ART OF PITCHING

Ballplayers have been hawking commercial products for a century and a half now, endorsing a dizzying array of products, from soap to cigarettes. Way back in 1874, George Wright—baseball's first superstar—was featured on a poster for Boston cigar makers Nichols & Macdonald, pitching their Red Stockings Cigars. History doesn't tell us how much he was paid, but this is the first known instance of an American athlete's endorsement of a commercial product.

Today, Los Angeles Dodgers two-way icon Shohei Ohtani is a global endorsement machine, having earned a reported $100 million in off-field deals in 2025 alone. That season, Ohtani led his club to a second consecutive World Series title while teaming up with more than twenty brand partners, including Japan Airlines, Panasonic, Seiko, Beats by Dre, and New Balance. His visage is especially ubiquitous in his native Japan, where he is the face of everything from Kose cosmetics to convenience store giant Family Mart, where he serves as an *onigiri* (rice ball) ambassador.

Modern American advertising and consumer culture began to take hold in the years following the Civil War. This coincided with the rise of professional baseball, which had become firmly entrenched in the American imagination by 1889, when two of the sport's biggest names posed for a lithograph that advertised E. & J. Burke's beers and ales. In it, Chicago third baseman Cap Anson, wearing his gray road uniform, is seen relaxing with a glass of pale ale, and New York Giants catcher Buck Ewing, clad in his home whites, is leaning back and unwinding with a stout. They are sitting in front of a striped tent, surrounded by barrels, cases, and discarded bottles of the product. Each man was given $300 and a case of ale for his backing.

In the first decades of the twentieth century, Deadball Era stars such as Ty Cobb and Honus Wagner attached their names and faces to a range of commercial goods, but Babe Ruth changed the game—both on and off the field of play. Aided by pioneering agent Christy Walsh, Ruth elevated the endorsement game to stratospheric levels, pitching a range of products that included underwear, gasoline, breakfast cereal, wristwatches, shoes, mattresses, automobiles, candy bars, and cigarettes. In 1934 the Babe inked a three-year deal with Quaker Oats which was worth a cool $62,788, an enormous sum at a time when the average big leaguer earned about $8,000 a season. The agreement included an obligation for him to autograph nine hundred baseballs every week for thirteen weeks, which was presumably worth the effort.

That same year, Ruth's Yankee teammate Lou Gehrig became the first athlete to be featured on a box of Wheaties, the "breakfast of champions." He has since been

joined by a deep roster of stars, including Cal Ripken Jr, Kirby Puckett, Dixie Walker, Jim Palmer, Jimmie Foxx, Fernando Valenzuela, and numerous others.

A wide range of notable ballplayers followed Ruth's example by endorsing tobacco products. Johnny Mize and Catfish Hunter promoted Red Man chewing tobacco, while Carlton Fisk was the frontman for Copenhagen. ("Just a pinch between my cheek and gum gives me rich tobacco flavor, without lighting up.") Chesterfield cigarettes were endorsed by Willie Mays, Joe DiMaggio, Ted Williams, Stan Musial, and Monte Irvin. Mel Ott was featured in print ads for Velvet pipe tobacco.

On a seemingly more healthy note, you have Yogi Berra, who was the public face of Yoo-hoo chocolate drink for decades. He was deeply connected to the brand and was a familiar presence at their factory in Carlstadt, New Jersey, not far from his longtime home in Montclair. In his 1989 autobiography, *Yogi: It Ain't Over*, Berra wrote: "One time I was in the office and the phone rang when no one else was around. I always answer a ringing phone, so I did. The woman who was calling asked if Yoo-hoo was hyphenated. I said, 'No ma'am, it's not even carbonated.'" Yogi also pitched Pringles potato chips, Aflac insurance, Miller beer, Stove Top stuffing, and Camel cigarettes.

For many in the 1970s and 1980s, Joe DiMaggio *was* Mr. Coffee, just as Pete Rose was slinging Aqua Velva and Kool-Aid. Ted Williams was the face of Moxie, a medicinal tasting beverage that was later named the official soft drink of the state of Maine. The company also produced Ted's Root Beer, a short-lived brand that featured a smiling Teddy Ballgame, bat in hand, on the bottle. Williams's successor in left field at Fenway Park, Carl Yastrzemski, was the frontman for Big Yaz bread and Yaz's Kielbasa Power sausages, and when his teammate, Red Sox pitcher Luis Tiant, moved from Boston to the Bronx in 1979, he appeared in ads for Yankee Franks, stating, "It's great to be with a wiener."

The list goes on and on: Ken Griffey Jr. for Pepsi, Darryl Strawberry and Mark McGwire for milk, and Reggie Jackson for Panasonic. Hank Aaron pitched Magnavox televisions, Rafael Palmeiro fronted for Viagra, and Nolan Ryan promoted Wrangler jeans, Justin boots, Advil, Southwest Airlines, and Whataburger.

Baseball has long been called "America's pastime," but consumerism may well be America's most defining characteristic. The combination of ballplayers and brands is something that's deeply embedded in our baseball culture, starting with George Wright's landmark cigar ad in 1874 and continuing forward to the present day, where Shohei Ohtani pitches footwear, headphones, and rice balls.

A STATUE FOR HONUS

Larger-than-life statues of legendary baseball players dot the major-league stadium landscape from coast to coast, commemorating heroic figures and milestone moments. There's a nine-and-a-half-foot tribute to Tony Gwynn outside of Petco Park in San Diego, and Tom Seaver holds forth at New York's Citi Field, depicted in the middle of his signature drop-and-drive delivery. Bud Selig has a statue in Milwaukee, and in Boston, Ted Williams, Bobby Doerr, Dom DiMaggio, and Johnny Pesky are forever remembered next to Fenway Park's Gate 5, bats on shoulders, honored as teammates and friends. But before any of these came a monument to one of the greatest baseball icons of yore, Honus Wagner. It now stands in front of the home-plate entrance of Pittsburgh's PNC Park, at the corner of West General Robinson Street and Mazeroski Way, it's third location.

The idea for a Wagner statue was first floated in January 1953, nearly a year after Wagner, a lifelong resident of the local community, retired as a Pirates coach after more than a half century with the organization. A group calling itself the Pittsburgh Professional Baseball Association was formed by former Bucs third baseman Frankie Gustine, and one of their efforts involved honoring Wagner with a permanent tribute. Gustine told the *Pittsburgh-Sun Telegram*, "We'd like to do something concrete while he's still around to smell the flowers."

They met with Bucs general manager Branch Rickey at Forbes Field and proposed that the ballpark be renamed in Wagner's honor, which was met with resistance. Another idea was that of a statuary tribute, a concept that was soon embraced by city leaders, including Pittsburgh mayor David Lawrence. In July 1953, the city's planning commission cleared the way for a Wagner statue, which was to be erected in Schenley Park, opposite Forbes Field's bleacher entrance.

Local sculptor Frank Vittor, an Italian native who studied in Paris under Auguste Rodin, was commissioned to create the sculpture, and the Pittsburgh Professional Baseball Association conducted a public campaign to raise $48,500 to fund the project. Cleveland Indians manager Al Lopez contributed $50, the B'nai B'rith Freedom Lodge 1780 raised $52, the Coraopolis Order of Moose sent in $10, and St. Louis Cardinals slugger Stan Musial mailed in a check for $100. One anonymous donor remitted $2, with a note that read, "In remembrance of many pleasant afternoons in the old Northside ball park." A steel tube with a list of contributors was eventually embedded in the base. Perhaps the only controversial item surrounding the plans involved the inscription on the statue's plinth, which was slated to simply read, "John Peter Wagner," with nary a Honus in sight. This was soon amended to "J. P. 'Honus' Wagner."

Vittor's portrayal of Wagner is powerful and colossal. He is depicted at bat, following through on a swing. His one-of-a-kind face, cast in bronze, seems perfectly at home in that medium. His massive forearms and thick-set knees are well articulated, and his baggy uniform includes period-specific details such as a collared jersey and high socks.

J.P. "HONUS"
WAGNER

The two-ton statue, which stands close to ten feet high, was fabricated by New York's Roman Bronze Works. It sits atop a mammoth twenty-one-ton granite base which was quarried by the Beck and Beck Company in Barre, Vermont. Frank's brother, Tony Vittori, created the relief work on the base, which depicts four children gazing up admiringly at Wagner. The lone girl in the group is Wagner's four-year-old granddaughter, Leslie Ann Blair.

Fundraising efforts included an exhibition game between the Pirates and the Philadelphia Athletics, which was played on August 9, 1954, at Forbes Field. Ninety-one-year-old A's owner Connie Mack paid a surprise visit to Wagner at his home in Carnegie that day—they'd first encountered one another during another exhibition game that was played fifty-nine summers earlier, when Mack was managing the Pirates and Wagner was hitting cleanup for a minor-league club based in Warren, Pennsylvania.

A group headed by US Steel board chairman Benjamin Fairless contributed the final $6,000 toward the effort in early March, and a dedication ceremony was planned for April 30, 1955. That day, a crowd of one thousand spectators gathered to pay tribute to the ailing Wagner, who sat in an open automobile in front of the speaker's stand. Attendees included Cy Young, commissioner Ford Frick, and Wagner's former manager Fred Clarke. Uniformed members of the Cincinnati Reds and Pittsburgh Pirates were there as well, including a twenty-year-old rookie named Roberto Clemente, who'd play the 10th game of his major-league career later that day. The Pittsburgh Police and Fireman's Band played "Take Me Out to the Ballgame" and the national anthem, and little Leslie Ann Blair pulled a cord to undrape the statue, which got stuck somewhere near the top. Former Pirates bullpen catcher Lenny Levy saved the day when he ascended the granite base and worked the cover free.

Honus Wagner passed away a little more than seven months later, on December 6, 1955, at the age of eighty-one. He was lauded as a modest, genial, and humble man, a pillar of his community who was loved and respected by generations of friends and fans. The Pirates abandoned Forbes Field for Three Rivers Stadium in 1970, and the statue was moved and rededicated there two years later, on July 21, 1972. Leslie Ann Blair did the honors yet again, and, as was the case seventeen years earlier, the Pirates played the Reds.

The statue's most recent move took place prior to the 2001 season, when the Bucs moved into PNC Park, which is located just a couple of blocks east of Exposition Park, where Wagner and his Pirates played before Forbes Field opened its gates in 1909. The words carved into the statue's granite plinth celebrate the Steel City's first superstar, whose legacy lives on more than a century after he last played.

Erected in 1955
by the fans of America in honor of a baseball immortal, a champion among champions, whose record on and off the playing field of the National Game will ever stand as a monument to his own greatness and as an example and inspiration to the youth of our country.

Sponsored by the Pittsburgh Professional Baseball Association

CAPS, COFFINS & COMMEMORATIVE COINS

Being a baseball fan requires a certain level of commitment. The season is a long one, stretching from spring training (which begins in February) all the way to the World Series (which can end in early November). It's a marathon, and the offseason can seem like a slog, but fans are gonna fan, 365 days a year, seven days a week. Lucky for us, we can pledge our allegiance to our teams by buying licensed merchandise that draws us closer to the field of play. The obvious offerings start with T-shirts, replica uniforms, and caps, but things quickly escalate to items such as dog collars, team-branded breakfast foods, barware, bandages, jewelry, and furniture.

Beginning in 2006 the true diehards among us could rest easy for all eternity in official MLB burial caskets, produced by the Eternal Image Group LLC who said that their products were "fitting for the lifelong baseball fan."

> *They are 18-gauge steel with a jet black exterior adorned with wood veneer, team emblems and the world-famous MLB™ Batter emblem. The velvet interior is trimmed with an additional team emblem and MLB™ Batter emblem, with a large team emblem on the interior headpanel. Official MLB™ Hologram sticker affixed to left, bottom corner of casket.*

If cremation is more your thing, then urns are an option. Yet it wasn't always this way.

Our now insatiable need for branded tchotchkes is a relatively recent phenomenon. Back in the really old days, fans could purchase a limited range of souvenirs, such as buttons and pennants, but licensing wasn't a thing until 1928. That's when sixteen-year-old Chicagoan David Warsaw, whose family owned a pottery business called the Stetson China Company, made history by creating an ashtray in the shape of Wrigley Field and included a Cubs logo on it. He then worked out an agreement with the team to sell the product at Wrigley—the Cubs got a percentage of the sale of each ashtray and, boom! Just like that, the sports licensing industry was born. Warsaw soon branched out to other products and named his business Sports Specialties Corporation. He patented the ceramic baseball player figurine with a nodding head that we now know as the bobblehead. When Warsaw died in 1996, he was justifiably lauded as an industry pioneer, "the father of the sports licensing industry," according to NBA commissioner David Stern.

Baseball's efforts to sell branded goods lagged behind their counterparts at the NFL. In 1959, Larry Kent, an executive at Roy Rogers Enterprises, contacted the Los Angeles Rams about marketing team merchandise through the "Roy Rogers Corral" at area Sears stores. Roy Rogers was famous for being Hollywood's "King of the Cowboys," but he was also the frontman for a licensing powerhouse. He started his merchandising arm in the early 1950s, and within a couple of years Roy Rogers Enterprises was producing an eighty-page catalog of officially licensed merch, grossing some $35 million annually.

Rogers and the league formed NFL Enterprises in October 1959 as a subsidiary of Roy Rogers Enterprises. Rogers received half the revenue, with NFL team owners splitting the rest of the pot. Their first venture was a deal with Standard Oil in the form of glassware with team logos, given away with fill-ups at Standard gas stations. A 1998 *Sports Illustrated* article said, "Within a year Rogers had lined up 45 manufacturers, churning out about 300 NFL products—cigarette lighters, dolls, vacuum bottles, ties, blankets, coats, pajamas and more. The strange marriage between branding iron and gridiron, however, didn't last. When the contract came up for renewal in 1962, Kent leaped from Roy Rogers Enterprises to the burgeoning NFL."

In 1963, the owners of the league's fourteen teams agreed to assign all rights to their team's trademarks, thus forming NFL Properties. That made baseball sit up and took notice, and, in December 1966, major-league owners

voted to form their own licensing arm, a joint venture of the twenty MLB clubs. This evolved into the Major League Baseball Promotions Corporation, which really ramped up their marketing efforts in anticipation of professional baseball's 100th anniversary season, in 1969.

Planning had begun the previous June, when MLB tapped advertising agency Batten, Barton, Durstine & Osborn to lead their marketing campaign. The agency assigned Tom Villante, a BBD&O vice president and former Yankees batboy, to manage the account. Major League Baseball had no official logo at this time, and Villante engaged Sandgren & Murtha, a New York–based design and marketing firm, to remedy that oversight. Designer Jerry Dior's silhouetted batter logo—baseball's first unified trademark—was released to the public in October 1968. His mark eschewed tradition, but he rendered it in red, white, and blue, which communicated the fact that baseball was *still* America's Pastime, even as the NFL was surpassing MLB in popularity, even as the Vietnam War slogged on, and even as America's identity itself was being questioned. The logo was simple and powerful, and it transitioned into the digital age with ease, a piece of art so well constructed and conceived that it never grew dated. More than half a century after its debut, it still says "baseball" to consumers all over the world.

The logo began to appear on the backs of team caps in 1992. MLB team-branded caps are now a global fashion staple, but with the exception of actual players, few people—especially adults—wore such things prior to the 1970s. Today, Buffalo, New York–based New Era rules the headwear roost. Founded in 1920, the company's first on-field client was the Cleveland Indians, who began to wear New Era caps back in 1934. Fan offerings didn't come until much later. Bostonian Tim McAuliffe began his career as a salesman for Spalding in 1924 and went into business for himself in 1941. He started concentrating on ballcaps in 1948, when Spalding closed its cap factory in Brooklyn, and by the mid-1950s he was the official headwear supplier for fourteen of MLB's sixteen clubs. McAuliffe also did a fairly brisk retail trade, selling caps via small ads in *The Sporting News* for many years. All these efforts were scattered and hardly lucrative, but today the baseball headwear business is a multibillion-dollar concern. Similarly, replica jerseys, which are now ubiquitous, were once a rarity off the field of play. That all changed in 1987, when Rawlings signed a five-year deal to become the official uniform supplier of Major League Baseball, an arrangement which allowed them to sell authentic replica jerseys at retail.

Nowadays, a visit to MLB's online shop (a Fanatics Experience!) reveals a multitude of items for sale, including phone cases, wireless keyboards, sandals, jars of game used dirt, commemorative coins, golf balls, signed photos, and lapel pins. Teams from baseball's past are represented too, just in case you need a Montréal Expos throw blanket or a Brooklyn Dodgers dual port USB car and home charger. Whatever one's level of fandom or team choice, there's something available for everyone, including those who want to continue their fandom into the great beyond.

BUY ME SOME PEANUTS AND PORK BAO BUNS

On the afternoon of Friday, June 15, 1894, John J. "Dasher" Troy, a former ballplayer who operated the food and beverage concessions at New York's Polo Grounds, attempted to bring three unticketed friends in with him to a game between the Giants and Pittsburgh Pirates. Ticket taker Harry Pittenger refused Troy's companions entry, and a scuffle quickly ensued. More specifically, as the *New York Evening World* reported, Troy "tried to push a grand-stand gatekeeper's nose through the back of his head." The Giants immediately stripped Troy of his concession privileges in favor of a new caterer named Harry M. Stevens. By the time Stevens died forty years later, he was fabulously wealthy, famous, and known to all as "the hot dog king."

Fans have been eating and drinking at baseball games since the sport's earliest days. An 1860 *New York Daily Herald* account of a game played in Brooklyn between the Atlantic and Excelsior clubs describes a huge, spill-over crowd which partook in lager beer, peanuts, apples, and pies. In 1867, the *Brooklyn Daily Eagle* talked about the fact that the "cocoanut-candy man" was becoming a fixture at the Union Grounds, baseball's first enclosed park, selling his wares at "fifteen cents a quarter of a pound—ten for five cents."

Some credit Chris Van Der Ahe, the owner of the American Association's St. Louis Browns, with being the first to sell hot dogs at games, but there's no hard evidence that confirms this. In contrast to the National League, the AA—termed the "Beer and Whiskey League"—sold alcohol at games, and Van Der Ahe's Sportsman's Park featured an open air beer garden in right field, complete with handball courts and lawn bowling—this was all originally part of the park's fair territory.

Back at the Polo Grounds, Dasher Troy, who was reputed to have been the first player ever signed by the Giants franchise, employed what the *New York Sun* described as "an army of waiters" who hawked peanuts and soft drinks in the stands. He also had his men peddling beer in the bleachers, which was a violation of the NL constitution. After the American Association and National League merged in 1892, beer became legal at NL parks, and Troy later operated a bar underneath the grandstand. His successor, Stevens, an English immigrant, started out selling scorecards at minor-league games in Columbus, Ohio, in 1887. He soon expanded his business eastward to Boston, Washington, Pittsburgh, and other big-league cities. Within a few short years, he was renowned as "the greatest of score-card sellers." Stevens was popular, well-connected, and hard-working, described as the "hustler of all hustlers" by the *Cincinnati Enquirer* in 1891, and his Polo Grounds contract launched what would become a sprawling empire, built on scorecards, sandwiches, ginger ale, beer, ice cream, peanuts, and, of course, hot dogs.

In 1919, Stevens introduced the "Stevens Fireless Frankfurter Cooker," an automated device which allowed vendors to deliver hot franks right to fans' seats. It was inspired by stew wagons used by European armies on battlefields during World War I. Customers inserted a dime on the side bearing a British flag and got a dog with English mustard. The other side featured a French tricolor flag, which vended a frank with French mustard—German mustard was strictly verboten.

Cracker Jack has been a baseball staple since the late nineteenth century. Its enduring connection to the sport was cemented by songwriters Jack Norworth and Albert Von Tilzer, who wrote "Take Me Out to the Ball Game" in 1908. Ballpark food settled into a predictable, sausage-forward routine for the next half century, but fans in the prosperous post–World War II era began demanding better and more varied options. The Cleveland Indians introduced pizza to their ballpark in 1958, and the Yankees upped their food game in 1964 when they brought aboard a new concessionaire and an expanded menu. The following year, the St. Louis Cardinals boasted a range of new offerings, including French fries, chicken fried steak, shrimp rolls, and Bavarian pretzels "baked right at the park." The Houston Colt .45s played outdoors in the stifling Texas heat for the first three years of their existence, selling corn dogs—along with five kinds of ice cream and seven kinds of beer—which must have helped cool things off a little bit. At New York's brand new Shea Stadium, the Mets sold knishes for a quarter each, a shrimp basket for 85 cents, and egg salad sandwiches for 45 cents. The Braves started selling Chick-fil-A sandwiches at their new stadium shortly after moving to Atlanta in 1966.

In 1975, the Texas Rangers introduced nachos to Arlington Stadium, and they were an immediate hit. That season they sold 90,000 orders, which included 11,000 pounds of cheese. The "father of ballpark nachos" was Frank Liberto, who ran a San Antonio concession supplier business. Liberto developed a quick-serve, ballpark-friendly solution to the already familiar Tex-Mex treat, rolling out a viscous cheese sauce that could be dispensed with little preparation. This was a revelation back in the late '70s. *Baytown Sun* (Texas) columnist Mike Finley expressed his surprise, writing, "Whoever heard of selling nachos at a baseball game?"

Philadelphia's Veterans Stadium switched concessionaires in 1986, and with that change came two new food courts—a nod to mall culture, which was all the rage at that particular time. The Phillies rolled out a bunch of new menu options, including cheesesteaks, meatball sandwiches, chalupas, and chicken tenders. Reviews were mixed. The *Philadelphia Inquirer* interviewed one Mets fan who had driven down from New York to see the home opener between the Phillies and the Mets. Commenting on the $1.50 pizza slices, he said, "The pizza tastes like a washcloth with pizza sauce," but added, "it's a crispier and better-tasting washcloth than at Shea."

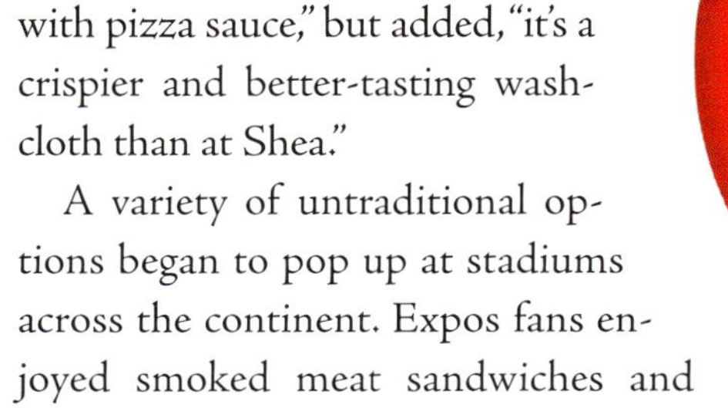

A variety of untraditional options began to pop up at stadiums across the continent. Expos fans enjoyed smoked meat sandwiches and poutine at Montréal's Olympic Stadium, crab cakes were available for sale at Baltimore's Memorial Stadium, and in Los Angeles, fans at Dodger Stadium could purchase Japanese rice bowls. San Diego Padres fans ate bagels and cream cheese at Jack Murphy Stadium, and the Florida Marlins sold arepas and Cuban sandwiches at Joe Robbie Stadium. When Coors Field opened in Denver in 1995, Rockies fans began to tuck in to locally sourced Bison burgers and Rocky Mountain oysters (feel free to go right ahead and look those up if you are not familiar with them). That same year, the Boston Red Sox rolled out clam chowder at Fenway Park.

Nowadays, fans can partake in an ever-expanding array of gastronomic offerings, from pork bao buns and chapulines (toasted grasshoppers) in Seattle to carne asada burrito bowls in San Francisco. In Pittsburgh, one can feast upon pierogis, and in Cincinnati you can tuck into a bowl of Skyline Chili. All across the land, baseball fans now enjoy an unprecedented variety of food choices, including the time-honored hot dog.

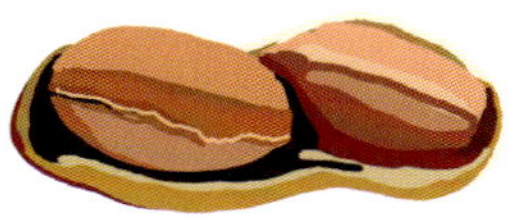

YOUR LAST STOP ON YOUR WAY HOME

A building housing the Boston Police Department currently sits at the corner of Ruggles Street and Tremont Avenue in Boston's Roxbury section. At the beginning of the twentieth century, it was the site of Michael T. McGreevy's Third Base Saloon, so named because "it was your last stop on your way home." It's been called "America's first sports bar," but that distinction really belongs to Nick Engel's Home Plate, a New York steakhouse that was both a hangout for and a shrine to the New York Giants of the late 1880s. Regardless, McGreevy's baseball-themed bar was unique and groundbreaking, a combination watering hole and museum devoted to America's pastime, conveniently located near both the South End Grounds, the home of the Boston Beaneaters (today's Atlanta Braves), and the Huntington Avenue Grounds, the first home of the Boston Red Sox.

The bar's proprietor was born in 1865, the first child of an Irish immigrant day laborer. He opened his first saloon in 1894, moving it to a new location at 940 Columbus Avenue in 1900. In September 1897, McGreevy organized a group of some two hundred diehard Beaneaters fans who journeyed by train to Baltimore, where they cheered on their team as they tangled with the Orioles for the National League pennant. The group later became known as the Royal Rooters, and they shifted their allegiance to the new American League club in town, the Red Sox, who were founded in 1901. The colorful and boisterous Rooters traveled back and forth between Pittsburgh and Boston for baseball's first modern World Series in 1903, gaining widespread fame. Abetted by the Boston Letter Carrier's Band, they serenaded their heroes and taunted their opponents with a popular Broadway tune from the musical, *The Silver Slipper*, "Tessie," which drove the Pirates mad. They set their sights on Bucs star Honus Wagner, transforming the line "Tessie, you make me feel so badly" into "Honus, why do you hit so badly." Almost sixty years later, when Pittsburgh infielder Tommy Leach was interviewed by author Lawrence Ritter for his book, *The Glory of Their Times*, he said, "I think those Boston fans actually won that Series for the Red Sox. We beat them three of the first four games, and then they started singing that damn *Tessie* song … sort of got on your nerves after a while. And before we knew what happened, we'd lost the World Series." After the Red Sox won the championship, the *Boston Globe* wrote, "'Tessie' will ever more stand well with the admirers of the American League and the royal rooters who took such a prominent part in landing Boston a winner." The cover of Boston's scorecard from that first World Series features images of the two opposing managers and an advertisement for McGreevy's, "On the Avenue," with an image of the bar's owner at top.

McGreevy was known to one and all as "Nuf Ced," a tribute to the signature expression that he employed to keep the peace and end barroom disputes, the final word which was delivered with a resolute "nuf ced!" and a pounded fist upon his establishment's oak bar. The tavern was a rendezvous for players and fans alike, the de facto headquarters for Boston baseball folks year round. It was decorated from floor to ceiling with baseball photographs and memorabilia—a veritable museum of baseball collectibles which included an extensive and impressive array of game-used equipment. Light fixtures, composed of illuminated frosted glass baseballs and game-used bats of stars such as Cap Anson, Cy Young, Nap Lajoie, and King Kelly, hung from the ceiling. McGreevy's most prized possession was a gold medal that was originally awarded by the *Boston Globe* to Kelly, an early Boston baseball legend, in 1887.

The gregarious McGreevy was a bona fide baseball celebrity, Boston's famed "first fan." He traveled to spring training in Hot Springs, Arkansas, with his beloved Sox, donning his own personal uniform and shagging fly balls. He was a fine athlete in his own right, too, a skilled bowler, ice skater, and handball player. McGreevy mixed with the famous and not so famous alike, including players, reporters, and politicians, among them congressman John F. "Honey Fitz" Fitzgerald, grandfather of future President John F. Kennedy, a Royal Rooter dating back to the Beaneaters days.

In 1912, the Red Sox notched their second World Series appearance—this time against the New York Giants—and the Rooters returned to the national stage. Accompanied by Fitzgerald, now the mayor of Boston, McGreevy led three hundred members of the group, including a thirty-piece brass band, to New York by rail. They reprised "Tessie" and watched their boys take Game One of the Series, 4–3. Up three games to two (with one tie), the series shifted to the Red Sox' new home, Fenway Park, where the Rooters expected their team to wrap things up.

Unfortunately, things did not go according to plan. The Rooters marched to Fenway for Game Seven and were astonished to find that the section of the left-field bleachers that had usually been reserved for them was occupied, with their usual seats having been sold out from under them. Frozen out, the group swarmed the field, where they were met by policemen. A fracas ensued, a section of the left-field fence was knocked down, and the game was delayed. The angry group was herded into a standing room only section, where they watched their team get thumped, 11–4. The disaffected Rooters boycotted the decisive eighth and final game the following day, when Boston wrapped up the Series. The Red Sox issued a formal apology to the group a couple of days after that, and the Rooters hit the road again two years later to watch the Boston Braves defeat the Philadelphia Athletics in the fall classic.

McGreevy moved his bar to its third and final location in 1915. Located just a couple blocks away, at Ruggles and Tremont, the saloon was done in by prohibition just five years after the move, in 1920. Three years later, he leased the bar to the Boston Public Library for $91.66 a month, and it was reborn as the Roxbury Crossing branch of the BPL. McGreevy donated his collection of photos to the library's print department, where it still resides today, described as "one of the most important collections of early baseball images in the United States." Part of his famed assemblage was displayed in a storefront window at Filene's department store in downtown Boston in 1939, in conjunction with baseball's centennial celebration.

McGreevy died at the age of seventy-seven on February 2, 1943. In 2008, the bar was revived at a new location on Boylston Street. The pub closed during the COVID-19 pandemic in 2020, but Michael T. McGreevy's legacy lives on. You can access his collection online via the Boston Public Library's website, which probably would have made Nuf Ced very happy.

940
WINE STO
M.T. McGREE
BOWLING
ALLEY
CONNECTED
40
BOSTON
LOYAL
"NUFFSAID"

EY & CO. IMPORTERS
ALE
STERLING ALE

AN ARCHITECT FOR THE FANS

Once upon a time, nearly half of our major-league stadiums were soulless, concrete multipurpose cookie cutter facilities. Cities such as Atlanta, Oakland, San Diego, and Seattle attracted new teams with these utilitarian stadiums, while historic urban parks were cast aside in places like St. Louis, Cincinnati, Philadelphia, and Pittsburgh. The new venues were uniformly gray, dreary, and circular, short on charm, comfort, and amenities, with a slew of them rising up in quick succession during the late 1960s and early '70s. National League infielder Richie Hebner reportedly said, "I stand at the plate in Philadelphia and I honestly don't know whether I'm in Pittsburgh, Cincinnati, St. Louis, or Philly," and fans who had the opportunity to have visited all of these places would wholeheartedly concur.

Then came Janet Marie Smith.

Smith, a native of Jackson, Mississippi, is a trained urban planner with a degree in architecture. Moreover, she is the most accomplished ballpark architect in the history of baseball. A champion of urban environments with a deep appreciation for history and thoughtful details, her love of the game permeates her work and has changed the way that we watch the sport, melding form and function as one for the benefit of the fan. Smith's influence on the game spans the continent—from Boston to San Diego to Atlanta to Los Angeles—but her magnum opus is and will always be Oriole Park at Camden Yards in Baltimore, a ballpark which set the standard for a wave of classically inspired baseball-only facilities after its 1992 opening.

Camden Yards is undeniably linked to its surrounding streets and the city beyond. It oozes architectural integrity, a throwback to baseball's intimate "jewel box" parks which emphasized steel and brick over drab concrete—and felt perfectly at home in their neighborhoods. All of these dynamics were quaint relics of a distant age when Smith, then in her early thirties, made a pit stop in Baltimore while on her way to a business trip in Philadelphia and decided to take in an Orioles game at Memorial Stadium. It was there that she overheard fans talking about a possible new stadium, after which she fired off what she called a "persuasive letter" to O's executive Larry Lucchino, a native of Pittsburgh whose childhood experiences of going to games at Forbes Field informed his affinity for the traditional, idiosyncratic, and intimate parks of yore.

Lucchino brough Smith in for an interview and dismissively asked her, "Which league has the designated hitter?" She rightfully took offense. Lucchino, to his credit, moved on with the discussion, and the rest is history. In June 1989, Smith was named vice president of new stadium planning and development for the Orioles. Their visionary partnership shifted from Baltimore to San Diego to Boston and Worcester, Massachusetts, continuing forward until Lucchino's death in 2024.

Smith became the public face of the Orioles' ballpark project, and the team's surprising vision for the place soon became clear, much to the delight of fans and media alike. Before it even opened, *The New York Times* architecture critic Paul Goldberger wrote, "This is a building capable of

ORIOLES
THE SUN
JANET MARIE
SMITH
NATIONAL
BOHEMIAN BEER
TEAM STORE
OLD BAY
SEASONING

wiping out in a single gesture fifty years of wretched stadium design, and of restoring the joyous possibility that a ball park might actually enhance the experience of watching the game of baseball." Asymmetrical outfield dimensions were in, and no detail was left untouched. Comfort was a priority as well. Seating at Camden Yards varied from 19 to 22 inches wide, as opposed to the average seat at Memorial Stadium (which was 18). The seats themselves were dark green in color, inspired by Chicago's Wrigley Field, and they were the first plastic stadium seats to be made with slats, a throwback look that took months of research and testing to get right. Literally capping all that off, 4,000 end caps of each row of seats included an ornate cast iron logo inspired by that of the 1890s Baltimore Orioles. The entire effort was executed by Kansas City–based architectural firm Hellmuth Obata & Kassabuam (HOK), along with Baltimore's David Ashton and Company, who created the park's graphics.

All those rich design details extended to the center-field scoreboard, which was topped off with a two-sided clock, echoing that of a nearby landmark, the Bromo Seltzer Tower. Some details are undeniably bigger than others. The decision to maintain and incorporate the landmark B&O warehouse into the ballpark defined the boundaries of the field itself. The 1,016-foot-long warehouse is the park's most visible feature, housing the Orioles' offices and a private club. The field of play was sunk eighteen feet below street level, which helped to keep the ballpark from hovering too high above the surrounding area. The ballpark faces north, which offers up a splendid view of downtown Baltimore. Eutaw Street, which runs between the park and the warehouse, was reimagined as a pedestrian walkway, a festive area where fans could meet, mingle, and marvel at the small brass baseballs that are embedded into the sidewalk, marking the spots where home runs soared up and over the right field fence. Smith forged an unlikely collaboration and friendship with Orioles manager Frank Robinson, an old-school baseball man who contributed his ideas about the designs of the playing field and clubhouse.

Camden Yards debuted on April 6, 1992, with Baltimore defeating Cleveland, 2–0, behind a complete-game shutout by Rick Sutcliffe. The stadium's planning and opening served as the catalyst for a generation of retro-inspired ballparks. Smith later moved on to Atlanta, where she was responsible for the transformation of that city's Olympic Stadium into the Braves' Turner Field. Her next stop after that was San Diego, where she again teamed up with Lucchino, this time helping out on the Padres' Petco Park. The two collaborated once again in Boston, where they worked to preserve, renovate, and expand venerable Fenway Park, a concept that was dismissed and given up for dead by the club's previous ownership.

Since then, Smith has overseen renovations at Pittsburgh's PNC Park, and has worked as an executive with the Los Angeles Dodgers, where she has overseen a series of upgrades to Dodger Stadium, a marvel of mid-century modern architecture. That ballpark opened exactly a half-century after Fenway and thirty years before Camden Yards. Her keen attention to detail now includes the sixteen shades of blue that are scattered throughout the stadium, something that the average fan would likely never, ever notice, but would be grateful for if they did.

Baseball owes a debt of gratitude to this remarkable visionary, a champion of cities and an architect for the fans.

FAMOUS FANS

On May 8, 2025, a column of white smoke billowed skyward from a chimney perched atop the Vatican's Sistine Chapel, signifying the election of a new pope: Chicago native Robert Francis Prevost. As far as we know, Pope Leo XIV is the first leader of the worldwide Roman Catholic Church who is also a fan of the Chicago White Sox—the future pope even attended Game One of the 2005 World Series clad in a pinstriped home Sox jersey. He was joined in attendance that night by Senator Barack Obama, a fellow Sox fan, who was elected President of the United States three years later. Your author was there, too.

Entertainers, politicians, artists, writers, and other celebrities have been rooting for their favorite players and teams since the very beginnings of the sport. President Ulysses S. Grant hosted baseball's first professional team, the Cincinnati Red Stockings, at the White House in 1869. Richard M. Nixon and Herbert Hoover were passionate, knowledgeable fans, and President William Howard Taft attended two major-league games in a single day, on May 4, 1910, when he saw part of a game between the Cardinals and Taft's hometown team, the Cincinnati Reds, at St. Louis' Robison Field, after which he watched the Browns take on Cleveland at Sportsman's Park. George W. Bush headed up a group of investors who purchased the Texas Rangers in 1989, and his father, President George H. W. Bush, was an avid supporter of the Houston Astros. Jimmy Carter followed the Atlanta Braves and a young Ronald Reagan called Chicago Cubs games on the radio.

How about writers and poets? Walt Whitman rhapsodized about baseball's connection to America's national character, stating that the sport was "our game: that's the chief fact in connection with it: America's game: has the snap, go, fling, of the American atmosphere." Poet Marianne Moore, an avid Brooklyn Dodgers fan, wrote "Hometown Piece for Messrs. Alston and Reese," which paid homage to her team's 1955 World Series win. Moore also penned a poem, entitled "Baseball and Writing," and she threw out the ceremonial first pitch at Yankee Stadum on Opening Day of the 1968 season. Novelist Tom Clancy owned a significant share of the Baltimore Orioles. John Updike wrote a famed essay for *The New Yorker* on Ted Williams's final game with the Boston Red Sox, "Hub Fans Bid Kid Adieu," and A. Bartlett Giamatti, a professor of English Renaissance literature and onetime president of Yale University, served as the seventh commissioner of Major League Baseball. A diehard Red Sox fan, Giamatti wrote extensively and eloquently about the sport. His captivating essay on the heartbreak of fandom and the last day of the Sox' 1977 season, "The Green Fields of the Mind," stands out.

A number of notable rock stars have been baseball fans, including Detroit native Alice Cooper, who grew up cheering for Al Kaline and the Tigers. He later moved to Phoenix and adopted the Diamondbacks as his National League team of choice. Rocker Joan Jett is a devoted Baltimore Orioles fan, Rush's Geddy Lee roots for the Toronto Blue Jays, and Pearl Jam's Eddie Vedder is a Cubs

SUITE ENTRANCE

diehard. Paul Simon roots for the Yankees, Jack White is a Tigers fan, and Green Day's Billie Joe Armstrong was a vocal supporter of his hometown Oakland Athletics before they left the Bay Area after the 2024 season.

Elton John, a most quintessential Englishman, purchased a home in Atlanta's Buckhead neighborhood in 1991, the year that the Braves broke through with the first of their five National League pennants in the '90s. Sir Elton became a devoted Braves supporter, following the team from afar while touring the world. He buttonholed manager Bobby Cox prior to a Braves-Cubs game at Wrigley Field in 1995, second-guessing the skipper's decision to drop Mark Lemke from the number two spot in the batting order in favor of Jeff Blauser while discussing the team's left field platoon of Ryan Klesko and Mike Kelly.

Visitors to Hoboken, New Jersey, are greeted by signs proclaiming it to be "the birthplace of baseball and Frank Sinatra." Sinatra grew up a New York Giants fan and was at the Polo Grounds on October 3, 1951, when Bobby Thomson hit the famous "Shot Heard 'Round the World" to defeat the Dodgers for the National League pennant. When both of those clubs moved to the West Coast in 1958, he switched sides and became a Dodgers diehard, palling around with manager and fellow Italian American Tommy Lasorda. Sinatra sang the National Anthem at Lasorda's first home opener in 1977. His familiar version of "New York, New York" remains a Yankee Stadium staple nearly three decades after his 1998 passing.

While hip hop and rap have traditionally been associated with basketball, baseball has connections in that community as well. Public Enemy frontman Chuck D is an avid and knowledgeable fan, the Beastie Boys name-checked both Phil Rizzuto and Sadaharu Oh in their songs, and the legendary Ice Cube rolled up to Dodger Stadium in a vintage blue Chevy Impala convertible on Opening Day 2025 to deliver the Commissioner's trophy to the defending world champs.

Stars of the stage and screen have been baseball fans since the sport's earliest days as well. Humphrey Bogart was a fan. Actress Tallulah Bankhead was a fervent New York Giants supporter, once observing, "There have been only two geniuses in the world, Willie Mays and Willie Shakespeare." Jerry Seinfeld loves the Mets, Bill Murray is a Cubs fanatic, Spike Lee is a Yankees diehard, and Ben Affleck and Matt Damon are Red Sox zealots. The late Donald Sutherland was a Montréal Expos superfan and a regular at Olympic Stadium. Kurt Russell played pro baseball before his acting career took off. The iconic entertainer Bob Hope, who spent most of his youth in Cleveland, bought a piece of the Indians in 1946. His frequent film partner Bing Crosby purchased a minority share in the Pittsburgh Pirates the same year, and Gene Autry, Hollywood's "Singing Cowboy," was the first principal owner of the Los Angeles Angels. Comedic actor and entertainer Danny Kaye became one of the owners of the expansion Seattle Mariners when they joined the American League in 1977.

While the Chicago White Sox may or may not have a direct pipeline to a higher authority, celebrities and stars are just like you and me, living and dying with their teams and following their favorite players with interest and passion. It really doesn't matter whether you are a peon, a president, a pope, or a pop star—we are all united by fandom.

POACHING THE PENNANT

Some 2,700 years ago, the Greek poet Homer wrote *The Odyssey*—an epic, sweeping tale which is, at its heart, centered around the themes of a long journey, loyalty, and vengeance. All of which, of course, brings us to Brooklyn in 1958, when the Dodgers pulled up stakes for Los Angeles, breaking the hearts of millions. Like Odysseus and his loyal band of supporters, retribution was eventually had by a select group of men. In this case, it was four sportswriters.

In 1959, the Dodgers won their first National League pennant since arriving on the West Coast. The World Series opened in Chicago, and then shifted to LA. It was there, on October 6, 1959, that the long arc of history settled upon a ballroom at the Biltmore Hotel, where the Dodgers sated the assembled with free food and liquor. There, hanging above a buffet table, was the holy grail itself: the physical manifestation of the Dodgers' lone World Series title to date, won by Brooklyn four years earlier. The Bums' historic world championship flag, a roughly 8-by-16-foot banner, was first raised at Ebbets Field prior to the team's 1956 home opener. Manager Walter Alson and captain Pee Wee Reese did the honors that day, assisted by fans Barbara Bilinski and Anthony Micari. The flag later moved west, along with the Dodgers franchise.

With the series about to shift back to Chicago after the White Sox' 1–0 Game Five victory, *Newsday* writers Stan Issacs and Jack Mann, Charley Sutton of the *Long Beach Independent*, and Steve Weller of the *Buffalo Evening News* set out to avenge injustice. As Issacs wrote in 1963, they were "disturbed that a pennant sweated for and won in Brooklyn—the only one of its kind—was hanging in Los Angeles in the possession of the blackguards who had betrayed the faithful." As the hospitality event ended and the ballroom emptied out, Isaacs, abetted by a couple of hotel busboys who helped out by stacking up some tables, climbed up and poached the pennant.

He later said that Sutton—the only local in the group—took it home, wrapped it in plastic, and brought it to the airport the following morning. Issacs and Mann then took it to Chicago for the final game of the series, after which they transported it back east.

The pennant sat in Issacs's basement in Roslyn Heights, Long Island, for close to seven years. In August 1966, Issacs traveled to Cooperstown and handed the flag over to Baseball Hall of Fame president Ken Smith, with the proviso that its stay there would be temporary, until it could be repatriated to a worthy place in Brooklyn. Despite its significance, the Hall never put it on public display. Thirty years after Isaacs and Co. liberated the pennant, he asked the Hall to release it to the Brooklyn Historical Society, which was in the process of assembling a collection of Dodgers memorabilia. Smith's successor, Bill Guilfoyle, refused, citing the lack of official written documentation of the gentlemen's agreement that originally landed the object in Cooperstown. Although possession is said to be nine-tenths of the law, Guilfoyle apparently felt the flag tech-

WORLD CHAMPIONS
1955
DODGERS

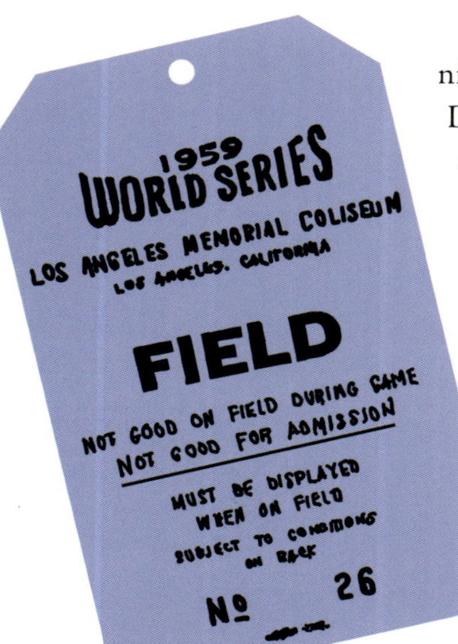

nically still belonged to the Dodgers, and that only they could effect a change in ownership.

The decades-long saga rolled forward, to the spring of 1995, when the Brooklyn Historical Society was getting ready to celebrate the fortieth anniversary of the Dodgers' historic 1955 win with a fundraising dinner, the theme of which was "A Blowout for Our Beloved Bums." The institution invited Dodgers owner Peter O'Malley, the son of the man who had inflicted so much pain on the borough. In a magnanimous gesture of reconciliation, the younger O'Malley agreed to ask the Hall to release the relic, saying, "It belongs in Brooklyn." He then donated it to the Historical Society, thus righting at least one small part of a historic wrong. A decade later, in 2005, the Textile Conservation Laboratory at the Cathedral of St. John the Divine spent three months restoring the banner, which had accumulated a half-century of dirt (which is called *schmutz* in Brooklyn). They repaired assorted holes and tears and mended portions of the huge pennant's Dodger blue border. That year, Dave Anderson, writing in *The New York Times*, quoted Issacs: "When somebody asked (Dodgers executive) Buzzie Bavasi years later about the 1955 pennant we stole … Buzzie said: 'It probably belongs in Brooklyn anyway, and the next time we needed a 1955 pennant, we got another one made up. It only cost $92.'"

Stan Issacs died on April 2, 2013, a week before the NBA's Brooklyn Nets marked the 100th anniversary of the first game at Ebbets Field with a rare public display of the championship banner that Isaacs and friends appropriated in 1959. Some odysseys end in ancient Ithaca, while others end in twenty-first century Brooklyn.

THE LOOK OF THE GAME

SEA	0	INNING	3	BALL
OAK	10	9	3	STRIKE
CLE	3		3	OUT
SD	2			

THE CINCINNATI GREENS

On March 17, 1978, the Cincinnati Reds became the Cincinnati Greens. That day, the Reds took batting practice in their usual red and white uniforms, then switched over to a set of green-trimmed outfits in celebration of St. Patrick's Day. A total of 7,043 fans were on hand at Tampa's Al Lopez Field for the spring-training matchup between Cincinnati and the defending World Series champion New York Yankees, and just about everyone there was surprised.

The Cincinnati franchise was long known for its stodgy, conservative reputation. In what was a particularly expressive era for baseball in just about every outward way, the Reds barred their players from sporting facial hair, white shoes, or high stirrups. As such, the players were shocked by the green uniforms. They were called into the clubhouse for what was described as a "team meeting," during which the uniforms were distributed by equipment manager Bernie Stowe. Outfielder George Foster, the reigning National League Most Valuable Player, said that he didn't even notice as he was colorblind. On the other hand, rookie infielder Mike Grace quipped, "I think I'm playing for the Boston Celtics." "Did we get traded to Oakland?" asked catcher Johnny Bench.

The club's transformation into "The Big Green Machine" was the work of their marketing executive, Roger Ruhl, who told the *Dayton Journal Herald*, "at first we talked about only green caps, but then (team president) Dick Wagner decided to go all the way." The club purchased fifty-two uniforms from Spalding, which included green-trimmed jerseys, pants, caps, and sweatshirts for a reported $105 per set. A green shamrock on the left sleeve of the jersey completed the look. One attention to detail was, however, neglected: the Reds wore their normal red batting helmets, which made for a very Christmas-y appearance when the team was up at bat.

This was not the first time that a big-league club went all in for St. Patrick's Day. On March 17, 1899, the Philadelphia Phillies similarly stunned their training camp when they broke out their new "bottle green and white" sweaters, described by the *Philadelphia Inquirer* as "a hue the like of which has never been seen this side of Ireland." The paper said that this marked "a fitting commemoration of the day."

This new, temporary look must have agreed with the Reds, because they thumped New York, 9–2. Yankees owner George M. Steinbrenner III, a Tampa resident, was on hand for the game, watching with a large group of friends. Steinbrenner, a man who demanded victory even in meaningless exhibition games, was none too happy with his team's performance. After the game, he told reporters, "I think the green uniforms that the Reds were wearing matched my complexion after seeing the inadequacies of the team that is supposed to be the world champions."

Cincinnati's stunt proved to be trendsetting. The following March 17, the Los Angeles Dodgers wore green caps to mark the day, and their field featured green bases. The Reds uniforms were immediately cited for their historic significance; they were displayed at the Hall of Fame in Cooperstown within a couple of years of their debut. Other clubs soon followed suit. In 1982, the Houston Astros took the field out in green pullovers with the words "Happy St. Patrick's Day" rendered on the back in script letterforms. Four years later, the Detroit Tigers wore white uniforms with green caps and socks, with their time-honored jerseys trimmed in green with a green Olde English "D." Every player wore number 30 that day—a nod to club owner Tom Monaghan, who also owned the Domino's pizza chain, which famously promised that their pizzas would be delivered in 30 minutes or less. The Twins and Phillies also wore green that day, and the floodgates soon opened wide with a bunch of clubs eventually clad in emerald for the holiday, including the Yankees, who have worn green caps in recent years to mark the occasion.

Every St. Patrick's Day, the city of Chicago dyes its namesake river green. While there are no regular-season games played in the middle of March, the Chicago White Sox annually commemorate "Halfway to St. Patrick's Day" in September, and, for several years beginning in 2005, they wore special uniforms which featured green pinstripes, green caps, green uniform lettering and, yes, green sox, an emerald-themed reminder of that spring day in Tampa in 1978 when the Reds pulled off a celebratory shenanigan that shocked the baseball world.

MADE IN JAPAN

In the late 1970s, America was buffeted by a series of tumultuous changes which deeply affected the national psyche. Economic, political, and societal upheaval characterized the moment. Soaring inflation, declining productivity, and the ongoing deterioration of America's industrial base contributed to the perception, both internally and globally, that America's best days had passed. This national malaise was starkly contrasted by the economic rise of Japan, which was driven by a surge in automobile and consumer electronic exports to the United States. American fears over Japan's economic might spilled out onto the baseball diamond in 1977, when the Pittsburgh Pirates ordered two new sets of uniforms from Osaka-based Descente Ltd., a French Japanese company that specialized in ski garments and apparel.

The Bucs' colorful new black-and-gold togs garnered a lot of attention, and the fact that two of the three sets were going to be made in Japan provoked broadly hostile reactions. Harold Wolfe of the National Association of Uniform Manufacturers told the Associated Press, "What could be more un-American than baseball uniforms made in another country at a time when this nation is experiencing such difficult economic times and when so many people are unemployed?" He urged baseball Commissioner Bowie Kuhn to pressure all clubs to adopt a "Made in America" policy. A snarky editorial in Ohio's *Springfield News-Sun* said, "The news that the Pittsburgh Pirates have bought uniforms from Japan is yet another sign that the American Century is being subcontracted out to foreigners."

In the wake of such backlash, the Pirates defended their decision to go overseas for their uniforms. Club vice president for business operations Joe O'Toole, in comments to the *Pittsburgh Post-Gazette*, said, "We didn't buy in Japan because it was cheaper. In fact, the Japanese uniforms are more expensive. They cost about $80 apiece and the Rawlings-made uniforms are slightly less. We talked to several manufacturers in the United States and they couldn't come up with a pinstripe uniform which was made in Japan." Bucs manager Chuck Tanner told the *New Castle News*, "It's a big joke. They're all upset about it. I'd like to walk into their homes and take a look at their Sony TVs and their Japanese cameras and make a big issue about that also."

Labor unions chimed in, boycotts were threatened, and people wrote angry letters to their local newspapers, but the controversy soon abated as fans turned their attention to the coming season. Pittsburgh fans harbored high hopes for their team, which featured a packed roster full of talent that included both speedsters and sluggers, fronted by Willie Stargell and Dave Parker. "The Lumber Company" wound up winning 96 games in 1977, good for a second place finish in the National League East, but the nucleus of the club went on to win the World Series in those same gaudy uniforms just two years later.

The mostly forgotten Japanese uniform kerfuffle flared up again in 1980, when the Baltimore Orioles contracted with Descente to produce their uniforms for the following season. General manager Hank Peters pushed back at all the negative press, noting that players were wearing shoes made in Europe and that the baseballs themselves were manufactured in Haiti. Some noted that half of all American flags at the time were manufactured overseas, and in February 1980, American Olympic speed skaters Eric and Beth Heiden were depicted on the cover of *Time* magazine with the Descente logo plastered right across their headgear.

Japan's economy continued to boom in the 1980s, and Japanese conglomerates went on a spending spree, buying a series of prominent and vital American companies from Hollywood to Wall Street. Mitsubishi's acquisition of New York's Rockefeller Center in 1989 provoked widespread outcry that the Japanese were taking over America, but the Japanese economy stagnated in the '90s, and nearly a half-century after the Pirates courted controversy by daring to import their uniforms from Japan, the sport's most celebrated superstar, Shohei Ohtani, hails from that country. The Japanese-made uniforms that the Pirates rolled out in 1977 are now fondly remembered as the garish look of a championship club. They are indelibly linked with a winner, and not with the fact that the club imported them from a menacing economic competitor half a world away.

THE YEAR OF THE PILLBOX CAP

The year 1976 was a moment of celebration for both America, which marked its bicentennial, and the National League, which observed its 100th anniversary that season. Every NL club (with the exception of Montréal) wore a commemorative National League centennial sleeve patch, designed by artist Dick Perez.* A handful of clubs decided to do something really, really special, in the form of striped throwback "pillbox" caps, an old-fashioned homage to what players wore on their noggins in the nineteenth century.

The Pittsburgh Pirates held a press conference on January 13, 1976, to show off their new headwear, which was modeled by players George "Doc" Medich and Bill Robinson, alongside manager Danny Murtaugh. Club officials pointed out that the Pirates were going to wear them for every game of the coming season. They had no idea at the time that the club would wind up wearing them for the next decade.

The New York Mets busted theirs out on Opening Day against the Expos. The *Daily News* ran a photo of the Montréal dugout, whose players were said to be "chuckling" over Mets manager Joe Frazier's cap, with a caption that noted, "They should laugh?" The Mets saved the pillboxes for select special occasions, which included their Fourth of July game against the Chicago Cubs.

That year, Philadelphia was the undisputed epicenter of all bicentennial festivities. The Phillies wore the pillboxes for the first two games of the season—both of which they lost to Pittsburgh—which, of course, brought them disfavor in the dugout. The big day, July 4, 1976, called for something special, and so the Phils wore them again when they split a doubleheader with the Pirates.

The St. Louis Cardinals were next up, on June 14, against Atlanta. The Redbirds were unique members of the flat-topped fraternity as they went all in with matching striped batting helmets, which were, unfortunately, rounded and not flat on top.

The National League All-Stars wore white flat-topped snapbacks that featured a jaunty script "N" during the pregame ceremonies in Philly on July 13, and they were joined by NL umpires, who sported navy pillboxes with an italicized "76" in white, backed by three white stripes. The umps also wore these during that year's World Series.

Finally, we have the case of the Expos—who wore them just once—in the first game of a doubleheader against the Phillies on September 26. These two games were the final ones at Jarry Park, which served as the Expos' home stadium for their first eight seasons. The team designated the event as Fan Appreciation Day and took out newspaper ads which noted the fact that they would be sporting the caps for this one and only occasion, after which they would be raffled off to the fans. There are no clear images of the Expos sporting these caps; however, we do have video evi-

* The Expos instead sported a patch that featured the logo of the 1976 Summer Olympic Games.

P

dence—which is poor in quality—yet conclusive. In the sixth inning, Philadelphia's Greg Luzinski launched a three-run homer that would clinch the National League East title. This was also the last home run in the history of the ballpark. The footage shows him as he rounds third base—at this point you can briefly make out two Expos players in the team's home bullpen, which was located in foul territory in left field. The caps are clearly all white, devoid of the team's signature blue and red panels, an incontrovertible Zapruder film–like snippet of evidence that confirms their usage.

When the centennial and bicentennial season ended, the popularity and mystique that surrounded the pillbox caps endured. The Pirates, of course, continued to wear them. In 1979, a group of San Francisco Giants players, led by pitcher Vida Blue, petitioned general manager Spec Richardson to let the team wear black-and-orange pillboxes, but he turned them down. Dissatisfied with their GM's reply, they ordered them anyway and wore them during batting practice that year. At the conclusion of the 1979 season, a group of MLB All-Stars traveled to Japan for a series of exhibition games, and a number of those players wore striped pillbox hats, including members of the Mets, Phillies, San Diego Padres, and Detroit Tigers.

The pillboxes' extended afterlife continued forward into the new decade. When the Pirates won the 1979 World Series, the caps were vaulted into icon status in the hearts and minds of baseball fans everywhere. In 1980, the Bucs planned on dropping them from their uniform rotation, but their distinctiveness—as well as their value to the team at the concession stands—kept them alive. A 1981 article in the *Minneapolis Tribune* centered on their popularity with young Black men in the Twin Cities, quoting a fifteen-year-old named Edwin Austin, who said, "I just wear it because the Pirates wear it ... they have a lot of Black people on the team." In 1987, Pittsburgh tweaked their logo and uniforms in conjunction with the club's 100th anniversary, and the pillboxes were ultimately eliminated. Outfielder Andy Van Slyke, who'd been traded to the club that offseason, made his feelings clear, telling the *Tampa Tribune-Times*, "I would have looked like Herman Munster in one of those old caps."

On July 9, 2003, the Pirates brought back their 1979 look (which included black pillbox caps) for a game in Milwaukee against the Brewers.[†] Thirteen years later, in 2016, the Pirates unveiled a new set of alternate Sunday uniforms, which included black pillboxes. That same season, the Phillies held a throwback night which featured their 1976 uniforms, including the flat-topped lids. As was the case with the Pirates' versions, these were not nearly as flat on top as the originals, but looked convincing enough.

The 1970s were a strange decade indeed, for many reasons, and the 1976 pillbox caps are part of that weird legacy. Born in the nineteenth century, popularized anew in the year of America's bicentennial, the pillboxes persist, a strange sartorial statement from a distant time.

† This is the game where Pittsburgh first baseman Randall Simon hit one of the Brewers' Racing Sausages with a bat, after which the mascot crumpled to the ground in a heap.

THE HALL OF JERSEYS

The aesthetic culture of baseball, which is most visibly conveyed via its uniforms, is deeply and sometimes insufferably rooted in tradition. Baseball's first professional club, the Cincinnati Red Stockings, were literally named for their hosiery, which became their visual calling card when they took the nation by storm in 1869. Today, the Red Sox' and White Sox' monikers pay homage to their socks, even if those are mostly hidden. Cincinnati's uniforms, described by the *Brooklyn Daily Eagle* as "white flannel trimmed with red, a red belt and stockings, the pants being fastened at the knee," essentially serve as the template for what teams still wear today.

How come players still wear belts? Why do baseball uniforms contain vestigial buttons? "Shield-front" bibbed jerseys, floppy collars, straight up "cadet collars," zippers, pullovers, and henleys have come and gone over the past century and a half, but buttons hang tough, baseball's version of the human appendix, a seemingly useless thing that somehow escaped evolution.

Some of baseball's earliest uniforms featured a shield or bib front, which was affixed to the garment by a series of buttons that encircled its perimeter. These were identical to the uniforms worn by firefighters of the time—indeed, some early clubs were offshoots of fire companies, including Mutual of New York, which was formed in 1857 by members of New York's Mutual Hook and Ladder Company No. 1, the city's first volunteer fire department. The Mutuals were also called the Green Stockings. They went pro in 1871 and became charter members of the National League in 1876 before being expelled after a single season as punishment for refusing to make a late-season road trip. By then, they were wearing brown stockings.

Some nineteenth-century baseball jerseys contained a front pocket, and others were accompanied by a tie which was tucked neatly into the placket. Lace-front jerseys, similar to traditional hockey sweaters, were also in style back then. New York Giants manager John McGraw, who tinkered with the look of his club on a seemingly annual basis, outfitted his club in collarless uniforms in 1906, a first. *New York Evening World* sportswriter Bozeman Bulger, who was a close friend of McGraw, kidded him in print, imagining what old-time star Cap Anson would have said "without a big collar to turn up around his neck and look tough?" He said that McGraw had always maintained that collars were useless on baseball jerseys, which was true, and indeed, this innovation eventually stuck. The 1909 Chicago Cubs went the other way, rolling out jerseys with tall military-inspired collars that fastened at the throat. These were popular for a while; just about every major-league club adopted the look before it fell out of fashion in the 1920s.

The Cubs introduced zippered jerseys in 1937 as part of a sartorial overhaul overseen by club art director Otis Shepard, who also reimagined the look of Wrigley Field that very same year. A number of big-league clubs later employed zippers, which were last worn on a regular basis by the 1986 Philadelphia Phillies. In 1940, the Cubs introduced gray sleeveless road jerseys—snug, form-fitting vests that were intended to provide better movement for the players' arms and shoulders. The following year the vests became powder blue instead of the usual gray, which elicited a torrent of sarcasm. The Camden, New Jersey, *Courier Post* ran a short article entitled, "Cubs Uniforms Bring Quips of la-de-da," saying that the club "looks worse than a girls softball team." "Have the Cubs developed a pantywaist inferiority complex?" asked *The Sporting News*. Appearances aside, the uniforms were made of a knitted fabric, instead of the usual heavy flannel, and the ballclub touted their elasticity, lightness, comfort, and coolness. Ultimately, the look was short-lived; the Cubs went back to gray jerseys with sleeves in 1943.

The following season, the Brooklyn Dodgers introduced satin uniforms for a handful of night games—white at home and powder blue on the road. Dodgers president Branch Rickey, a famously conservative man in just about every respect, had attended an All-American Girls Professional Baseball League game the previous season and was struck by the way the players' shiny skirts shimmered under the lights. Those uniforms were designed by the Cubs' Shepard, who was assisted by Chicago softball player Ann Harnett. A couple of other clubs also experimented with satins for some night games at one time or another during the '40s.

Teams continued to experiment with lighter weight fabrics during the postwar era, but the graphics and the basic look of the uniform remained stuck in the Roaring Twenties. Critics howled and players grumbled when Bill Veeck's White Sox added names to the backs of their road jerseys in 1960, but today every club sports them on one unform or another, with the exception of the uber-traditional (some might even say pretentious) Yankees.

In 1963, Kansas City Athletics owner Charles O. Finley decked his club out in "Tulane Gold" and kelly green togs, saying "My feeling is that baseball should do everything possible to add color to the game." The outfits were called clownish, bizarre, bush league, and worse, but Finley got the last laugh when the sport finally caught up with him about a decade later, just as the A's were winning back-to-back-to-back world championships.

In 1970, the Pittsburgh Pirates became the first club to wear pullover jerseys and beltless pants, kicking off a decade when the look of the sport went wild. Within a few short years the Cleveland Indians were clad in red, the Orioles were wearing orange, the Padres were resplendent in brown and yellow, and the Braves hit the road in handsome royal-blue jerseys. By 1980, eleven of MLB's twenty-six teams wore powder blue on the road, which probably would have caused those snarky observers of the 1941 Cubs uniforms to have an apoplectic fit.

The election of Ronald Reagan as President of the United States in 1980 brought forth an era of conservatism that was reflected on diamonds all across the land. Teams began to shun pullovers in favor of buttons, and belts were back in style. In 1987, eight of MLB's twenty-six clubs adopted new uniform designs, and the majority of them embodied a return to baseball's mythical past, with one Associated Press story noting, "everything old is new when it comes to duds on the diamonds." The 1990s featured some outlandish looks, but the core of the time-honored uniform remained intact—buttons, belts, and stirrups, which were largely covered up by long pants.

As the millennium ebbed, the Seattle Mariners looked not to the past, but to the future. In 1998, they turned the clock ahead to the year 2027, imagining what the club would look like during its yet-distant fiftieth anniversary season. The resulting promotion saw the team garbed in sleeveless black jerseys with outsized graphics and italicized player numbers. The following season, MLB embarked upon a "Turn Ahead the Clock" campaign, sponsored by the Century 21 real estate firm, which catapulted baseball into the year 2021, when the look of most clubs would align with Seattle's vision of the future. The Yankees, perennially "on brand," opted out, with club owner George M. Steinbrenner reportedly quipping that the Yankees were already wearing their uniforms of the future. With 2021 safely behind us at the time of publication, we can state with all certainty that this look, as fun as it was, did not in fact happen.

The twenty-first century is now one quarter over, and baseball uniforms continue to make headlines. Nike took over as official supplier of MLB uniforms in 2020 and promptly added their swoosh logo to the fronts of every jersey, including those of the Yankees. The following season, seven clubs—led by the Boston Red Sox—rolled out "City Connect" uniforms, a unified marketing initiative that MLB described as "a celebration of the powerful synergy between teams and the cities that support them." Boston wore yellow jerseys, the Cubs and Dodgers were outfitted in blue from head to toe, and the Marlins took the field in red with uniforms that paid homage to the old minor-league Havana Sugar Kings.

Advertisements were added to the sleeves of major-league jerseys in 2023, a move that had been discussed for a quarter century, and, in 2024, fans revolted when Nike and MLB introduced new templated uniforms that shrunk the size of player names and standardized colors across clubs. Players weren't happy, either. Philadelphia Phillies shortstop Trea Turner told the AP, "Everyone hates them." Sweat stains, see-through pants, mismatched gray colors, and cheap embellishments added to the perception that things had gone off the rails for no good reason, and the players association wound up issuing a memo accusing Nike of "innovating something that didn't need to be innovated." Nike and MLB reversed course and started to move back to the previous template and details the following year.

It's safe to assume that trends will come and go and that new innovations will take root as the years roll forward. Some may wish to compile a list of the best- or worst-looking jerseys of all time, but aesthetics are invariably subjective—beauty, as always, is in the eye of the beholder. Generations see these things differently. Somewhere there's a boomer Tigers or Giants fan arguing with his or her Gen Z niece, nephew, grandchild, or whoever, who is a huge fan of what the Marlins or Angels once wore. Get off their lawn and take your damned City Connects with you! Instead, how about a callout of twelve important, influential, or interesting jerseys that help tell the story of how we got from the bewhiskered Red Stockings to today? Here we go.

1876 HARTFORD DARK BLUES

Hartford wore these "shield front" jerseys during the National League's inaugural season, 1876. Typical of the era, they are straightforward, with only the name of the club's home city featured. Lace-up jerseys soon became the favored style, a trend that carried over into the early twentieth century.

1906 NEW YORK GIANTS

John McGraw's 1906 Giants strutted out onto the field in these audacious jerseys, but there was innovation lurking beneath all the boastfulness. These were the first major-league jerseys to not include collars, a look that soon caught on and which is still worn today.

1909 CHICAGO CUBS

The 1909 Chicago Cubs wore these jerseys on the road, which are noteworthy for two reasons. They were the first major-league jerseys to feature "cadet-style" or standing collars, which quickly became a fad. These are also the first Cubs jerseys to showcase an oversized "C" with the letters "UBS" nested within.

1936 NEW YORK YANKEES

Fact: Babe Ruth never played a game with the Yankees' famed "NY" logo on his pinstriped jersey. These uniforms, introduced in 1936, are similar to those still worn at home today. They are also the successors to jerseys that utilized the mark on either sleeves or fronts from 1909 through 1916.

1941 CHICAGO CUBS

The Chicago Cubs wore these sleeveless zippered powder blue jerseys on the road in 1941. The look was widely ridiculed, but players applauded the flexibility that they offered. A number of clubs picked up on vests in the '50s and '60s, and again in the early '90s.

1944 BROOKLYN DODGERS

The Brooklyn Dodgers wore these snazzy satin jerseys for select night games, starting in 1944. The intent was to produce a dazzling visual effect under the arc lights, along with increased visibility, but players disliked them and they were soon discontinued.

1963 KANSAS CITY A'S

Owner Charles O. Finley's Kansas City Athletics rocked baseball's sartorial world in 1963, when they first sported these "Tulane Gold" and kelly green flannels. Many observers tarred them as garish, but they were profoundly influential, the first volley in a color revolution that later transformed the look of the sport.

1971 PITTSBURGH PIRATES

Much to the surprise of just about everybody in attendance, the Pittsburgh Pirates took the field at brand-new Three Rivers Stadium on July 16, 1970, wearing these form-fitting pullover jerseys, which were paired with beltless pants, a major-league first.

The Houston Astros broke the mold when they rolled out these expressive, colorful jerseys in 1975. The "rainbows" or "tequila sunrises" were worn both at home and on the road, a sharp departure from tradition. This look has been both celebrated and reviled, a franchise staple and a source of civic pride.

1976 CHICAGO WHITE SOX

The 1976 Chicago White Sox, owned by marketing genius Bill Veeck, rolled up in these collared jerseys, which were worn untucked, pajama style, and originally paired with shorts for hot weather games. Veeck touted the "practical and utilitarian" nature of these iconic togs, which were worn through 1981.

1987 OAKLAND ATHLETICS

In 1987, eight of the twenty-six MLB clubs changed uniforms, including the Oakland Athletics, who abandoned their mix-and-match green-and-gold pullovers for a refined, retro-inspired look, which included buttons. This return to tradition also included clubs such as Atlanta, Seattle, Houston, and the White Sox.

2021 BOSTON RED SOX

On April 17, 2021, the Boston Red Sox became the first team to wear a Nike City Connect uniform. The program—a league-wide marketing initiative—was created to celebrate "the bond between each team and its city." The Nike swoosh logo first appeared on all MLB uniforms in 2020.

ALSO BY TODD RADOM

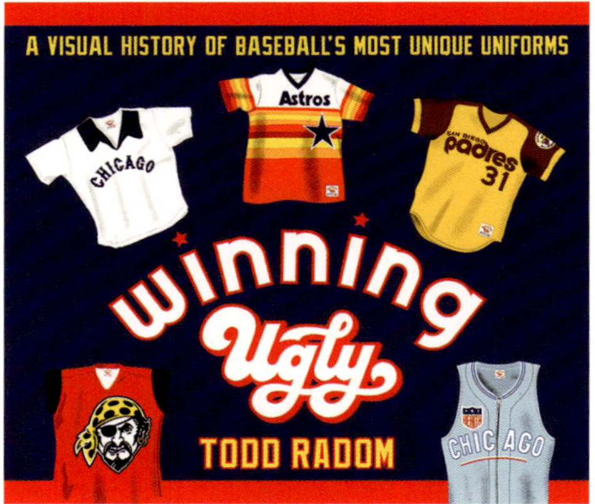

WINNING UGLY: A VISUAL HISTORY OF BASEBALL'S MOST UNIQUE UNIFORMS

Todd Radom

Baseball, our national pastime. All fans have great memories of their teams. We also remember those things that we wish we could forget: the errors, the mental mistakes . . . and the ugly uniforms.

In an ode to those eyesores, Todd Radom has collected and chronicled some of the swing-and-misses we've seen on the baseball diamond. Remember when the Chicago White Sox thought wearing shorts in 1977 was a good idea? How about when the Baltimore Orioles wore their all-orange jerseys in 1971? Do you remember the 1999 "Turn Ahead the Clock" campaign? Or the most recent all-camo jerseys of the San Diego Padres?

Yes, there is much to talk about when it comes to the odd uniform decisions teams have made over the years. But just like there's love out there for French bulldogs or Christmas sweaters, ugly uniforms hold a warm place in the heart of all baseball fans, and *Winning Ugly* is just that: an ode to our favorites from today and yesterday that bring smiles and sighs to all baseball fans.

Sure they didn't affect wins and losses (unless you mention Chris Sale), but a fan's love and ire goes well beyond the current standings. So whether your team appears in *Winning Ugly* or not, fans of the sport will enjoy reliving the moments most teams would like to forget.

$19.99 • Paperback • ISBN: 978-1-68358-395-0

ALSO BY TODD RADOM

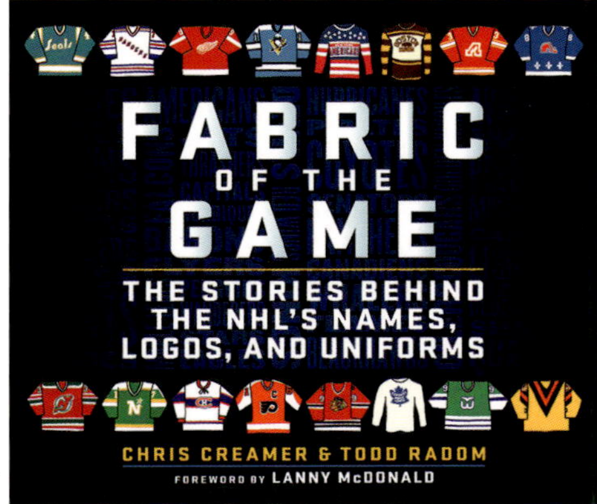

FABRIC OF THE GAME: THE STORIES BEHIND THE NHL'S NAMES, LOGOS, AND UNIFORMS

Chris Creamer and Todd Radom
Foreword by Lanny McDonald

Nothing unites or divides fans quite like their favorite hockey team. The passion they hold within them for the New York Rangers, Toronto Maple Leafs, Montreal Canadiens, or Boston Bruins allows them to look past any differences and channels it into a powerful, shared admiration for their team.

We decorate our lives with their logos, stock our wardrobe with their jerseys, and, in some cases, even tattoo our bodies with their iconography and colors. They're so ingrained in our lives we don't even think to ask ourselves why Los Angeles celebrates royalty or why Buffalo cheers for not one, but two massive cavalry swords.

All that and more is explored in *Fabric of the Game*, authored by two of the sports world's leading experts in team branding and design: Chris Creamer and Todd Radom. Tapping into their vast knowledge of the whys and hows, Creamer and Radom explore and share the origin stories behind these and more, talking directly to those involved in the decision processes and designs of the NHL's team names, logos, and uniforms. Learn more about the historied Detroit Red Wings and Chicago Blackhawks, as well as the lost but not forgotten Hartford Whalers and Quebec Nordiques, all the way to the lesser-known Kansas City Scouts and Philadelphia Quakers. Whichever team you pledge allegiance, *Fabric of the Game* covers them in-depth with research and knowledge for any hockey fan to enjoy.

$29.99 • Hardcover • ISBN: 978-1-68358-384-4

REACH
MARK
REG. IN U.S. PAT. OFF.
OFFICIAL
American League Ball
PAT'D. MAR. 17-25
WARRANTED
The Cushioned Cork Center
9 IN. 5 OZ.

RAIN CHECK
THE PHILADELPHIA NATIONAL LEAGUE CLUB
CONNIE MACK STADIUM
DELUXE BOX
56
S. F.
AUGUST 27, 1967
ENTER GATES 22 TO 26 ROTUNDA
LOWER STAND
EBBETS FIELD
BROOKLYN
NIGHT GAME
SAN DIEGO padres BASEBALL CLUB
LOS ANGELES DODGERS TUE. EVE.
APR. 29
MEZZANINE BOX
BALTIMORE ORIOLES
Championship Series 1969
$7.00
1949 SEASON
J 15190
RAIN CHECK
GRAND STAND
AUDIT STUB
SEP. 14 1979 NIGHT
SOX
LOWER DECK BOX $6.00
DO NOT DETACH
ALL STAR GAME
JULY 8, 1952
NATIONAL LEAGUE STARS vs AMERICAN LEAGUE STARS
Upper Grandstand $4.00
1st BASE RES. BENCH
$7.50
Tues. SEP. 10
Hilldale Base Ball
RAIN CHECK
BREWERS VS SEA. MARINERS
ENTER GATE C
09 24 57
SEC. ROW SEAT
LOWER STAND $2.00
Dodgers
TUESDAY SEPT. 24 1957
EBBETS FIELD
ASTROS EXPOS
JEUDI - 8:05 - THURSDAY
AUG. 17 1972
GARDER CE TALON
RETAIN THIS STUB
expos
ENTER AT GATE
LOWER BOX
10 3 6
CINCINNATI REDS
CROSLEY FIELD
LOWER BOX $10.25
JUNE 14 1978
UPPER RESERVED
RAIN CHECK
California
Angels
UPPER RESERVED $3.25
WORLD SERIES
AMERICAN LEAGUE vs. NATIONAL LEAGUE
1973
baseball
SECOND DECK
$10.00
NATIONAL LEAGUE
OAKLAND A's
GAME 6
OAKLAND-ALAMEDA COUNTY COLISEUM
BOWIE KUHN
ADMIT ONE
AMERICAN LEAGUE CHAMPIONSHIP
METROPOLITAN STADIUM, BLOOMINGTON, MINN.
DIVISION WEST vs. DIVISION EAST
MINNESOTA TWINS
DO NOT DETACH THIS COUPON FROM RAIN CHECK
GAME 3
ADMISSION
GAME 15
ENTER ANY GATE
02376
CINCINNATI
MAY 6, 1983
FRI 8:05 PM
SHEA STADIUM
Mets
$3.00
RAINCHECK
RAIN CHECK
JULY 28 1957
Upper Deck Box
MILWAUKEE BRAVES
BLEACHERS